SOVIET POLICY

TOWARDS

PAKISTAN & BANGLADESH

BY THE SAME AUTHOR

Documentary Study of the Warsaw Pact

China Pakistan and Bangladesh

India and Disarmament, Vol. I
Nehru Era : An Analytical Study

Nuclear India : Vol. I

Nuclear India : Vol. II

Soviet Policy
Towards
Pakistan
and
Bangladesh

J. P. Jain

Visiting Associate Professor
Centre for International
Politics and Organization,
Jawaharlal Nehru University

Radiant Publishers

Distributed by:
South Asia Books
Box 502
Columbia, MO 65201

ISBN 0 88386 482 7

First Published 1974 by
RADIANT PUBLISHERS
E-155, Kalkaji, New Delhi-19.

Printed in India by
RAJAM PRINTERS
7A/12, W.E.A. Karol Bagh, New Delhi-5.

Preface

The present book is a sequel to my earlier study *China Pakistan and Bangladesh*. It is concerned with the foreign policy objectives of the Soviet Union in the changing international environment and the political, economic and strategic interests of the USSR in the Indian subcontinent. It examines the motivations behind various diplomatic moves made by the Kremlin to woo Pakistan and the attitude adopted by it during the Indo-Pak Conflicts of 1965 and 1971. Moscow's role in the emergence of Bangladesh and the pattern of its relations with the Republic of Bangladesh are also discussed in detail.

The book, at the same time, deals with the considerations which led Pakistan to befriend the USSR. The impact of Sino-US rapprochement and the Indo-Soviet Treaty of Friendship, Cooperation and Peace on USSR-Pak relations and the inter-play of Soviet and Chinese policies in the region are also analyzed in depth.

The views expressed in the study are entirely my own personal views and are not to be attributed to any institution, agency or organization. I thank my son Rajendra for his help in editing and reading the proofs and my wife, Sheila Devi Jain, who has rendered assistance of various kinds.

New Delhi   **J.P. JAIN**

Contents

Preface   *v*

1 Background   1

2 USSR-Pak Relations 1947-53   25

3 USSR-Pak Relations 1954-64   43

4 Indo-Pakistan Conflict of 1965   69

5 After Tashkent   83

6 The Bangladesh Crisis and the Indo-Pakistan
  War of 1971   113

7 USSR-Pak Relations After 1971   148

8 USSR and Bangladesh   170

9 Conclusion   195

Notes   213

Appendices

A. Tashkent Declaration   228

B. Simla Agreement   231

*C. Exchange of Visits Between USSR and
   Pakistan*   234

D. Agreements Between USSR and Pakistan   237

E. Pakistan's Trade with USSR   241

*F. Exchange of Visits Between USSR and
   Bangladesh*   242

G. Agreements Between USSR and Bangladesh   243

Select Bibliography   245

Index   253

1
Background

IN a book entitled *Pakistan : Ideology—Constitution—Laws—Foreign Policy* the author, Samin Khan, has described Pakistan as an "ideological State." The book was published in Karachi in early 1961 and carried a Foreword by Z.A. Bhutto, then Minister for National Reconstruction and Information of Pakistan. The "ideological State" has been distinguished by Samin from the "territorial State" over which it is said to enjoy great advantage. The latter does not have the weapons to retaliate the "ideological onslaughts" of the former and is always on the defensive, he states. None of the institutions of an ideological State, Samin Khan observes, "are more important than its ideology, for the ideology is sacred, supreme and inviolable." According to him, the ideology provides the underlying philosophy of the country or the "Ultimate National Objective," which, in the case of Pakistan, meant unity of the Islamic World. This, at the same time, also provides an "ideological camouflage" for the foreign policy of Pakistan, which is considered essential for the promotion of "expansionist tendencies" in the world. "The expansionist policy of ideological States," he remarks, "can be cloaked under ideology which it tries to propagate." To that end, such a State should continue to be "infused with a certain degree of dynamism," as he put it. Otherwise, there was danger of its becoming reactionary and nationalistic.

Having, thus, laid the infrastructure of Pakistan's foreign policy, *i.e.* the projection and propagation of the national ideology—Islam—as an "ideal" on the international plane, Samin Khan went on to establish the claims of Pakistan for leadership, if not indeed "monopoly," in protecting the interests of the Islamic World. The birth of Pakistan, he observed, "was the greatest event in the Islamic World since the downfall of the orthodox Caliphate." The creation of Pakistan, he stated, was a significant victory of the forces of Islam and the concept of the ideological state over those of "territorial nationalism and secularism." It was, thus, obvious, he pointed out, that "the destiny of Pakistan is inevitably linked with the ideology that was instrumental in the creation of Pakistan, that is Islam." Being the largest Muslim State in the world and "the only State created on the basis of Islam, it is the duty and responsibility of Pakistan to lead these forces." He went on to add :

> So our objective in foreign policy should be to accumulate, control, channelise these forces so as to serve the interests of the entire Islamic World. Our foreign policy thus cannot confine itself to the narrow limits of our own national interests. It would be a betrayal of not only the Islamicists in the Muslim World (if we follow such a policy) but also a betrayal of the ideology of Pakistan itself.[1]

True to the principles enunciated by the author mentioned above, Bhutto, as Foreign Minister of Pakistan, declared from the platform of the United Nations, a few years later, that "the ideology of Pakistan is truly founded on Islam."[2] The Minister for Information and Broadcasting, Pir Ali Mohammed, in his speech before the Constituent Assembly of Pakistan, stated :

> Hitherto, throughout the last 1300 years, many Muslim units fought shy of taking the name of Islam in constitutional and governmental fields. True to the basic concept of Pakistan we have tried to translate into action the basic values of Islam.[3]

President Ayub Khan, in his Election Manifesto, undertook "to advance the ideology of Muslim nationalism," to support "all liberal causes" and to provide "whatever assistance may be possible to such *people or communities* as may be in bondage..."[4] Thus, there can hardly be any doubt that the first and foremost consideration, in the eyes of Pakistani leaders, was for the cause of Muslims—who were regarded as a separate entity from other communities or people in the world. The strategy, as conceived by the originators of the idea of Pakistan and upheld subsequently by its leaders, was to declare the "political, cultural and economic interests" of the Muslim community as quite distinct from and irreconcilable with those of other communities; to uphold as "command of God" the basic allegiance or "first Duty" to the Muslim cause over and above loyalty to the State; and to seek to protect the rights and interests of a Muslim community even by resorting to 'civil war' within a country to establish a separate homeland for the Muslims.[5] Allama Sheikh Mohammed Iqbal, the father of the idea of Pakistan, not only proclaimed "the formation of a consolidated North West Indian Muslim State," to which he later added "Bengal," the final destiny of Muslims" of at least these areas, and "a redistribution of the country on the lines of racial, religious and linguistic affinities" as "the only way to a peaceful India," but also proclaimed the right of "self-determination" for Muslim majority areas "outside India."[6]

The demand for the protection of the rights and interests of Muslims in order "to save Muslims from the domination of non-Muslims" does not always come to an end with the partition of a country into Muslim and non-Muslim homelands. At times, it goes to the extent of claiming control of the Muslim community over the whole length and breadth of the country, thereby bringing non-Muslims under the domination of Muslims. Thus, as late as March 1965, an article in *Dawn* linked the idea of a Muslim homeland with the "Jehad Movement" whose objective was "to re-establish a Muslim state on the sub-continent."[7] This objective was not completely lost sight of by Bhutto. In his statement on 25 October 1965, he abused India and reminded members of the Security Council of 800 years of Muslim domination in India.[8] "The demand for Pakistan," declared Pakistan's Minister for Education, A.T.M. Mustafa, "is the expression of the deepest inner yearning of the Muslim to live—as a Muslim—in his own historical cultural connotations." He spurned "all the concepts of text-book nationalism" as well as the idea of the modern State. Instead, he averred the religious basis of nationhood and the universal concept of the State underlying the ideology of "Muslim nationalism," enshrined in Pakistan, whose nationalism was not defined by "rivers, mountains or climatic zones." To quote him further :

> The universal concept of State underlies the basic concep-
> tion of Pakistan—and Pakistan is a State of universal con-
> cept in miniature, transcending the barriers of geography,
> race, language, colour, class and secular creed.

Mustafa went on to state that Pakistan was conceived "in the ideals of its origin and dedicated to its goal." He added : "The destiny of Pakistan is interlinked with the historical role of this ideal and with the success or failure of its life-view."

Like Marxism, the Education Minister of Pakistan con-sidered Pakistan both as an embodiment of a universal concept with its own life-view and "a movement" of great significance for the transformation and salvation of entire humanity. Of the four living civilizations in the world today—the Muslim, the Western, the Communist and the Indian—(the order of listing is not without significance), he said, "it seems that the Muslim civilization is *materially* the weakest lacking in strength, cohesiveness and requisite homegeneity in a heterogeneous world society of a composite character. Pakistan is the flag-bearer of this civilisation today." Accordingly, Pakistan was described as "the most important thing" that had happened to the Muslims after the Holy Prophet and Khulafa-e-Rashedeen. The creation of Pakistan—"the land of the Pure"—and the conclusion of the Istanbul Pact (Regional Cooperation Deve-lopment comprising Pakistan, Iran and Turkey) were hailed as "one of the greatest achievements of President Ayub Khan." They were said to make possible the emergence of "a sixth continent of Muslim nations occupying the middle world, representing the middle path between the giants astride this planet." Further elaborating the ideological moorings, aspira-tions and the basic concept underlying the historic Pakistan movement, Pakistan's Education Minister Mustafa observed :

> The concept of Pakistan taken to its logical conclusion, and
> the Istanbul Pact is a logical extension of the basic assump-
> tions underlying Pakistan, may possibly have the signifi-
> cant historical destiny of *uniting the Muslim peoples and the
> Muslim Nations* under the common banner of Islam in
> defence of their basic life-view and life perspective in its
> essential fundamental : their common historical heritage,

traditions and culture, their common values, regulative principles of life and doctrinal institutions, their common concepts, convictions and beliefs, and the small disunited, weak, vulnerable Muslim countries of today, may, in the historical process of a contracting world, be transformed into the mighty giant of a Muslim Commonwealth tomorrow. It may and probably does sound unpractical and visionary to a practical politician. But so was Pakistan a vision and a dream only two decades ago. If ever the Muslims recapture the vision of Islam, rediscover the ideals of the Holy Prophet and recapture the vision of a Muslim Millat indivisible, united and one as the Holy Quran ordained, we shall represent not only the revolutionary theoretical concepts of Islam in the world scene, contending for the heart and soul of man in competition with the rest of the theoretical life concepts in the world today; we may also transform ourselves into a mighty and powerful human combination capable of projecting ourselves adequately enough to meet the challenge of our common problems— the challenge of life and of this Atomic Age and carve for ourselves a place of honour and dignity in this ruthless world and evoke the respect and attention vouchsafed to us by our 'FAITH'.[9]

Foreign policy, to quote Samin Khan again, "is invariably the instrument through which the conflicts, problems and the ideology of a country are intentionally and unintentionally exported abroad."[10] Thus, one very important and powerful motivating factor in Pakistan's foreign relations, that had nothing in common with India's secular nationalism,[11] had been the belief in the concept of the two-nation theory and its projection on the world arena. As distinguished from the efforts to build communal harmony and a multi-religious society in India, Pakistan's approach had been one of treating Muslims as a separate—and privileged—class from others. In fact, the origins of Pakistan can be traced, as the Education Minister of India, Mohemmedali Currim Chagla, once pointed out, "to religious apartheid"—a manifestation of which was the two-nation theory, that is, Muslims and others are separate nations.[12]

Implicit in this concept of the two-nation theory is the demand of redrawing the political boundaries "with due regard to cultural and geographical realities."[13] The use of force for the accomplishment of this objective was fully justified in the name of *Jehad* or holy war and the cry of "Islam in danger" was often raised.[14] In support of this demand, the principle of self-determination and the idea of complete freedom from foreign rule were also advanced and for its realization the support of international forces invoked. "Islam," the Prime Minister of Pakistan, Khwaja Nazimuddin, said in October 1951, "is a body and the Moslem States represent the limbs of this body." The assertion of the right of religious minorities to statehood, accompanied as it was with clamour for international support, would hardly be conducive to peace in the world. Such an approach was likely to result in prolonged struggles, leading to frequent civil wars and, possibly, the break-up of multi-national States.

Concern for Muslims in Other Lands

Pakistan's concern for Muslims in Kashmir and other parts of India was not the only offshoot of this communal approach projected by Pakistan in international relations. This approach was also considered for application to the Muslims in Ceylon, Burma, China, the Soviet Union and other countries of Asia and was quite in consonance with the philosophy on which Pakistan was based. Addressing a student meeting in Dacca on 9 December 1956, Prime Minister of Pakistan, H.S. Suhrawardy, declared :

> There is that Muslim sentiment in all our hearts which goes out whenever we find any brother Muslim anywhere else being subjected to some kind of pressure or attack. It is something which is inborn in us.

Suhrawardy desired that the Muslim countries should sit together, consult and act together for a common cause.[15]

In an editorial on 24 March 1965, the *Morning News* of Pakistan called it "an encouraging sign of our time" that Islam which had been thrown in the backwaters for the last 200 years was now emerging as a force in world affairs. The editorial was commenting on the "Afro-Asian Muslim Conference" in which about 33 Muslim countries "including representatives from Muslim populations under non-Muslim control" were said to have participated. The Conference appealed to Muslim peoples all over the world to come closer and to know each other's problems. It "supported the cause of self-determination and the application of human rights in respect of Muslim peoples" throughout the world. The resolutions passed at the Conference "demanded protection of Muslim minorities in non-Muslim countries against crimes of genocide and political, economic and cultural discrimination or any other violation of fundamental human rights." A permanent organization to achieve the objective was also established by the Conference.[16]

Choudhury Rahmat Ali, in a study *Pakistan : The Fatherland of Pak Nation*, declared that, as a Muslim land, Pakistan's "fate and fortune are indissolubly linked" with the Muslim world. (He even coined a new word "Pakasians" or "Pure Asians.") He pleaded for the integration of Muslims of Western Ceylon and the Ameen Islands into Safistan, the integration of Muslims of Eastern Ceylon into Nasaristan and such other integrations in other nations, for the purpose of uniting all these nations later into a Pak Commonwealth of Nations. He said : "To us, the Pakasians, union is not only a source of strength, but also a sacred duty." He added :

> Hence this commandment, which means we must bring together in an inter-national organization at least our ten countries—Pakistan, Bangistan, Osmanistan, Siddiqistan, Faruqistan, Haideristan, Muinistan, Safistan and Nasaristan.

He then ordained : "Secure the Millat, and above all re-establish the cause of Islam throughout Pakasia."[17]

Muslims in Burma

The so-called future of Northern Arakan became a subject of burning controversy between Pakistan and Burma because Pakistan would not give up its support to the cause of its Muslim brethren. In Northern Arakan, which is contiguous to the border of Pakistan, the Muslims form 60 percent of the population of Buthidaung township and 45 per cent of the township of Maungdaw. These Muslims were classified in the Burmese census as Pakistanis but the External Affairs Department of the Pakistan Government disagreed with this view. The rivalry between the two communities was intensified during World War II. A section of the Burmese population rendered assistance to the Japenese and the Muslims came to be armed by the British for guerilla warfare. Even after the attainment of independence by Burma and Pakistan, the guerilla activities of Muslims did not cease but continued under the name of "Mujahid Movement" which resisted Burmese central government control. The Burmese press accused Pakistan a number of times of giving not only sanctuary to the rebels in East Pakistan but also of rendering material and moral assistance to them. The issue of "Mujahids" or the so-called "freedom-fighters," headed by Kasim, was the subject of heated discussion in the Burmese Parliament and was also referred to by Pakistan's Foreign Minister Hamidul Huq Chowdhury in the National Assembly on 26 March 1956. Chowdhury informed the Assembly of the despatch of a Pakistani delegation to Burma "to discuss and settle certain matters of mutual interest." He described "the problem of the Arakanese Muslims" as "an off-shoot of the Mujahid problem." He called upon the Burmese Government to "do their utmost to create a sense of confidence and security in the mind of the Arakani Muslims now living in Arakan" and to take back all Arakanese refugees staying in East Bengal.[18]

Maulvi Zahiruddin Ahmad, who was "President" of a 'Republic' of the Buthidaung and Maungdaw areas during the days of resistance to the Japanese invaders in World War II, asserted that 99 per cent of the population of northern Arakan had close cultural, racial and religious affinities with the people of Chittagong and that, during the War, the Burmese were hostile to the Muslims of this area and indulged in mass massacres. He, therefore, suggested that the people of northern Arakan be given the right of self-determination and that a plebiscite be held to determine whether the area, inhabited by Muslims, should continue to be a part of Burma or be merged with Bengal.

The author of *The Basis of Pakistan* endorsed this demand when he stated : "Obviously, a very democratic process has been suggested." He went on to remark :

Northern Arakan is important to Bengal as a granary and in the event of the establishment of Pakistan, its economic and strategic significance will be great. U. Aung San has recently discussed the matter with Mr. Jinnah in Karachi and the 'status quo' has been accepted for the time being, but this is an issue which is likely to crop up for decision later on.[19]

In December 1951, it was reported in the *New York Times* that during the last three years nearly 250,000 Arakan Muslims had crossed into East Bengal. The latest influx, which started in May 1951, resulted in the entry of 30,000 more Muslims. The continued influx of these Arakan Muslims into East Bengal, the newspaper report said, was the subject of a strong protest note addressed by the Pakistan Government to the Burmese Government warning it against the possibility of disturbances by the refugees on the international border. The note also asked for the immediate repatriation of Arakan Muslims.[20] In the summer of 1959, about 10,000 Muslims were said to have crossed into East Pakistan. However, so far as Burmese newspapers and authorities were concerned, the problem was one of illegal entry of Pakistanis into Burma and their repatriation. Columnist U Yan Gon wrote in the Burmese paper, *Rangoon Daily*, on 17 January 1964 :

> There are some 200,000 people who have illegally migrated from Pakistan into Burma. A large number of these illegal immigrants have been interned and fed in the Akyab prison by the Burmese Government as the Pakistan Government refused to recognise them as its citizens. It is surprising that Pakistan did not accept them, although they actually belong to that country. We are afraid that the illicit Pakistanis' entry into Burma may in future become a problem like the illegal migration of Pakistanis into India. These people have moved into Assam, Tripura and West Bengal.

The Burmese columnist denied the existence of a problem like the Kashmir issue between Pakistan and Burma. However, he expressed serious concern about Pakistani infiltration into Akyab district. Speaking of the Arakan Muslims, W. Norman Brown observed :

> The community has felt itself insufficiently represented in Burma government affairs, considered itself discriminated against by the majority Buddhist community—as did the Muslims of India in relation to the Hindus—and some of its members have indicated a desire to be a part of Pakistan.[21]

There had been many areas of friction between Burma and

Pakistan, for instance, the smuggling of rice from Burma into East Pakistan, which resulted in the loss of foreign exchange to Burma and the border problem, which was the subject of much discussion between the two governments from 1959 onwards. However, it was the demand of the Muslim community on the Arakan coast for separation from Burma and merger with Pakistan that demonstrated the desire of Pakistan to inject its two-nation theory into all neighbouring areas.

Muslims in Soviet Central Asia

Pakistan was no less concerned with the fate of millions of Muslims of Turkistan in the Asiatic part of the Soviet Union. (A British writer put the figure at approximately twenty-four and a half millions.[22]) These Muslims, living in the five Republics of Kazakhstan, Uzbekistan, Tajikistan, Kirghizia and Turkmenia, with Karakalpakistan as an "Autonomous" S.S.R. within Uzbekistan, were seen not only as totally distinct from the Russians but also as discriminated against and trampled upon by the latter (a Western writer called the reduction in the Kazak population 'genocide'[23]) and aspiring for their national independence from the Soviet yoke. "Pakistanis," Sarwar Hasan observed, "were profoundly interested in the Republics of Central Asia, the Turkistan of the pre-Soviet days, with which they had not only religious but deep racial, cultural and historical ties." He asked : "Were not the arches and domes of Samarkand the prototypes of those of Lahore ?" and added, "and Turkistan was just a few miles from Pakistan's frontier." Although the Soviet achievements in agricultural and industrial development amid social conditions similar to those obtaining in Pakistan were considered "impressive," it was, at the same time, asserted that "development is not everything."

Sarwar Hasan recalled the famous appeal, issued by Lenin and Stalin in December 1917, to all "toiling and disinherited Moslems of Russia and the East." In that appeal, all those whose mosques and prayer houses were destroyed and whose religion and customs trampled upon by the Russian Czars and tyrants were assured that henceforward their beliefs and customs, their "national and cultural institutions are declared free and inviolable ! Build your national life freely and without hindrance." The famous Declaration of Rights, issued earlier over the names of Lenin and of Stalin, had declared "equality and sovereignty of the nations of Russia" and their right to "free self-determination, including the right to secede and form independent states..." Despite all that, Sarwar Hasan expressed doubt about the sincerity of Soviet rulers. He observed :

> Pakistan wondered to what extent the faith and customs and national and cultural institutions of the Muslims of Turkistan were free and whether they had really been able to build up their national life unhindered.[24]

It may be recalled that during the difficult and uneasy period between the October Revolution of 1917 and the consolidation of Soviet power in 1924, three autonomous States were said to have been set up within Turkistan-Kokand (in Farghana), Bukhara and Alash Orda (on the Kazak steppe). The second Turkistan Muslim Congress, held in Samarkand in April 1922, adopted a resolution which, *inter alia,* declared : "Should the Soviet Government not restore to them [Muslims] their political and cultural rights, we the Muslims of Turkistan, with or without arms, will wage war on the Soviet Government to the last drop of our blood." In 1937, the Prime Minister of Uzbekistan, Faizullah Khan, and the First Secretary of the Communist Party of Uzbekistan, Ikram, who were accused, among other things, of 'nationalism' and of being British agents and were executed, admitted that they had worked for the independence of Turkistan from Soviet rule.[25] As was to be expected, Moscow could not accede to any demand for separation of its territory. Stalin considered the principle of self-determination and the right of secession inapplicable in the USSR. He "bluntly" declared that the right of self-determination could not and "must not serve as an obstacle to the exercise by the working class of its right to dictatorship" and must give way to the latter.[26]

With the participation of Pakistan in Western military alliances, an attempt was made to find some common ground between the ideology of Pakistan and that of Western democracies against communism. Thus, in a study of the Pakistan Institute of International Affairs, G.W. Choudhury asserted :

> The ideology of Pakistan is based on the principles of

Islam, just as the broad ideals of Judeo-Christian ethics have provided the basic notions of the Western democracies. The similarity between the two makes intercourse between Pakistan and the West easy and natural. On the other hand, the ethics of communism are based upon power and materialism.

He then quoted Richard N. Frye as saying :

Communism has a blueprint for salvation which makes society or state a higher plane of reality than the individual. In spite of the social and legal aspects of the Judeo-Christian tradition and of Islam, it is the individual soul which is important in the three great religions. If communism and Christianity are incompatible, so are communism and Islam...for communism usurps for man the rights of God.[27]

In 1961, Samin Khan, referring to Pakistan's attitude towards the Soviet Union, observed that both Pakistan and the USSR were ideological States "with obvious territorial ambitions." Conflict between the two was, therefore, "inevitable." The ideology represented by the Soviet Union, he said, was more acceptable to the people of Asia and Africa than the ideologies of the West. It was, however, no longer revolutionary and was experiencing 'bourgeois' decadence. He said that inter-continental ballistic missiles and other scientific achievements had diminished the chances of war between the Soviet Union and the West and the constant "inter-action of ideologies" would result in the disappearance of conflict between them. After thus appraising the ideological and other factors, Samin Khan declared :

Our policy towards the Soviet Union should be based on this important principle, that we have to 'liberate' the Muslims in the U.S.S.R. from Soviet domination. If the West is prepared to help in 'liberating' these Muslims living in a strategic area, then we should make common cause with the West. However if the West wants to involve us in the cold war without any commitment on their part, then we should, for the time being and until we are strong, remain neutral in the cold war *vis-a-vis* Central Asia. Anyhow the international situation is such that the West, cornered as it is now and on the defensive both ideologically and militarily, has no other alternative than to accept this demand of ours.[28]

Some of the members of the Pakistani delegations, that visited the USSR, spoke in critical terms about the treatment of Muslims in Central Asia and Azerbaidzhan on their return to Pakistan. Thus, Maulana Wahab stated : "The Muslims have little or no voice in the Central Government and Administration ; their Republics are slaves and serfs of Moscow."[29]

Pakistan's concern for the large Muslim population in China was no less acute. This has been discussed in detail in the author's book *China, Pakistan and Bangladesh*.[30]

To his Muslim brethren in India, Ceylon, Burma, Soviet Central Asia, Sinkiang (China) or other areas, therefore, the moral that the very creation and existence of Pakistan conveyed was that if they were repressed by the majority community and two communities could not live together, then the Muslim minority had every right to have their own separate state. This was considered necessary "to save Islam from complete annihilation" in the country, to use the words of Quaid-e-Azam Jinnah.[31] Thus, the creation of separate Muslim states and the survival of Islam were considered as two facets of the same problem.

Relations with India

Before Pakistan came into existence, the leaders of the Muslim League often talked of striving for good neighbourly relations between India and Pakistan. The author of the book entitled *The Basis of Pakistan*, written on the eve of the partition of India, observed that "in a condition of discord and civil war none can retain their freedom." H.S. Suhrawardy, the Muslim League Premier of Bengal who later became Prime Minister of Pakistan, underscored that view in the Foreword he wrote to that book. He said : "It is impossible now to visualize that Hindustan and Pakistan will always exist in a perpetual state of hatred and conflict."[32] Three years earlier, Jinnah, in an interview with newspaper correspondents on 5 October 1944, stated that Pakistan would have good neighbourly relations with post-partition India. He added : "We will say 'hands off India' to all outsiders." He went on to say that Pakistan would not tolerate any outside design or aggression on the sub-continent and that Pakistan would observe something like the Monroe doctrine so far as the Indo-Pakistan sub-continent was concerned.[33]

The author of *The Basis of Pakistan* elaborated this idea of the founder of Pakistan. He observed : "When the passions of the moment die out, Pakistan and Hindustan, while remaining independent, may work out a system of joint defence on the basis of common interest." The US, Canadian and Pan-American defence were cited as instances in point. He also endorsed the idea put forward by K.M. Panikkar, the Indian author of the book *The Future of South-East Asia*, that India, Pakistan and Burma should organize themselves for common defence and peace in Southeast Asia. A similar idea of South Asiatic solidarity, he said, was stressed by H.H. The Aga Khan. In an interview in Bombay in February 1946, Aga Khan stated : "I envisage a Pakistan as part of an Indian and South Asiatic Confederation, to include Burma and Siam, in the east, probably Afghanistan and possibly Iran in the West and certainly Ceylon in the South—a great Asiatic Confederation." Amplifying his idea, he added :

> This confederation would have no frontiers between its constituent members in the normal sense of the word, each state being a unit, like the units of the British Commonwealth. All those things which affected the confederation as a whole would have to be handled by a body representing all the units of the federation, while in other matters each unit would look after its own affairs and would work out its own social, economic and intellectual life.[34]

All such ideas, based as they were on the concept of territorial nationalism, obviously militated against the ideological bases of Pakistan and, therefore, were soon abandoned. The restraint in speech concerning good neighbourly relations with India was probably the result of tactical considerations, and it disappeared with the attainment of the objective, *i.e.* the establishment of Pakistan. Once the decision to incorporate Jammu & Kashmir in Pakistan by force was taken, hostility towards India became such an important factor in Pakistan's foreign policy that it came to colour every aspect thereof, including relations with the Soviet Union.

In the early years of their independent career, the leaders of Pakistan set out to formulate the internal and external policies of Pakistan in terms, which, in some ways, were not the same as they emerged in the second half of the 1950s. It was then considered that there would be a great measure of state control, if not the immediate establishment of socialism. As early as 8 November 1945, in an interview to an Associated Press of America correspondent, Jinnah categorically declared that Pakistan would be a democracy in which major industries and public utilities would be socialized. At the Civil Aviation Conference, held in New Delhi in February 1947, the (Muslim League) Member for Communications in the Interim Government, Sardar Abdur Rab Nishtar, stated that he had never concealed his preference for nationalization. The draft manifesto of the Bengal Provincial Muslim League spoke of the immediate nationalization of all key industries beginning with transport, abolition of the Permanent Zamindari Settlement and rigid control of all forms of vested interests "whether on land or in capital."[35] The presence of Birla and Tata, on the other hand, was considered as an obstacle in the way of state planning on socialist lines in India.

In the external field, Pakistan was not so committed to the Western bloc as it became after its acceptance of US military aid. Pakistan was the only non-communist country to vote against the resolution recommending that the Interim Committee, the creation of which in 1947 was supported by Pakistan but strongly opposed by the Soviet bloc, be continued for an indefinite period. In 1950, Pakistan voted in favour of the representation of China in the UN General Assembly. In the same year, the Deputy Foreign Minister of Pakistan, Mahmud Hussain, stated that the basic aspiration of Pakistan's foreign policy was to preserve good relations with both the Soviet and Western blocs. Despite Commonwealth ties, he said, "we do not regard ourselves as members of either or any bloc." He was also reported to have remarked that Karachi had intended to recognize the Bao Dai regime in Indo-China but was now holding off for a while as "recent trends indicate it might not be there to stay and we don't wish to recognize a regime that will fall."[36]

Relations with the West

But on certain important issues between the East and the

West, Pakistan's attitude was definitely more favourably inclined towards the Western Powers. Thus, Pakistan became a
member of the Balkan Committee, which the Russians boy-
cotted, and the Commission for the Rehabilitation and Unification of Korea. Pakistan also voted in favour of the "Uniting
for Peace" resolution and the General Assembly resolution
on the initial action in Korea. American prospectors were
invited to locate oil in Baluchistan as early as 1948. In the
beginning of 1949, the *Times* (London) wrote that "neither
Communism nor Socialism is in a position to challenge the
present right-wing theocratic regime" in Pakistan. Communism, it said, was less of a threat in Pakistan than in most
countries east of Suez and, significantly enough, Pakistan had
not yet responded to Soviet overtures for an exchange of
representatives. The Commonwealth, that is Britain, promised all possible help in developing Pakistan's economy and
there existed "remarkable rapprochement between Pakistan
and British civil servants."[37]

In 1951, Pakistan unhesitatingly lined up with the United
States and its allies against the Soviet Union and China when
it signed the San Francisco Peace Treaty with Japan. Zaf-
rulla Khan described that Treaty as the embodiment of "justice and reconciliation." The alignment with the Western
Powers gave Pakistan some bargaining position over them,
especially *vis-a-vis* India. Thus, according to the London
Times the Pakistani Prime Minister's threat to postpone his
departure to London to attend the Commonwealth Premiers'
Conference unless the Kashmir issue was put on its agenda
succeeded and the British bowed down.[38] Robert Trumbull,
while reporting about the firm alignment of Pakistan with the
United States in signing the Peace Treaty with Japan, considered the grant of a $190 million loan to India for the purchase
of grain as "an irritant to Pakistan" and warned against the
cooling off of Pakistan towards the West in the following
words :

> If Pakistan's foreign policy should take the direction that
> increasingly is being advocated here [Karachi], the United
> States will have lost her one sure friend in South Asia..... .
> Pakistan, as part of the world strategic picture, happens to
> involve Khyber Pass, historic invasion route to India, the

important port and air base of Karachi, which was key staging point for United States forces in World War II; an army of about 250,000 crack troops and a population of about 80,000,000, who form one of the few Asian nations self-sufficient in food.[39]

Khwaja Nazimuddin, who became Prime Minister of Pakistan after Liaquat Ali Khan's assassination, in a speech on 21 October 1951, declared :

Besides the Moslem States, we have friendly relations with other countries. I count among these states the countries of the Commonwealth. I include America and, in addition to these, other countries of the world.

The omission here of the Soviet Union, China, India, of course, and other Afro-Asian countries is significant. Nazimuddin was also reported to have stated that Pakistan would "favourably consider" sending troops to join the United Nations force in Korea if the Kashmir issue was settled to Pakistan's satisfaction.

The years 1952-53 may be said to be the turning point in Pakistan's foreign policy as during the next eight years—a period coinciding with Republican rule in the United States—the international posture of Pakistan changed considerably. The motivating factor was its obsession with Kashmir and animosity towards India. Pakistan accepted United States' military assistance and entered into such alliances as the SEATO and the Baghdad Pact (renamed CENTO in August 1959)—thereby effectively committing itself to the side of the Western Powers. In these circumstances, Pakistan came to support Western policies on the question of Hungary and disarmament. In 1956, the Pakistani Foreign Minister referred to Pakistan's relations with the West as "bound by closest ties of mutual understanding." Premier Suhrawardy gave the most powerful support to the Baghdad Pact during the Suez crisis when anti-Western feelings were running high in other Muslim countries. The special study mission of the House Foreign Affairs Committee of the United States in 1955 found Pakistan "the largest and strongest military force allied with the Free World between Turkey and Taiwan."

Washington offered economic aid to Pakistan in November

1950 which was accepted in February 1951. It has now been revealed that as early as August 1951, the Commander-in-Chief of the Pakistan army, General Ayub Khan, suggested that Pakistan join in military alliance with powerful United States.[40] It has also recently come to light that, long before John Foster Dulles publicly broached the idea of "Northern Tier" nations in the Middle East, the Pentagon was seriously thinking of filling the gap in its system of military bases and "defensive organizations" in the Middle East area. The Editor-in-Chief of *Al Ahram*, Mohammed Hassanein Heikal, recalls in his Cairo paper that he had heard of the idea of an Islamic Pact, for the first time, in 1952 from the Director of Military Aid Projects, General Olmstead, in the course of an interview with him in Washington at the Pentagon. General Olmstead asked Heikal about filling the vacuum in the Middle East with an "Islamic Pact" which was to have three axes : Turkey—the strongest Islamic country; Pakistan—the most populous; and Egypt—the most influential, considering that *Al Azhar* was in its capital. "Such a pact," he said, "would not only resist communism but would also attract the attention of a hundred millions in China and the Soviet Union.[41] It was thought that Egypt, as a leading country in the Middle East, might feel attracted towards this scheme. In a pamphlet, *The Philosophy of the Egyptian Revolution*, Col. Nasser wrote as follows :

> I often think of the 80 million Moslems in Indonesia, the 50 millions in China, the several millions in Malaya, Siam and Burma, the close on 100 millions in Pakistan, the more than 100 millions in the Middle East, the 40 millions inside the U.S S.R. and the several million others scattered in various parts of the world. When I consider these hundreds of millions united by the same faith, I get a powerful impression of the immense possibilities which could be realised by the cooperation of all Moslems. This cooperation would naturally not negate their loyalty to their countries of origin. But it would insure them all an illimitable force.

Thus, while Col. Nasser sympathized with the idea of "cooperation of all Moslems" in the world, he did not sacrifice either territorial nationalism or "loyalty to the Arab race" at the altar of Islamic ideology in its universal concept, as conceived by Pakistan. For Pakistan, which believed that Islam

itself was a nationality, such ideas as those of Nasser seemed
both strange and dangerous—strange because "the racial distinction" between an Arab and non-Arab country had never
existed in Islamic history and dangerous because for a Muslim
country to discard the Islamic ideology in favour of "outmoded racialism" was bound to provoke "reaction within the
Islamic civilization and further intensify divisions" and, finally,
lead to its disintegration. To Pakistan, the ideas of Col. Nasser
were "ulcers of racialism and geographical nationalism" that
had become engrafted on the body politic of Islam, eating into
its vitals, while that of General Olmstead seemed appealing.
The author of *Pakistan Seeks Security* observes :

> Already Central Asia is lost ; Bokhara and Merv are no
> longer Muslim ; part of the Islamic homeland is lost to the
> Jews. If things continue moving as at present, part of the
> Muslim homeland will be blown up and the other part
> bound down by allegiance, cultural or total.[42]

The contrast between the views of Pakistan, based as they
are on religious fanaticism, and those of other Muslim countries is described by Keith Callard in the following words :

> In fact the political upsurge elsewhere was based largely on
> territorial and racial nationalism, anti-Western, anti-White.
> Religion played a part in this, but it was a lesser part than
> colour, language and a political theory of violent opposition
> to 'colonialism' and 'exploitation'. For many Muslims
> elsewhere it has been more important to align Asians and
> Africans against the colonial powers than to defend Muslim
> causes against non-Muslims....
> Pakistan was less tempted than certain other countries by
> the concept of Asian (or non-white) solidarity.
> Pakistan was founded on the basis of the vital [religious]
> difference between groups of Asians, and her leaders can
> perceive much more dangerous potential enemies than the
> colonial powers of Europe.[43]

It was, therefore, hardly surprising that no sooner than
Pakistan came into existence, it started projecting its philosophy
and ideology. Pakistan took early steps to foster closer links
with the Muslim world. In 1949, the Pakistan Government
proposed holding a general Islamic Conference. The plan,
however, failed to materialize. Towards the end of that year

the first International Islamic Economic Conference was held in Karachi. In 1949 and 1951 the *Motamar-i-Alam-i-Islami*, a local group, held (so-called) World Muslim Conferences at Karachi which did succeed in attracting delegates from several Muslim countries, but a more ambitious plan for a permanent consultative organization of Muslim States had to be abandoned because of the reluctance of some of the invited governments. Arab nationalism proved strong enough to scuttle the moves towards an Islamic alliance. In the wake of the Arab-Israeli Conflict of 1967, however, the idea of regular periodic Islamic Conferences and the establishment of Islamic Secretariat did succeed in making much headway. Nasser's successor, Sadat, had to depend on the subsidy provided by Saudi Arabia and others. The Muslim states deemed it necessary to unite their efforts for the defence and promotion of their interests, particularly the Arab interests against Israel.

In the early part of 1952, Pakistan tried to show sympathy for the cause of Arab states in order to make success of the meeting of twelve Muslim states, whose Prime Ministers it had invited to meet in Karachi in April 1952 to discuss matters of mutual interest. The idea behind that meeting was to establish Pakistan as the leading Power among Islamic nations. Thus, the Foreign Minister of Pakistan, Zafrullah Khan, declared in Karachi on 21 March 1952 that Arab states must have satisfaction on the problems of the Arab refugees and the frontier with Israel before they could cooperate in a Middle East defence pact.[44] After Mohammad Ali came to power, a definite swing in Pakistan's policy towards the United States was noticeable. In April 1953, he had proposed a friendship pact with Washington. On the very first day of his becoming Prime Minister of Pakistan, Mohammed Ali declared that his country would "welcome opportunities to discuss with the Western Powers the immediate restoration of peace in this part of the world, including the Middle East." Karachi, which served 15 international airlines and was "the closest of all airbases of the free Asian countries to the Russian border," loomed large in Western strategic calculation. Asked about permitting the establishment of American and British air bases in Karachi, Mohammed Ali replied : "If we feel that our security is threatened, we certainly would prepare to consider all questions of guaranteeing that security with the countries that also think democratically." He declined to answer a question whether he would accept aid from the Soviet Union.[45]

Soon after the signing of the SEATO pact with his Western allies, Mohammed Ali visited Washington. From there, he brought back "substantial military aid" and economic assistance amounting to $105 million by the end of June 1955. The economic aid offered by the United States, he said in a broadcast to the nation on his return, was "five times as much as we have received in any previous year." As for military aid, he stated that it was not expedient for him "to disclose its extent or its nature." He, however, assured his countrymen that "it would be substantial and will powerfully reinforce and strengthen the defences of our country." Pakistan, he declared, had "a vital interest in the security and prosperity both of the Middle East and of South East Asia." He expressed a desire "to strengthen brotherly relations with all Muslim countries," but, at the same time, asserted that this would be without prejudice to his "belief in collective security" and his disdain of the policy of neutrality, which he considered "impracticable and unrealistic." For India, he had nothing but "bitterness and tension" until the "monstrously unjust" situation of denial of the right of self-determination for the people of Kashmir was remedied.[46] The proposed United States' military aid to Pakistan was described by Afghanistan's Prime Minister on 30 December 1954 as "a grave danger to the security and peace of Afghanistan."

With the signing of the Mutual Defence Assistance Agreement on 19 May 1954, US military aid began to pour in Pakistan. It might be recalled that Pakistan's Governor-General and Commander-in-Chief had visited Washington in November 1953. US military aid continued to increase after Pakistan joined the SEATO in September 1954 and became a member of the Baghdad Pact a year later. In December 1960, the US Consul-General in Lahore estimated that his country had made available to Pakistan $1,292 million for economic requirements since February 1951.[47] Although the extent of military aid had not been officially disclosed (at Pakistan's request), it was estimated that it had been of the order of $3 billion, of which no less than $1,300 million had been in military hardware.[48]

It is often asserted that Pakistan was forced to accept United States' assistance because of its critical economic situation. In support of this argument, it is said that in 1952 Pakistan had a deficit of Rs.321 million in its balance of trade and that in 1953 Pakistan faced a desperate food situation, which was overcome by a gift of 610,000 tons of wheat worth $67.2 million from the United States. Here, it should not be forgotten that in 1953 Pakistan had a surplus of Rs. 295 million in its balance of trade. Moreover, the so-called critical economic situation could hardly be said to be a justification for the acceptance of military assistance. Nor should the fact be ignored that much of Pakistan's economic ills could very well be traced to heavy defence expenditure—running as high as 75 per cent of the budget. The real reasons for the close relationship between the United States and Pakistan are aptly described by Keith Callard in the following words :

> In 1953 two changes took place. In the United States, Eisenhowever was installed as President with J.F. Dulles as Secretary of State; in Pakistan, Ghulam Mohammad dismissed Nazimuddin and replaced him as Prime Minister by Mohammed Ali, formerly Ambassador in Washington. Mr. Dulles wanted pacts; Mr. Mohammed Ali liked Americans. Pakistan wanted money and arms.[49]

What is probably ignored by Callard is the fact that Pakistan desired arms from the Western Powers primarily, if not solely, to strengthen itself against India. The Prime Minister of Pakistan, Feroz Khan Noon, emphatically stated, before the National Assembly, that the purpose of defensive pacts was to provide security against India. If they did not achieve that end, he was even prepared to break those pacts and work with the countries against whom they were allegedly directed.[50] What Noon said verbally was later proved by Pakistan's actions—it used arms and equipment, obtained from the US, against India in the Rann of Kutch in April 1965 and again during the Indo-Pak conflict of August-September 1965. Islamabad, thus, violated the categorical assurances and solemn guarantees publicly given by the leaders of the United States that American arms and equipment supplied to Pakistan would not be used against India. The assurances given by Pakistan's Prime Minister to Chou-En-lai at Bandung also proved beyond doubt what Pakistan's real motive was in joining the pacts.[51] In this connection, the following remark of the Pakistani author of *Pakistan's External Relations* is quite significant. He observes :

> The security which Pakistan was searching for since she came into existence in 1947 was security against Indian aggression. SEATO does not cover, as has been pointed out, non-communist aggression. But the Baghdad Pact does not make any distinction between Communist or non-Communist aggression.[52]

With the participation of Pakistan in Western alliances, a political affinity came to be established between Pakistan and the Western Powers. If Dulles considered neutrality "immoral," the Foreign Minister of Pakistan no less held in derision the concept of neutralism.[53] Along with its Western friends, Pakistan considered the Soviet Union to be an expansionist Power bent on having an outlet in an ice-free port on the Indian Ocean. In that regard, it was said that Russia attempted to negotiate with Nazi Germany, during World War II, for certain advantages. Clause IV of draft Soviet protocol I, for instance, stated : "The Soviet Union declares that its territorial aspirations centre south of the national territory of the Soviet Union in the direction of the Indian Ocean." Soviet moves against Turkey and Iran, immediately after World War II, were also cited in support of that view. In support of these interests of the USSR, Arnold Toynbee considered Karachi a "tempting bait" which could not have failed to suggest "dangerous thoughts" to calculating Russian minds. This warning, as also Toynbee's idea regarding "a future empire builder from Central Asia," it seemed, was enthusiastically taken to heart by Pakistan. Just as Western nations endeavoured to free Eastern Europe from the influence of the Soviet Union, Pakistan aspired for the liberation of its Muslim brethren in Central Asia. Believing firmly in ideological homogeneity, based on Islam, and criticizing Egypt for not supporting "Kashmiri Muslims" in the manner desired by Pakistan, the author of *Pakistan Seeks Security* observes :

The Muslims of Central Asia have of course been forgotten. Were they not a source of strength to every Muslim country? Have they not a right to expect some recognition or moral support from every heartland and rimland Muslim country? Immediate kinship is so easy to recognise; but it is useful for every Muslim country to glance occasionally at the horizon and learn to appreciate and recognise ideological allies scattered all around. Narrowing of interests is a sure sign of decline which one should try to overcome.[54]

2
USSR-Pak Relations 1947-53

LIKE that of any other state, the foreign policy of the USSR is also basically motivated by its national interests. If the Marxist-Leninist ideology is said to be the guiding principle of Soviet state policy, it is because it serves as a cover or camouflage for promoting its national interests. The wearing of an ideological mask by the USSR—the first socialist state in the world—enables Moscow to exercise influence over the international communist movement. It gives the Kremlin a powerful leverage over both communist and non-communist regimes. Ideology, thus, is the handmaid of Soviet state policy.

The new regime in Soviet Russia, which was established after the 1917 October Revolution, found itself in capitalist encirclement. It had to face intervention by imperialist Powers. The requirements of survival dictated that it should seek common cause with the national liberation struggles in the colonies. The Comintern (Communist International) which was established in Moscow in 1919 to promote and guide the International Communist Movement in the world was said to be an organ of international communism and not of the Soviet state as such. But the colonial question, which became the major plank of Comintern's policy, gave sustenance to the Soviet policy of awakening the masses and stirring up unrest in colonies—the backyard of imperialist Powers. Since India was the mainstay of British imperialism, her struggle for independence was considered as directed against a common enemy. Accordingly, the Soviet leaders looked upon that struggle as a natural ally of the

Soviet Union. After Moscow became involved in a life and
death struggle against Nazi Germany, the Comintern was seen
as hampering close cooperation between the USSR and the
Allied Powers and was, therefore, abruptly dissolved in 1943.

Thus, in the first phase of the Second World War, when
Hitler was fighting against the Western Powers and had not
attacked the USSR (it had rather come to an understanding
with Stalin by signing a non-aggression Pact in 1939), Moscow
saw in the Indian struggle for freedom a positive development
aimed at weakening British power. The Muslim League, which
looked towards Britain for sustenance and support, was
castigated as a reactionary communal organization. A state
based on religion ran counter to the Marxist approach to the
question of defining a nation and the two-nation theory of
Jinnah had grave implications for the USSR, which had a
sizeable Muslim population in close proximity to the Indian
sub-continent. Moreover, the Muslim League was regarded as
"pro-imperialist" because the British encouraged its separatist
tendencies in every manner possible.[1]

V. Balabushevich and A. Dyakov, in an article published in
December 1940 in *Mirove Khoziaistvo*, criticized the Muslim
League for "disrupting the front of the struggle of the Indian
people for its independence." The Soviet scholars favourably
commented on those sections of the Muslim community in
India which lent support to the Indian National Congress. The
Soviet Union, thus, appeared contemptuous of the Muslim
League because of its communal outlook and also because of
its negative role which threatened to weaken the national libera-
tion movement directed against British imperialism.[2]

After Hitler invaded Russia and Moscow became engaged
in mortal combat with Nazi Germany, a certain change occurred in the Soviet attitude towards the Muslim League. Considerations of solidifying the wartime alliance with Britain
and intensification of the war efforts in India led Moscow to
modify its earlier stance towards the Congress and the League.
The Indian National Congress' refusal to support the British
war efforts in India, without a firm commitment on the part of
London to grant freedom to India soon after the War, was
viewed by the Soviet Union as an intransigent attitude. The

Communist Party of India (CPI) was prevailed upon to pursue a "pro-war line" and "united front" tactics.[3] The British war effort in the "People's War" against fascism thus came to be supported by the CPI. The British, on their part, removed, in July 1942, the ban they had imposed on the legality of the CPI two years earlier.

In these circumstances, the CPI dissociated itself from the Indian freedom struggle, directed as it was against an ally of the Soviet Union. In appreciation of the Muslim League's decision to support the war efforts of the British Government, the CPI gave up its earlier stand which regarded Congress as the main political party embodying the aspirations of the Indian people, Hindus and Muslims alike, for national independence.[4] The Muslim League was characterized as "the premier political organization of the second largest community in our country." The CPI leader P.C. Joshi, stated that the Congress had "some responsibility," along with the League, for the lack of communal unity and that it was "wrong and unrealistic" to denounce the Muslim League as a reactionary communal organization, which exercised influence over a large section of the Muslim population. He even desired that the Congress should concede the Muslim League's demand for a "separate state."[5]

The increasing warmth of the CPI for the Muslim League manifested itself not only in its approval of the League's aspirations but also in its criticism of the "Quit India" resolution of the Indian National Congress as "misguided" and "pernicious." By mid-1942, the CPI had begun to question the concept that India was a single nation and to support recognition of the principle of self-determination, including the right of separation, for "all the nationalities" that were said to inhabit the great Indian sub-continent. It thereby conceded to the Muslims the right to form their own autonomous state or states within the free Indian union or federation and even to secede therefrom if they so desired. A year later, the CPI described "the demand for Muslim self-determination or Pakistan" as "a just, progressive and national demand."[6] The changed CPI policy towards the Muslim League was adopted partly to secure a foothold among the Muslim masses and partly to cater to the war-time needs of Moscow. Soviet commentators also dealt sympathetically with the Muslim League. Support to the Quit India Movement was withheld and it was stated that a settlement of the Indian problem must await the defeat of Germany and Japan.[7]

After World War II, Stalin was pre-occupied with East Europe and internal economic reconstruction. He could not, therefore, pay much attention to developments in the Indian sub-continent. Moreover, greater awareness of the intricate situation in India led Moscow to adopt a cautious approach. Writing in 1946, the leading Soviet Indologist, A. Dyakov, described the Indian National Congress as "the most influential" of the national political organizations fighting for the attainment of "full independence." Under conditions obtaining in India, the social and economic programme of the Congress was considered progressive. At the same time, he adopted an equally sympathetic attitude towards the Muslim League which was regarded as the "most influential Muslim organization." The Congress, dominated by Hindus, he stated, had "paid little heed to the needs of Muslims." On the crucial question of Pakistan, however, Dyakov was cautious and, in a way, non-committal. On the one hand, he blamed the Congress for not acknowledging "the right of secession" in its programme as advocated by C. Rajagopalachari and some organizations, including the CPI. On the other hand, he stated that "many progressive Indian leaders consider that partition of India would not solve the Hindu-Muslim problem and would weaken India." Dyakov did not appear to expressly support the CPI line on partition but seemingly approved the Congress solution of transforming India into a loose federation with considerable political and administrative power remaining in the hands of the provinces rather than its division on a communal basis into two or even three separate states.[8]

By August 1946, the CPI position on the partition of India underwent some change. The demand for Pakistan was considered as an attempt on the part of the "Muslim bourgeoisie and feudal vested interests" to seek "a compromise with imperialism for a share of administration." The CPI resolution of August 1946 further asserted that the Indian masses supporting the Congress "rightly oppose the partition of India on a religious and undemocratic basis and correctly desire a single Union." It stated that the Muslims should agree to Congress-League unity "without making the acceptance of Pakistan a pre-condition."[9]

Despite certain apprehensions about the right-wing elements of the bourgeois National Congress making a bargain with the British authorities,[10] Nehru was praised, after the formation of the Interim Government under his leadership, as a "left-wing progressive."[11] Moreover, the establishment of diplomatic relations between the USSR and India in April 1947 was hailed as "a sign that India is moving towards an independent policy."[12] Yet Moscow looked with suspicion at the Asian Relations Conference, organized by Nehru in New Delhi in February 1947. E. Zhukov, a member of the Soviet delegation to that Conference, spoke of the positive contribution of Egypt, Indonesia, Indo-China and Burma. However, he attacked Nehru for his pro-British sentiments, which accounted for his eagerness to conciliate the West and failure to organize Asia in opposition to Western imperialism, as well as for his Pan-Asianism in which he suspected harbouring of expansionist ambitions in Asia. The prospect of India and China, either separately or in collaboration, filling up the power vacuum in Asia created by the defeat of Japan did not escape his attention.[13] India's policy of so-called strict neutrality in the conflict between the two blocs did not satisfy Zhukov. In reality, the theory about neutrality, he said, justified India's closeness with British imperialism. In that connection, he referred to a report presented at the Asian Relations Conference on "India and Inter-Asian Communications" by an official of the Transport Department of the Government of India. In the course of the report, the official made a statement : "The growth of Soviet power and its closeness to India necessitates the urgency to build roads in certain strategic places." According to Zhukov, that was not an isolated incident but reflected Indian subjugation to British political and military plans.[14]

After the acceptance of the Mountbatten Plan on the partition of India by the leaders of both the Congress and the Muslim League in June 1947, a clear change in Soviet policy was

visible. That plan, Dyakov stated, was accepted "under the
pressure of wealthy classes who would exploit the domestic
market, and avert *a real democratic revolution*."[15] Under the
impact of the Cold War, and the deterioration of UK-Soviet
relations in 1947, Moscow was adopting a hard line and
making things difficult for imperialist Western countries in
their erstwhile colonies. The Kremlin, therefore, disliked the
deal struck between British imperialism, on the one hand,
and the Congress and the Muslim League, on the other. In the
opinion of the Soviet Union, the leadership of both the major
parties in India was considered as representing big bourgeoisie. The political settlement that was effected as a result
of that deal was described as a new form of economic and
political dependence of the two dominions on British imperialism. The USSR saw in the Mountbatten Plan a clear
manoeuvre by the British authorities to retain India and Pakistan in a state of total dependence on themselves and to perpetuate their political and economic interests in the sub-continent.[16]

Thus, India and Pakistan, which attained independence in
August 1947, were looked upon by Moscow as appendages of
British imperialism. The Kremlin had doubts about their
being genuinely independent entities. "The partition of India,"
the *Great Soviet Encyclopaedia* observed, "enabled British
imperialism to weaken the economy of the country, and the
inflaming of differences between India and Pakistan has facilitated British domination in both dominions."[17] As a matter
of fact, India and Pakistan were described as "parts of the
British Empire, former British colonies, retaining to a different degree their dependence on Great Britain and...members
of the so-called British Commonwealth of Nations."[18]

In these circumstances, it is hardly surprising that the
Soviet publicity media paid no attention whatsoever to the
proclamation of Indian independence. The Kremlin did not
deem it necessary to extend felicitations to Pakistani leaders
on the occasion of the formal inaguration of their State. "How
primitive it is to create a State on the basis of religion," Stalin
told an Indian diplomat. He even expressed the view that a
federation between India and Pakistan "would be the ideal

solution."[19]   Soviet commentators had serious doubts about the prospect of Pakistan surviving as an independent State. Not only did Pakistan consist of geographically two separate and disunited parts, but the two wings of the country were also culturally, racially and linguistically distinct from each other.   Thus, A. Dyakov described Pakistan as an "artificial State" and observed that the "sole link" between its two parts was "a common religion."[20]

Besides, the economic base of the nation (Pakistan) was also not strong.   It had no large industrial centres and was extremely poor in mineral resources.   It was "an agrarian country and its economy bears a colonial character," remarked Dyakov.[21]   British capital investments in Pakistan were estimated at Rs. 1,000 million[22] and British monopolies held dominating positions in Pakistan's industry, foreign trade and finance.   Three of the four provincial Governors were British. British officials also occupied other key positions, both civil and military, in the administrative machinery of Pakistan. The British, thus, wielded considerable influence in Pakistan.   The partisan attitude adopted by the British on the Kashmir question gave additional leverage to them in Pakistan.   A Soviet writer described Pakistan as "a British bridgehead in the East...a second Trans-Jordan of enormous dimensions" and accused the reactionary ruling circles of Pakistan of allowing the continuance of British military bases in its territory.   The reactionary Muslim League was said to retain its influence over the masses by whipping their "pan-Islamic" and "anti-Hindustan" sentiments.[23]

Despite its criticism of Pakistani leadership, the Kremlin deemed it necessary to establish Soviet diplomatic presence in Karachi. Relations at the ambassadorial level were established with India as early as 28 June 1947. As for Pakistan, *Tass* announced on 2 May 1948, that the governments of the USSR and Pakistan had agreed to establish diplomatic relations. But the actual exchange of ambassadors encountered certain difficulties, although even the names of the ambassadors of Pakistan and the USSR were announced in October-November 1949. Since the Soviet Ambassador-designate, M. Ivan Nikolaevich, had held, from 1943 to 1947, the post of Soviet

Ambassador to Afghanistan, with whom Pakistan has a serious dispute over Pakhtoonistan, he was not acceptable to Karachi. Therefore, A.G. Stetsenko, the former Chancellor of the Soviet Embassy in London, was named in his place and he assumed office in Karachi on 15 March 1950—nearly three years after Pakistan achieved its independence.

Although quite a few Soviet delegations had visited Pakistan in 1949, the relations between USSR and Pakistan during the Stalin Era remained at a low ebb. The *New Times* comment that Pakistan was being made use of by Britain for establishing military bases near Soviet borders evoked strong resentment in Pakistani circles.[24] In the Commonwealth Relations Conference of 1949, the Pakistani delegate agreed with others that the Soviet Union was the potential enemy of Pakistan and suggested that long-term defence planning of the Commonwealth should be based on that assumption.[25]

The visit of the Russian trade delegation to Pakistan in 1949 was a failure. The leader and four members of the Soviet delegation were withdrawn before any agreement could be reached, and the remaining members of the delegation were unable to achieve any results by the end of 1949. The Rawalpindi Conspiracy Case, as a result of which two top-ranking Pakistani Communist leaders were jailed, and the Soviet condemnation of the convening of the first Islamic Economic Conference further exacerbated relations between the Soviet Union and Pakistan. The visit of four American Senators to the Khyber Pass and other places in Pakistan at the end of 1949 was interpreted in Moscow as indicating that "the American and British imperialists are interested in Pakistan not only as a market and field of investment, they are out to make it one of their military bases."[26] Pakistan's attitude in the Korean War—extending full support to the UN, condemning North Korean action as a clear case of aggression and its offer of 5,000 tons of wheat as a gift to the UN for use in South Korea—was also disliked by Moscow. The Kremlin was well aware of Pakistan already coming closer to the Western side in view of the support being given to Pakistan by the USA and the UK on the Kashmir issue.

An important episode in the early relations between Pakistan and the USSR was that a friendly invitation from the Soviet Union for Liaquat Ali Khan, Prime Minister of Pakistan, to visit Moscow was rebuffed despite its formal acceptance. The acceptance of the Moscow visit was regarded a popular step, and there was great jubilation among the masses. Though it was considered to be a counter-move to Indian Prime Minister Nehru's trip to the USA in 1949, it later turned out to be merely a ruse to draw the attention of the Western Powers towards Pakistan. Khan Abdul Qayum Khan, Premier of North-West Frontier Province, described the proposed visit to Moscow a great event. "A free and sovereign State such as ours," he said, "could not possibly carry on without contacts with the USSR,"[27] which is separated from Pakistan by a few miles of Afghanistan's Wakhan corridor. Liaquat Ali Khan also considered it "a friendly visit to a neighbouring country" and stated that Pakistan stood to gain from Soviet experience and assistance in the field of agriculture. He expressed the hope that he would avail of the invitation, which would be good for both countries, "as soon as possible."[28] A well-known Pakistani author, writing after the receipt of the invitation but before the visit was put aside in favour of a tour of the USA, observed that conflict between Pakistan and the USSR was neither imminent nor inevitable since the Soviet Union generally practised the doctrine that regions should be settled according to the wishes of the inhabitants.[29]

During his visit to the United States, Liaquat Ali Khan, in his speeches, made a determined attempt to attract the sympathy of Americans for Pakistan by inviting foreign investments and laying stress on respect for the rights of the individual enshrined in both Islam and Christianity.[30] The Pakistani Prime Minister's devotion to the encouragement of private enterprise and his conviction that communism was incompatible with Pakistan's Islamic way of life evoked a much more favourable response from the American Congress and Press than Nehru's exposition of non-alignment.[31]

An attempt to explain the rebuff—Pakistani rejection of the Soviet invitation to Liaquat Ali Khan—was made in a group study of the Pakistan Institute of International Affairs published in 1956. The explanation gave three reasons to prove that an alliance between the Soviet Union and Pakistan was "*ab initio* improbable."[32] One was based on the dogma that Marx and Allah cannot coexist together—that Pakistan's Islamic faith, which is "theistic and individualistic," has nothing in common with atheistic communism that "takes no account of the personality or the rights of the individual."[33] This reason can hardly be regarded as tenable, as many Muslim countries have friendly relations with the Soviet Union. The second attributes expansionist and imperialist motives to Soviet policy. "Pakistan had noticed the subservience which was forced upon the allies of the Soviet Union." Pakistan's independence, it added, had been won "after too profound a struggle for its loss to be risked." To say that Pakistan's independence was "won" after "too profound a struggle" is hardly true. Those possessing even an elementary knowledge of India's freedom struggle are well aware that Pakistan was the result of the Muslim League's complicity, if not conspiracy, with the British rulers and not of any freedom struggle waged against the British. Soviet experts on India were aware of that fact and as such the Muslim League was criticized by them in 1940 for disrupting "the front of the struggle of the Indian people for its independence." Khrushchov, in his speech in Srinagar in 1955, observed :

> If I may, I should like to state my opinion generally concerning the division of India into two States. We, the friends of India, were convinced that the imperialist forces succeeded in dividing India into two parts : India and Pakistan.[34]

The third reason given was that the Soviet Union could not have supplied the aid, both material and technical, which Pakistan so urgently required. It might be that Soviet assistance to Pakistan could not have been on the scale likely to be given by the United States. That was, however, no justification that Pakistan's Premier should not have availed of the invitation to visit Moscow after it had been accepted. If the reasons given were convincing to Pakistani leaders, then the question arises as to why they were overlooked at the time of the acceptance of the invitation. Thus, either the desire of Pakistan to use that invitation to extort the maximum advantage from the

USA or pressure on the part of the Western Powers seems to have been the reason for the change of mind of the Pakistani leaders regarding the Soviet invitation. The invitation was said to have caused a flutter in Western circles, the United Kingdom in particular, and Pakistan's becoming "a satellite of Russia,"[35] began to be talked about.

Liaquat Ali Khan's visit to the US proved highly rewarding. US economic (and later military) aid began to pour in Pakistan and with that Pakistan's policy started moving rapidly towards greater alignment with the West. The reason for Pakistan's acceptance of US assistance is sometimes said to be the adverse economic situation that Pakistan faced in 1952. However, this was the result of a highly inflated defence expenditure for as much as 70 per cent of the revenue budget went to the armed forces. Mustaq Ahmad tried to put things in proper perspective when he observed : "The impact of the economic crisis which hit the country in 1952 would not have been disastrous had the defence expenditure not been so enormous."[36] The acceptance of US military aid and participation of Pakistan in the SEATO and the CENTO, which followed in quick succession, were the cause of protest notes from both India and the Soviet Union. The Chinese Government, however, maintained studied silence and did not deliver any official protest to Pakistan.[37]

USSR-Pak relations were subjected to severe strains and stresses in the early part of the 1950s and relations between the two deteriorated steadily as rapport between the United States and Pakistan developed further. The Soviet disquiet and concern were aired in the Soviet press and other news media. Virulent personal attacks were levelled against Liaquat Ali Khan and his policy. The gift of 5,000 tons of wheat to the UN for use in South Korea was dubbed as "Liaquat Ali Khan's servile zeal."[38] Another Soviet magazine branded Liaquat Ali Khan as the "Pakistan type of Syngman Rhee" and strongly denounced his "zealous subservience to Washington." He was accused of turning Pakistan from a "British colony" to "an American colony." The Soviet magazine stated : "Liaquat Ali Khan returned to Karachi after assuring his American bosses that he would assist their plans for the enslavement of Pakistan and converting it into a political, economic and strategic Asian base

for Wall Street."[39] The Soviet weekly, *New Times,* described
Liaquat Ali Khan as the "agent of Anglo-American imperialism to promote its interest in the Middle East and Southeast Asia in return for American arms and equipment." Not
only was Pakistan strongly condemned for its support of the
US position in Korea but also warned of "deplorable consequences" if such a policy was pursued.[40]

Moscow denounced, in no uncertain terms, Pakistani efforts
in the direction of Pan-Islamism—the forging of closer links
among the Muslim States by organizing an All-Muslim Conference, which was held in Karachi in February 1949, and
the International Economic Conferences in 1949 and 1950.
It was Moscow's contention that Muslim politicians of that
sort were "plotting against the national liberation movement
in Asia and the Middle East and supporting the anti-Soviet
military schemes of the US and British imperialists" under
the cloak of religious, cultural and economic cooperation.
It was alleged that the US Embassy in Karachi had borne the
expenses incurred by the President of the Muslim League of
Pakistan during his visit to the Middle East countries to can-
vass support for the creation of a Pan-Islamic State. To
line up an "anti-communist bloc" was said to be the primary
object of the two Economic Conferences.[41] Commenting on the
Second World Muslim Conference, which was held in Karachi
in February 1950, the Soviet journal, *New Times,* observed
that under the cloak of a "League of Moslem countries," the
obvious purpose of the Pan-Islam organization seemed to be to
set up a "military and political bloc." Pakistan wanted to
obtain the leadership of the Muslim countries, it said. It
also desired to strengthen its prestige in the international
field and its position *vis-a-vis* India.[42]

The Pan-Islamic movement, based as it was on religion,
was criticized by the Soviet leaders as reactionary and harmful partly because it threatened to retard the progress towards
democratization of Muslim countries and stand in the way of
the spread of communism and partly because it had grave
political implications for the USSR, which had a sizeable
Muslim population, particularly in its Central Asian region.
But the virulent attack which the Soviet press and radio mount-

ed against Pakistani efforts in popularising the Pan-Islamic movement was hardly "conducive to help an improvement of relations between the Soviet Union and Pakistan."[43]

The Pakistan Government's attempt to crush the communist movement within Pakistan and the Soviet denunciation of those attempts created further strains in the relations between the two countries. In October 1950, *Pravda* supported the programme of the Communist Party of Pakistan (formed in in March 1948). That programme called for Pakistan's withdrawal from the British Commonwealth of Nations and the sterling bloc; the dismissal of all British officers from the Pakistan army and the Civil Service; the nationalization of all Pakistani industry; and the establishment of friendly relations with the USSR, China and People's Democracies.[44] Earlier in June 1950, a Moscow broadcast supported the agitation launched by the Pakistan Communist Party in West Punjab and Sind and said that "the present movement against the landlords is on the upswing."[45]

In March 1951, Prime Minister Liaquat Ali Khan announced the unearthing of an anti-Government conspiracy, in which the army officers of Pakistan were said to be in league with the Communists. The conspirators, he stated, had planned to invite advisory missions from "a certain foreign country" to set up a communist State.[46] In April-May 1951, the Pakistan Government launched a round-up of communists, who were charged with anti-State activities and subversive plotting. All this was the subject of much adverse criticism in the Soviet press. The whole story of a "conspiracy" was stated to have been cooked up by the "reactionary ruling circles of Pakistan," who were accused of creating an atmosphere of terror and anti-communist hysteria in the country. The Soviet journal, *New Times*, observed : "The Government, mortally afraid of the people, hatched this controversy against the people." It added : "People are being poisoned systematically by reactionary propaganda dished in religious jargon."[47] Subsequently, *Pravda* condemned the "notorious" Law of Public Safety under which a number of Communists were put under arrest without a fair chance of defending themselves.[48]

The Soviet Union was also very critical of Pakistan toeing the line of the Western Powers on various international
issues. The USSR's criticism of Pakistan's stand on the
Korean question has already been noted. The Pakistan
Government was taken to task for its acceptance of Western
foreign capital and for not effecting democratic agrarian
reforms.[49] Pakistan's support to Washington on the question of a separate peace treaty with Japan was stated to
have given rise to unequivocal praise from the directors of
US foreign policy and was obviously the subject of much
criticism in the Soviet press. Furthermore, Pakistan's involvement in the US scheme of Middle East Command, it was
stated, would "mean the political enslavement of Pakistan
and constitute a direct threat to its independence." In short,
Pakistan's foreign policy was contemptuously described as
"reactionary" and condemned as being influenced by the mon-
opolistic American and British circles, interested in establishing their "stranglehold" over Pakistan.[50]

Moscow had taken a neutral attitude by abstaining on the
Kashmir question in the Security Council debate in 1948-49,
but thereafter, it began to give expression to its sensitivity about
Anglo-US machinations in Kashmir and, to a certain extent,
to tilt its attitude in favour of India. Thus, on 30 April
1951, Malik, the representative of the Soviet Union, voiced
criticism of the nomination by the UK and the USA of Frank
P. Graham for appointment as the United Nations' Representative for India and Pakistan. He also criticized Washington for complicating the Kashmir issue and for habour-
ing strategic interests in the area. A month later, Malik
disapproved of the text of the letter to be sent by the
President to the Security Council to the Governments of
India and Pakistan, the main purpose of which was to prevent the Kashmir Constituent Assembly from expressing
its opinion on the question of accession. In 1952, the
Soviet delegate opposed the introduction of foreign troops in
Kashmir and desired the status of Kashmir to be decided by
its Constituent Assembly. Malik stated that the emphasis
laid by the USA and the UK on "assistance through the
United Nations" was a mere pretext for an annexationist,

imperialistic design to convert Kashmir "into an Anglo-American colony and a military and strategic base."[51] In December 1952, the Soviet representative, V. Zorin, repeated the substance of Malik's earlier speech and virulently criticized the British and American Governments for interfering in the Indo-Pakistan dispute and rendering its solution more difficult.[52]

By persisting in a more or less non-committal stand in the matter, the Kremlin was probably trying to impress upon the people of both Pakistan and India that, unlike the imperialist Powers, the Soviet Union had no desire to intervene in the Indo-Pakistan dispute left over by history. Moscow favoured the settlement of the Kashmir dispute by peaceful means through bilateral negotiations. The Karachi meeting between the Prime Ministers of India and Pakistan in July 1953 was, thus, applauded in the Soviet press. "Inspite of the will of the enemies of peace," I. Alexandrov wrote in *Pravda* on 1 August 1953, "the [Karachi] meeting occurred without any so-called mediation." It "signified the begining of direct conversations between interested sides as the sole method which in our times can be used to settle controversial international problems and conflicts."[53]

In short, throughout the Stalin Era, USSR-Pak relations were far from cordial. Stalin's pre-occupation with Europe and his bi-polar view of the world was responsible for his not paying sufficient attention to the Third World countries, Pakistan included. He felt particular detestation for Pakistan because of its so-called Islamic ideology which had serious implications for the Muslim population in the Central Asian Republics of the USSR and also because of its toeing the line of the Western Powers on a number of international issues. Pakistan's zeal for Pan-Islamism was the subject of much criticism in the Soviet press and the Pakistan Government's clampdown on Communists in Pakistan created further complications in USSR-Pak relations. Karachi complained of a Soviet hand in the conspiracy to overthrow the Government, while, to the Kremlin, Pakistan appeared to be gradually sliding into the Western camp.

The deterioration in USSR-Pak relations actually took place in the early 1950s rather than in the late 1940s. Stalin's detestation for Pakistan's Islamic zeal did not mean that he should have refrained from establishing friendly relations with a neighbouring state, Pakistan for instance. The Kremlin's presence in Karachi could have helped Moscow in various ways : in preventing Pakistan from moving too close to the Western Powers ; in acquiring a position of influence in Pakistan ; and in gaining access to the Indian Ocean. Besides, by developing fruitful relations with a leading Muslim country on its periphery, the USSR could hope to pacify its own Muslim population. So far as the question of Pakistan trying to foment disaffection or encourage separatist tendencies among the Muslims of Central Asian Republics was concerned, the problem was not unmanageable. The powerful Communist dictator was quite confident of meeting any challenge in that regard. He was, at the same time, in a better position to take advantage of progressive and democratic forces and the Communist Party within Pakistan.

USSR-Pak relations during 1947-53 were said to be characterized by an attitude of indifference and coolness. But the primary question is : who was to blame for this "attitude of indifference and coolness"—the USSR or Pakistan or both. Some believe, as indeed an Indian researcher seems to think, that Stalin was averse to cultivating meaningful relations with Pakistan,[54] and therefore, is primarily to be held responsible for the sorry state of affairs in the relations between the two countries. Let us, for a moment, see how India figured in the calculations of the Soviet dictator. For him, there existed only two camps in the world—a socialist camp and a capitalist camp. India's non-alignment had no meaning, appeal or significance whatsoever for him. India, like Pakistan, was the target of Soviet criticism for her being a member of the British Commonwealth and remaining in the "English sterling bloc and imperial defence system."[55]

While in the first two or three years of Pakistan's existence the Kremlin could see some hopeful features in the domestic and foreign policies of Pakistan, the situation in India appeared quite bleak from Moscow's point of view. Most of the news concerning India carried in the Soviet press during 1948-49 was about strikes and the arrests and repressions of Indian Communists. The "terrorist anti-communist activities" of the Government of India were said to be guided by the desire of the ruling Congress to clear the way "to tie down the country economically and politically to the U.S.A."[56]

The hold of big bourgeoisie was considered to be stronger in India than in Pakistan. Sardar Patel "the all-powerful Minister for Home Affairs, whom many regard as India's future dictator" was stated in the Soviet press to be dependent on Birla Bros. Ltd., to whom he "owes his career." Another bigshot, Dr. John Mathai, "a top administrator in the Government of India" during and before World War II and subsequently Minister of Transport and Railways in the Nehru Cabinet, was said to be on the payroll of Tata Sons Ltd., having been one of the directors of that firm.[57] In Pakistan, on the other hand, there were no such Birlas or Tatas who could be thought of as scuttling State planning on socialist lines.

Besides, during 1948-49, the Nehru Government was also accused of deliberately pursuing anti-Soviet policies, exemplified in the ban imposed on Soviet films,[58] the banning of the Conference of "Progressive Writers," refusal to give permission to Soviet writers to come to India and participate therein,[59] and the alleged refusal of the Indian Government to issue *visas* for 15 Russians connected with anti-fascist organizations to participate in a conference organized by the All-India Students Federation.[60] The Indian constitution, which was adopted by the Constitutent Assembly on 26 November 1949, was said to embody the characteristics of all bourgeois constitutions—"the private ownership of land, forests, factories, mills and other means of production," etc.,[61] and was considered to "strengthen the interests of the bourgeoisie and capitalists."[62] Above all, Nehru's visit to the USA was seen as a sure indication of India being lured into becoming "a special base of Anglo-American imperialistic plans in the East."[63]

In these circumstances, it was not surprising that Stalin, the Soviet dictator, deemed it necessary to cultivate Pakistan. A number of delegations, including a trade delegation, were despatched to Pakistan. Moreover, with a view to establish rapport at the highest level with the rulers of Pakistan, an invitation was extended to Prime Minister Liaquat Ali Khan to visit Moscow. The latter move signified that the Kremlin seemed inclined to counter Anglo-American *demarches* towards India by taking initiative to draw Pakistan closer to itself. It might be that because of Pakistan's greater proximity to Soviet borders and its strategic location, Stalin deemed it prudent to assign a higher priority to Karachi than to New Delhi. Or it may be that by extending an invitation to Liaquat Ali Khan, Moscow actually sought to convey its dislike to New Delhi for the latter's moving closer to the Western Powers and also a warning that such a step was fraught with dangers and obvious risks, which India should not forget. Whatever it might have been, one cannot possibly claim that the Kremlin was indifferent to its national interests, ignorant of the geo-political importance of Pakistan—a neighbouring state—and not inclined to cultivate relations with Pakistan. If nothing came out of Moscow's overtures, it was primarily due to lack of response on the part of Pakistan. Karachi not only spurned the Soviet invitation but, thereafter, also began to look with high hopes towards the Western Powers for sustenance and support. Thus, it appears that in the late 1940s, the Kremlin seemed to be better disposed towards Pakistan than towards India. It was only in the early 1950s that USSR-Pak relations began to deteriorate, for which the rulers of Pakistan were no less, if not to a greater degree, responsible than Stalin.

3

USSR-Pak Relations 1954-64

WHILE India's refusal to take part in the San Francisco Conference on a Peace Treaty with Japan and her independent role in the Korean War impressed the Kremlin, Pakistan's performance on both these counts could hardly have appealed to the Soviet Union. After Pakistan joined the Anglo-American alliance system, USSR-Pak relations were characterized by heightened tension and much bitterness. Soviet relations with India, on the other hand, showed a marked improvement. Both countries were opposed to Western-sponsored military pacts. India's anti-imperialist posture and her policy of non-alignment were considered a positive force by Moscow. This facilitated Indo-Soviet collaboration in economic, cultural, political and foreign policy matters.

During Stalin's time, the USSR had remained practically isolated from the Third World countries. Khrushchov, therefore, realized the importance of cultivating those nations with the dual purpose of undermining the Western Powers' influence there and increasing the prestige and influence of Moscow in the uncommitted world. He thereby sought to broaden the base of Soviet foreign policy.

Moscow supported India's stand on the Kashmir question and Afghanistan's viewpoint on the Pakhtoonistan issue—the two most vital problems facing Pakistan. Yet, given the geographical proximity of Pakistan to Soviet borders, the Kremlin could not completely write off Pakistan. Economic and technical assistance was, therefore, offered to Pakistan several times. But considerations of displeasing its Western allies, as also feelings of suspicion and mistrust with regard to Soviet motives, prevented Pakistan from responding favourably to Soviet overtures. The pro-West orientation of the Ayub regime was proved by the bilateral defence agreement which Pakistan concluded with the USA in 1959.

Even when Pakistan had not aligned itself with the West, its ruling elite considered the USSR as posing the main threat to its existence and to its way of life. Consequently, they showed a marked preference for the United States and Britain. While accepting the credentials of the first US Ambassador, the founder of Pakistan and its first Governor-General (Jinnah) spoke of the American and Pakistani people as "standing shoulder to shoulder in defence of democracy" during the two World Wars. Pakistan's Minister for Commerce, Fazlul Rahman, declared in October 1947 that the United States and Pakistan shared a similar ideological outlook and, therefore, his country would not tolerate communism.[1] After Pakistan entered into a military agreement with the USA, it openly castigated the USSR as an imperialist and expansionist Power, implying, at times, that it was "more anti-communist than the United States itself."[2] All along, Karachi made a distinction between the USSR and China. Speaking at Bandung, Mohammed Ali, the Prime Minister of Pakistan, called the USSR "an imperialist nation with satellites which had brought many people under its heel." As for China, he gave expression to his conviction regarding its peaceful motives and added that Peking was "certainly not imperialistic."[3] Later in March 1963, Foreign Minister Z.A. Bhutto had remarked that "given geography and the power realities of the nuclear age, the military threat to us, if there is one, would come more from the Soviet Union than from China."[4]

The differential treatment meted out to the Soviet Union and China by Pakistan was reflected in the differing attitudes of the two Communist countries towards Islamabad. While Peking maintained more or less a neutral attitude on Kashmir, Moscow came out firmly in support of India on the issue. Likewise, China officially maintained studied silence about Pakistan's participation in the Western military alliances, while the USSR did not hesitate to deliver official protest notes to Pakistan in that regard. Evidently, Moscow appeared more concerned about the presence of US bases on Pakistani territory, especially the Peshawar base in West Pakistan. That base was being used by Washington for the highly secret U-2 operations, which enabled the USA to gather information about the nature and location of Soviet targets as also about its military preparations.

During their visit to India in the winter of 1955-56, the Soviet leaders—Bulganin and Khrushchov—endorsed the Indian stand on the Kashmir question. The creation of Pakistan was attributed to imperialist manipulation. Khrushchov dismissed Pakistan's concept of the two-nation theory and upheld India's secularism when he observed : "Religion has never been the chief consideration when any State was established." In stating that Kashmir was one of the constituent States of India and that fact "has been decided by the people of Kashmir," Khrushchov totally aligned himself with India. He also ridiculed the cry of *Jehad*. He declared that the partition was a decided issue and that it was scarcely necessary "now to redraw" the boundaries of India and Pakistan as certain Powers would like to do. "We know that changes of frontiers are always a painful process and involve bloodshed," he added.[5] The Soviet leader was obviously criticizing unsatiated Powers like Pakistan and China who harped on their right to modify the established boundaries especially with India and the Soviet Union. Changes of boundaries are, indeed, fraught with serious dangers for international peace and security.

Speaking at a dinner hosted by the Prime Minister of Afghanistan in Kabul on 16 December 1955, Premier Bulganin expressed sympathy for Afghanistan's policy on the Pakhtoonistan issue. The Soviet Union, he stated, stood for a just settlement of the Pakhtoonistan question which could be properly solved "only if the vital interests of the peoples inhabiting Pushtunistan are taken into account."[6] Thus, the Kremlin went to the extent of extending its unequivocal support to Kabul in its dispute with Pakistan on the Pakhtoonistan issue. It is significant to recall that before 1955, Moscow had taken a non-committal stand in the matter.

Thus, during the Khrushchov-Bulganin visit to India and Afghanistan, Soviet leaders extended their support to the stands of the two non-aligned states in their disputes with Pakistan. This was, indeed, a reaction to Pakistan's policy of joining "the notorious Baghdad Pact," and allowing Washington to establish bases on its territory, i.e. in close proximity to the borders of the USSR. In the beginning of 1957, the Soviet Union vetoed a Pakistani proposal in the Security Council relating to the introduction of a UN Force into Kashmir. The veto, no doubt, relieved India of great anxiety and furthered her political and security interests, but the Soviet attitude in that regard was, at the same time, determined by considerations of its own national interests. The prospect of the presence of UN forces, composed as they would have been of "imperialist" Western Powers or their supporters and located near Soviet borders, was detrimental to Soviet interests. When Moscow was strongly criticizing the establishment of US bases in Pakistan, how could it possibly have entertained the idea of the presence of Western troops, in the garb of UN forces, in Kashmir—a region so close to its own borders ?

It is, however, quite significant to note that although the Soviet representative saw no useful purpose being served by the inclusion in the Security Council resolution of a clause providing for the holding of a plebiscite in Kashmir, he did not deem it necessary to veto other resolutions on the Kashmir question, which made a reference to both plebiscite and demilitarization. Only the resolution, which sought to station UN forces in Kashmir was considered directly impinging on Soviet national interests and, consequently, requiring the use of the veto. With a view to soften Pakistan's ruffled feelings in the matter, the Soviet representative left unanswered the criticism levelled against the Soviet veto by the Foreign Minister of Pakistan.

Pakistan, on its part, continued to follow a policy which could hardly be considered friendly by the Soviet Union. At the Colombo Conference of five Asian Prime Ministers, Mohammed Ali of Pakistan asserted that the greater menace to the region was international communism rather than Western colonialism which was in the process of liquidation. On 5 July 1954, the Communist Party was outlawed in East Pakistan and the ban became national on 24 July 1954 when similar action was taken in West Pakistan. The mass arrests of comunists, which followed, greatly strained USSR-Pak relations. The repressive policy of the Pakistan Government was denounced in the Soviet press. It was stated that persons who spoke "in opposition to the US-Pakistan military agreement and the anti-national policy of the Muslim League" were persecuted on the charge of "subversive activity."[7] Serious concern was also expressed over the US' economic assistance to Pakistan.[8]

On 27 July 1954, Soviet diplomats and their families were restricted to a 35-mile radius from the centre of Karachi, much in the same way as the two-man Pakistan embassy staff was bound in Moscow. On 14 September 1954, six days after Pakistan initialled the SEATO pact with the Western Powers, the Pakistan Government cancelled the five-month old licence of the Soviet Government's foreign insurance department, which had been operating since April 1954 a marine and fire underwriting company, known as *Ingosstrakh*, in Pakistan. Besides this cancellation, the Soviet Union was instructed to refund premiums sold by that company and, if this order was not complied with by 10 October, the Pakistan Government threatened to pay off the claimants from the "security" fund deposited by the company when the licence was issued. These actions were taken on the plea that the Soviet Government did not allow foreign insurance companies to operate in its territory. The Minister of Interior of Pakistan was also reported at the time to be looking into violations of espionage laws.[9]

At the Bandung Conference of Asian and African countries in April 1955, Ceylon's Prime Minister, Sir John Kotelawala, referred to "Russian satellites" in Europe and desired condemnation of colonialism, old and new. While the charges levelled against the Soviet Union were denied by Chou En-lai and Nehru, who affirmed that the East European countries were independent states, Kotelawala had the full support of the Pakistani Premier. It is significant to recall that while supporting his colleague from Ceylon, Pakistan's Prime Minister made it clear that his country did not regard China as imperialistic, for Peking had no satellites. He added that he was convinced of the peaceful motives of China.[10]

All these utterances and actions on the part of the Pakistani Government leaders, coupled as they were with Pakistan's firm commitment to Western military alliance systems, *viz.* the SEATO and the CENTO, put a "severe strain" on Pakistan's relations with the Soviet Union. The Foreign Minister of Pakistan, Hamidul Huq Chowdhury, in his speech before the National Assembly of Pakistan on 25 March 1956, laid the blame for the sorry state of affairs on "certain pronouncements" of Soviet leaders "on matters of vital concern" to Pakistan and termed them as unfriendly acts. Though diplomatic relations were not ruptured, Pakistan recalled its Ambassador from Moscow. The visit of the First Deputy Prime Minister of the USSR, Mikoyan, to participate in Pakistan's Republic Day ceremonies, was, however, welcomed and Chowdhury even spoke of Pakistan's willingness to normalize its relations with the Soviet Union and to remove "in course of time all our misunderstandings." He observed : "We shall soon send our Ambassador to Moscow where the post has remained vacant for some time."[11]

While in Karachi, Mikoyan invited a Pakistani parliamentary delegation to visit the Soviet Union and also extended an invitation to the Speaker of the National Assembly on behalf of the Supreme Soviet. He told reporters that he could say nothing about his country's offer to Pakistan of economic assistance and a steel plant because he had left Moscow when the offer was made by Molotov. "We give assistance only to those who want it from us, we do not impose assistance," he said.[12]

After the Awami League came into power in September 1956, Premier Suhrawardy sent Sheikh Mujibur Rahman as his representative on a visit to the Soviet Union. There was, however, no change in the Pakistani attitude towards the Soviet Union. Speaking before students in Dacca on 9 December 1956, Prime Minister Suhrawardy criticized the USSR in very strong terms. He laid the blame at Moscow's door for starting the Cold War. He condemmed the USSR for "the tragedy of Hungary" and for maintaining its armed forces in the "satellite countries" of East Germany, Poland and Czechoslovakia. He gave no credence to Soviet protestations against Western imperialism when it perpetrated its own imperialism—"the New Imperialism" as he called it—or to Moscow's tirades against Western military alliances when it forged "between Russia and its satellite countries," the Warsaw Pact, which was "absolutely a military alliance."[13]

During the discussion on the Hungarian crisis in the UN, Pakistan completely aligned itself with Washington. It sponsored a resolution which described the Soviet action in Hungary as "violent repression" of the Hungarian people. It voted in favour of another US-sponsored resolution which condemned the Soviet Union for depriving Hungary of its independence and called upon Moscow to withdraw all its armed forces from Hungary without delay. Pakistan also supported yet another resolution which asked for the holding of free elections in Hungary, under the auspices of the United Nations. Pakistan's policy of strongly denouncing the Soviet action in Hungary and its helpful attitude towards the West in the Suez crisis was in marked contrast to that of India. New Delhi was extremely critical of the Anglo-French invasion of Egypt and quite restrained in its criticism of the Soviet action in Hungary.

Thus, whatever hopes Moscow might have entertained about the East Pakistan Awami League ("once perhaps the most popular political party in the country," as one Soviet commentary put it) of bringing about a change in Pakistan's foreign policy and improving relations with the USSR, were dashed to the ground. The Awami League, it was said, had succeeded in defeating the Muslim League due to the support of "progressive organizations." It was also pointed out that in its 1953, 1955 and 1956 resolutions, the Awami League had condemned military pacts. However, after it was able to form a non-Muslim League Government in Pakistan, its leader, Suhrawardy, zealously defended his country's membership of the SEATO and the Baghdad Pact. The Soviet Union, therefore, described Suhrawardy's attitude as "anti-national" and extolled Maulana Bhashani, one of the Awami League's prominent leaders, as "a man who enjoys wide esteem throughout the country." His resignation from the Awami League was approved in the Soviet commentary, as also his remarks that

he resigned because the Suhrawardy faction was "ignoring
the will of the people" and, for all practical purposes, had
abandoned the Party's programme. Referring to the plans
about forming a new party, Bhashani was quoted as saying :
"The fight must continue...to make Pakistan an independent
and sovereign State, free of all the restrictions imposed by
membership in imperialist military blocs...and solve the economic problems of our oppressed people." In this connection,
the Soviet commentary noted with satisfaction the "wide support" enjoyed by the movement to form a new party and the
establishment of a coordinating committee in West Pakistan
"to unite the democratic forces of both parts of the country."[14]
Another commentary in the *Mirovaiia Ekonomika* in July 1958
criticized Suhrawardy for reducing Pakistan to a "full-fledged
American colony."[15]

The military *coup* in Pakistan, which brought Ayub into
power, was considered by Soviet leaders as an attempt to
crush the popular movement represented by the National
Awami Party. That Party was said to be enjoying "particular
popularity in Pakistan, especially in her eastern province."
Its meetings were considered "regular demonstrations" against
the pro-American policy of Pakistani rulers. The Soviet commentator, D. Volsky, spoke highly of Maulana Bhashani. The
latter was described as a "prominent political leader" and one
of the founders of the national peasant organization, which
championed the peasant struggle against landowners and "at
the same time works for the country's genuine independence
and against its pro-American policy." The reactionary forces
in Pakistan were said to have joined hands with US imperialists
in a bid to restrict the democratic rights of the people and to
scuttle the demand for the country's "genuine independence."
The struggle against imperialism was said to have been joined
by a part of the national bourgeoisie leading to the formation
of a wide anti-imperialist front. D. Volsky asserted : "The
political parties demanding independence of the United States
became an influential force." Ayub's military dictatorship was
criticized for repressing those forces.[16] Khrushchov, in his
report to the 21st Congress of the CPSU, saw in the ushering of the Ayub regime by Washington an attempt to crush

democratic forces.[17] The Soviet press exposed the reactionary character of the military rule in Pakistan. Ayub's foreign policy was described as being hostile not only to its "peaceful neighbour," India, but to the USSR as well.[18]

In marked contrast to China, the Soviet Union continued to send protest notes to Pakistan against the increasing collaboration with the Western Powers in the military field under the Western alliance system. As early as 30 November 1953, a Soviet protest note was addressed to the Pakistan Government. It referred to press reports about negotiations between the Governments of Pakistan and the USA on the conclusion of an agreement to set up American bases on Pakistani territory. The note stated that Moscow could not remain indifferent to such reports as the establishment of US air bases in close proximity to Soviet borders and that Pakistan's adherence to the so-called Middle Eastern bloc had "a direct bearing on the security of the Soviet Union."[19] Bases in Pakistan, Moscow Radio observed, would strengthen the American position and ultimately result in the subjugation of Pakistan to US interests.[20] Pakistan's reply of 18 December 1953[21] did not satisfy Moscow and the relations between the two countries continued to deteriorate. In the opinion of the *New Times*, the Turko-Pakistani Pact of 1954 bore "all the hallmarks of American imperialist aggression which threatens the security and independence of many countries."[22]

On 26 March 1954 a second Soviet protest note was handed over to the Pakistani *Charge d'Affaires* in Moscow. It repeated the charge that Pakistan had granted military bases to the United States and had joined America in creating a military bloc in the Middle East, which was directed against the Soviet Union and the peace-loving countries of Asia. It also warned that Pakistani activities would harm its "relations" with the USSR and that "responsibility for such a situation" would rest squarely upon Pakistan.[23] *Dawn*, the influential Pakistani paper, dismissed the Soviet protest note as "rubbish"[24] while the Pakistan Government, in its reply of 4 May 1954, rejected it outright. The acceptance of US military aid, the Pakistani note said, did not signify that the Pakistan Army would be placed under foreign command. It was further stated that there was no basis for the "unjustified conclusion" that had been drawn by the Soviet Government.[25]

The second half of the 1950s witnessed considerable deterioration in USSR-Pak relations. The Soviet protest note of 14 April 1958 warned that in view of its geographical proximity to the Soviet Union "grave consequences" would inevitably await Pakistan "if its territory will be allowed to be used for the establishment of military bases for the purpose of using them against the Soviet Union." Attention was drawn to the construction of launching grounds for guided missiles and rockets, and of military installations and runways for landing modern bombers of strategic aviation. It was emphasized that, since Pakistan did not possess these weapons, the facilities would be used by the United States and its other allies. Moreover, it was pointed out that at the Ankara CENTO meeting, Pakistan had asked for the arming of the Treaty countries with rockets and atomic weapons.[26]

The Pakistan Government's note in reply, handed over to the Soviet Ambassador on 24 May 1958, stated that Soviet objections to Pakistan's participation in collective security arrangements were "not comprehensible" in view of the USSR's own association in a politico-military alliance, *viz.* the Warsaw Pact. It was further stated that by its membership of the SEATO and the CENTO, Pakistan was trying to make aggression against it unprofitable, thereby imputing aggressive motives to the Soviet Union. The note denied the existence of launching sites for guided missiles or rocket missiles in Pakistan. On the other hand, the USSR was criticized for keeping all types of military bases and weapons in close proximity to Pakistan. The Pakistani note termed Soviet criticism of foreign military bases in Pakistan as "baseless allegations." It asserted that the "partisan attitude" of the Soviet Union on the Kashmir problem had created "greater bitterness and disappointment in Pakistan" and "indeed throughout the Muslim world." It further called upon the USSR to change its attitude in that regard and added :

The exercise of the right of veto in the Security Council to frustrate the solution of certain disputes has prevented improvement of the relations between nations in the region and contributed to the maintenance of tension and lack of security.[27]

The Soviet *Aide Memoire* of 26 December 1958 expressed concern over the negotiations for a bilateral agreement between Pakistan and the United States. It stated that the agreement "cannot but infringe the interests of the Soviet Union's security." It also warned Pakistan of "possible consequences." In its reply of 7 January 1959, Pakistan asserted its sovereign right to bolster up its defence capacity. Reference was also made to Moscow's nefarious activities in the countries adjacent to Pakistan, *e.g.* Afghanistan, to which it had supplied arms, built roads, constructed airfields and other military installations. Pakistan requested the Soviet Union to use its great influence in helping to reduce tensions in the regions of South East Asia and the Middle East by assisting in the solution of disputes.[28] Moscow was not at all convinced by the arguments advanced by Karachi to justify "the aggressive character of the military blocs" to which the latter belonged. Consequently, the Soviet Government sent another *Aide Memoire* on 18 February 1959 to which the Pakistan Government replied on 27 February 1959. Therein, Karachi observed :

> The Soviet Government, although repeating their assertion that Collective Security Pacts aggravate tension in the regions, have remained silent on the request of the Government of Pakistan that the Soviet Government assist in the solution of disputes which constitute a threat to international peace and security in the region.[29]

Moscow was not satisfied with Pakistan's explanations. A Soviet Government delegation, visiting India in March 1959, described the US-Pakistan bilateral military agreement as directed not only against the Soviet Union but "first of all against the neighbours of Pakistan—India and Afghanistan." Since no one threatened Pakistan, Iran and Turkey, the new military agreements with the USA were said to have been concluded by their governments for the purpose of intimidating their own peoples. According to the statement issued to the press by the Soviet delegation on 19 March 1959, Washington needed those pacts "for turning the territories of these countries into military and atomic bases against the peaceful nations of Asia." Moscow, the statement added, could not remain indifferent to the intrigues of the aggressive circles of the US in aggravating the situation in Asia, particularly when they were occurring near the borders of the Soviet Union.[30]

The Soviet Government's statement of 25 March 1959 referred to Pakistan's reply of 27 February 1959 in which it was declared that it would not allow the use of its territory for aggressive purposes by any other Power. It was then pointed out that the facts showed that the new military agreement between Pakistan and the USA made for greater "dependence of Pakistani army and of Pakistan herself as a state on the aggressive plans of the United States." The arrival of a great number of American military advisers, engineers and other personnel and the construction of military bases and missile launching ramps was cited in support of the Soviet contention. The conclusion of military agreements in Ankara by Iran, Turkey and Pakistan with the United States was described as "a hostile act against the Soviet Union." Those agreements were said to aggravate the situation in the vast area "stretching along the southern frontiers of the Soviet Union or in direct proximity to them." Those agreements, the Soviet statement added, had been rightly assessed in China, India, Afghanistan, Iraq and in other peace-loving countries as "a profoundly hostile act against those countries." The Soviet Government statement spoke of Moscow taking all the necessary steps towards safeguarding the security of Soviet frontiers and maintaining peace. It also pointed out that in concluding those agreements the Governments of Iran, Turkey and Pakistan were obviously showing "too little concern for the real security and independence of their states." The three Governments were said to be principally concerned with adapting their foreign and other policies more and more to "the strategic and colonialist plans of the aggressive military blocs whipped together under the aegis of the United States."[31]

The flight of the American U-2 plane (that took off from the airport of Peshawar in Pakistan and was shot down over Soviet territory on 1 May 1960) provoked another protest note from Moscow. That note described the intrusion of the US espionage plane as "a gross violation of the Soviet State frontier." Pakistan was blamed for its complicity in the "hostile mission." The protest note recalled earlier Soviet statements in the matter and accused Pakistan of lending its territory for purposes of committing aggressive actions against the Soviet Union. After thus denouncing Pakistan's role of an accomplice in those actions, the Soviet protest note warned that "if such actions are repeated from Pakistani territory," Moscow would be compelled to take proper retaliatory measures. The USSR, it said, had the "means to render harmless" the bases used for "aggressive actions" against the Soviet Union. It, thus, indirectly threatened the obliteration of the Peshawar and other airfields.[32] Pakistan denied that it had played any part in the preparations for and the execution of the flight of any aircraft for the purpose of military intelligence over the Soviet Union. It accused Moscow of violating Pakistani air space several times. Karachi, however, took the precaution of tightening its control of the use of Pakistani airfields by US aircraft.[33]

Speaking at a news conference on 23 October 1959, President Ayub described Khrushchov's proposal for total disarmament rather "unrealistic." He stated :

Unless conflicts and fears and their causes were removed, total disarmament could not be achieved, because armaments are the result of fears and conflicts. However, it should be seen as to how much of the proposal could be accepted and implemented.[34]

In an interview with a British author, President Ayub observed :

In four or five years time the development of communications that is taking place in Afghanistan by the Russians and also of the bases being constructed by the Chinese in Tibet, will present us with a new situation. It is not inconceivable that one of the dangers is that the communist world will have the power and facility to bring direct military pressure to bear. This is self-evident. They have the capacity. I do not say that is their intention.[35]

In November 1959, the President of Pakistan expressed concern about the growing Russian influence in Afghanistan, and warned his Western allies that "a Russian-Chinese drive to the Indian Ocean is a major aim in the communist drive for world domination."[36] On 20 November 1959, President Ayub stated that Pakistan, Iran and Turkey were "acting as a shield of security for the entire Middle East, South Asia and the African continent."[37]

US aid to Pakistan came to be severely criticized in mid-1959 in the course of the hearings on Mutual Security Legislation and discussions in the Senate Foreign Relations Committee. Congressional critics pointed out that Pakistan was receiving too much military aid and that its army was practically of no use to the United States in a war with Russia. Replying to such critics, Ayub referred to the Soviet and Chinese pressures on the north and the hardly friendly Afghan attitude towards Pakistan and the West. On 22 June 1959, he deemed it necessary to issue a formal statement to assure Washington. "Our American friends," he declared, "will find us dependable and trustworthy." In an interview with Robert R. Brunn, Ayub described the sub-continent as vulnerable and talked of "mutual military defence" between India and Pakistan.[38] He expressed a similar view in an article in *Foreign Affairs*. "As a student of war and strategy," he stated in that article, he saw "quite clearly the inexorable push of the north in the direction of the warm waters of the Indian Ocean." He added that that could be checkmated if India and Pakistan stop squabbling with each other, "resolve our problems" and "disengage our armed forces from facing inwards as they do today, and face them outwards."[39]

All such offers of "joint defence" with India, emanating from Pakistan were conditional on the settlement of the Kashmir problem to the satisfaction of Pakistan. The joint defence proposal, it seemed, was designed as a sop to US critics of Pakistan in order to maintain the flow of massive economic and military aid from Washington. That proposal was also aimed at disarming India so that on any suitable occasion Pakistan could proceed to occupy the whole of Kashmir, as was amply proved by the events of August-September 1965. The so-called offer of joint defence might also have been intended as a tempting bait to lure India with a view to malign her policy of non-alignment and to jeopardize her relations with the Communist countries, especially with the Soviet Union. That the offers of joint defence were devoid of good faith was proved not only by their conditional nature but also by the continued refusal of Pakistan to enter into a no-war pact with India. It has recently been revealed that the idea behind the joint defence proposal was to grab the whole of Jammu and Kashmir. In an informal interview given to the Urdu weekly, *Lail-o-Nihar* (Lahore), three days before his death on 20 April 1974, Ayub disclosed : "Under the garb of 'joint defence' we wanted to send our forces across the cease-fire line. Once our army was stationed in Srinagar, India would have been forced to hold a plebiscite in Kashmir."[40]

Khrushchov's visit to India and Afghanistan, in the beginning of 1960, was looked upon with concern in Pakistan. The Soviet-Afghan communique of 4 March 1960 proposed the implementation of the principle of self-determination on the basis of the Charter of the United Nations to settle the destiny of the Pathan people. Manzur Qadir, the Foreign Minister of Pakistan, deemed it interference in the internal affairs of Pakistan. President Ayub criticized Soviet support to what he called the "totally unjustifiable claim" of Afghanistan in the following words :

> To us the object is quite clear. It is first of all to aggravate problems in this part of the world and secondly to pave the way for the age-old attempt of the North to dominate the Indo-Pakistan sub-continent and the areas surrounding it.[41]

In an address to the Pakistan Institute of International Affairs on 11 March 1960, Foreign Minister Manzur Qadir described alliance with the West as "the sheet anchor of Pakistan's foreign policy." He observed :

> There are certain attitudes which are inherent and implicit in the fact that we have chosen to be allies of the West. Those attitudes will continue to manifest themselves because alliance with the West is the sheet anchor of Pakistan's foreign policy. If there are any implications arising from it, or ramifications flowing from it, they are there. In the Western alignment is implicit the guarantee of our sovereignty and independence.[42]

Pakistan's Ambassador to the United States, Aziz Ahmed, in an address in Philadelphia on 8 April 1960, described Pakistan as "the most allied of America's Asian allies." He rejected the policy of neutrality as "shortsighted." He denounced the USSR for its veto on Kashmir and "open incitement by it of Afghanistan to lay claim to Pakistani territory." He criticized those Americans who advocated a policy of neutrality for Asian countries situated along the Communist perimeter and stated that Pakistan would not tolerate any premium being put on neutrality. Aziz Ahmed emphasized the value of the alliances and said that if they were of little consequence the "countries whose expansionist ambitions they are designed to thwart would not continue to denounce them so violently or work so sedulously for their undoing." He cited, in that connection, the intense Soviet pressure on Iran which was a member of the Western alliance system. He added :

> Similarly, one cannot help ponder the fact that the Chinese should not attempt to seize a small island like Formosa but should quietly bite of a sizeable portion of Ladakh and take forcible possession of Longju, despite the non-aggression treaty and friendship which bound them to India. Was it perhaps because India, although a far bigger and stronger country than Formosa, was alone militarily?[43]

Throughout 1952-60, Moscow repeatedly expressed its desire to develop trade, economic and cultural relations with Pakistan but the latter's response was far from encouraging. In 1952, a barter agreement was concluded. It provided for the exchange of 150,000 tons of wheat from the Soviet Union for 22,000 tons of jute and 13,000 bales of cotton from Pakistan. In January 1954, Soviet representatives participated in a conference of Pakistani scientists and preliminary talks on concluding a trade agreement (similar to that between the USSR and India) took place between the two countries. The question of Soviet technical assistance was also discussed. In February 1954, the leader of the Soviet delegation to the ECAFE meeting invited 12 countries, including Pakistan, to send delegations to visit the USSR to study his country's industrial, agricultural, scientific and social achievements. A 16-member Soviet cultural good-will mission came to Pakistan in March-April 1954 and, at the invitation of the Kremlin, a delegation of Pakistani industrialists and businessmen visited the USSR in October 1954. Later, Pakistan's Secretary in the Ministry of Economic Afairs, Said Hasan, went to Moscow as the leader of that delegation to participate in the talks.

A trade agreement was signed on 27 June 1956. It provided for payments in Pakistani rupees. Under the agreement, the two nations also agreed to extend the most-favoured-nation treatment to each other in matters of trade. The Soviet Union appointed a trade representative in Karachi and opened a show room there. There was relatively increased trade between the two countries during 1957-58.

In February 1956, Marshal Bulganin offered Soviet technical assistance in the peaceful uses of atomic energy to Pakistan. He saw sufficient possibility of mutually beneficial economic cooperation between the USSR and Pakistan. On the occasion of the Republic Day reception by the Pakistani Embassy in Moscow in March 1956, Soviet Foreign Minister Molotov offered to construct a steel mill in Pakistan, similar to the one the Soviet Union had built for India.[44] On 15 June 1956, Moscow announced a gift of 16,500 tons of rice to help Pakistan tide over its food crisis. The Soviet offer of technical and economic assistance was made in February 1958 by the leader of the Soviet Parliamentary Delegation, I.A. Benediktov. It was repeated in March 1958 by the Soviet Ambassador in Pakistan. It was stated that such assistance could be arranged on a bilateral basis or channelled through the United Nations. Agricultural and other machinery could be given on a credit basis. Moscow was prepared to assist Pakistan in easing its foreign exchange difficulties by trading in Pakistani rupees. It also expressed its inclination to assist Pakistan in the fields of agriculture, irrigation, control of floods, salination and land erosion.

In November 1958, a month after the establishment of the martial regime in Pakistan, Moscow offered assistance in the exploration of mineral resources, including the much-needed oil. Pakistan's response was again far from encouraging. It was only when the American Senate drastically curtailed the extent of the military allocations proposed by President Eisenhower in the budget that Pakistan began to express its interest in Soviet aid. Senator Wayne Morse (Democrat) declared that he was not in favour of giving any economic assistance to Pakistan since he believed that such aid would "fall into Russian hands if the Russian Juggernaut decided to move."[45]

Thus, Pakistan's Minister, Zulfikar Ali Bhutto, remarked in July 1959 that "special attention has been given to promoting trade with the USSR, the East European countries, including Yugoslavia and the Chinese Mainland." He also expressed the hope that regular trade relationship with these countries would be developed.[46] Encouraged by those remarks, the Kremlin extended an invitation to Bhutto to visit Moscow for discussing trade proposals between the two countries. The invitation, sent in January 1960, was meant both to improve USSR-Pak relations as also to exploit the growing anti-Western sentiments in Pakistan, to its advantage.

President Ayub threatened to turn to "other Powers" for help if the United States continued to underestimate Pakistan's needs. He observed : "The camp opposed to the Americans attaches great importance to our country both militarily and politically and persistently makes advances to us."[47] The *Pakistan Times* referred to repeated offers of "substantial aid without political strings" from "other states" and remarked that "America should have no grouse if we turn to those countries to make up the shortfall between our needs and the aid available to us from our major allies."[48]

In marked departure from its previous stand, Pakistan accepted, in August 1960, the Soviet offer of assistance in the exploration of mineral resources, including oil. While in New York, Pakistan's Minister of Industries and Natural Resources, Z.A. Bhutto, stated that his country would seek funds from the Western allies rather than borrow from the Communist countries at a low rate of interest.[49] Nevertheless, negotiations on the exploration of oil and other mineral resources began in Karachi on 10 September 1960 and were continued in Moscow. On his return from Moscow, Bhutto disclosed (11 January 1961) that Russia had offered unconditional economic assistance to Pakistan in any field the latter desired and that the extent of such aid would depend on Pakistan's requirements.[50] In March 1961, Pakistan and the Soviet Union signed an agreement for the supply of Soviet equipment and services of experts for oil and gas exploration in Pakistan to the extent of $30 million. The loan was to be repaid in 12 years at an interest of $2\frac{1}{2}$ per cent. Prices for the equipment and material to be supplied to Pakistan under the agreement were to be fixed on the basis of world market prices. Repayment of credit and payment of interest was to be made in Pakistani rupees. Talking to pressmen after signing the agreement, Dr. Kapitsa observed that the agreement was "an evidence of Soviet intentions" and expressed the hope that there would be close cooperation between Pakistan and the USSR in the economic and cultural spheres.[51]

As Western assistance for Pakistan's Second Five Year Plan (1960-65) fell short of Pakistan's foreign exchange needs, its Minister of Industries categorically stated, on 11 June 1961, that his country would accept aid from any friendly quarter to finance the Plan. If there was such an offer from the Soviet Union, he added, Pakistan would unhesitatingly accept it.[52] This declaration was in marked contrast to Pakistan's earlier stand of caution and delay in accepting Soviet offers of economic and technical assistance and reflected Pakistan's dissatisfaction with the Western Powers, the United States in particular. Premier Khrushchov was quoted by the Soviet Ambassador to Pakistan as having said that the USSR would consider active economic collaboration with Pakistan if the latter pursued a policy of non-alignment. It was evident from this remark that large-scale economic assistance to Pakistan would be given only after Pakistan withdrew from "anti-Soviet" military pacts.[53] The oil pact of March 1961 was followed in August 1963 by a barter agreement providing for a total trade of Rs. 10 million. On 7 October 1963, an air transport agreement was concluded under which the Soviet Union, for the first time, granted rights to an airline to operate services through Moscow to points beyond.[54] In June 1964, an agreement on a cultural and scientific exchange programme for 1964, and a credit agreement providing for a Soviet loan of $11 million were signed. The latter indicated Moscow's willingness to participate in Pakistan's efforts to accelerate its economic development.[55] Concerned as the Soviet Union was about the presence of hostile bases in close proximity to its borders, it was, at the same time, inclined to normalize its relations with its neighbours, on its southern periphery, viz. Iran, Turkey and Pakistan. Moscow, therefore, often expressed its willingness to improve relations with Pakistan not only in the economic sphere but also on the political plane as well. Thus, in his report to the Supreme Soviet in 1955, Bulganin observed that Moscow would "continue to exert efforts to improve our relations with Pakistan."[56] *Izvestia* suggested that Pakistan was not yet altogether lost to the Western Powers because of its membership of the SEATO and the CENTO. It still pinned its hopes on the "progressive forces" in Pakistan which were said to be making every effort to extricate the country from its position of dependence and re-orient its foreign policy on more independent lines.[57] The defeat of the Muslim League in the elections of East Pakistan, where it could secure only 7 out of 237 seats, was interpreted in the Soviet press as a strong and clear disapproval by the people of Pakistan's military collusion with the United States.[58]

In the report of the Central Committee of the CPSU to the 20th Party Congress, it was stated that the USSR would strive unswervingly for improving relations with Iran, Turkey and Pakistan. It also expressed the Soviet Union's willingness to conclude, with them, "non-aggression treaties or treaties of friendship" which, it was emphasized, "would help remove existing suspicion and mistrust in relations between countries and normalise the international situation."[59] In 1959, the Soviet Ambassador to Pakistan was reported to have remarked that only 10 per cent of the problems between the USSR and Pakistan were controversial in nature and that on the remaining 90 per cent "there is a possibility of developing friendly relations."[60] These remarks, an Indian researcher observes, might have been made to probe the minds of the new Pakistani leaders. The Kremlin, he adds, must have been aware of the pressures that were likely to build on the new government for a reconciliation with the Soviet Union.[61] However, nothing tangible came out of these efforts.

There was no response from Pakistan to Soviet overtures and, therefore, Moscow often criticized the rulers of Pakistan. At the 22nd Congress of the CPSU in 1961, Khrushchov singled out Pakistan for attack saying that the "sorry fate of Pakistan gives cause for thought to the public of other countries, where influential forces are destroying national unity and are oppressing progressive leaders—in the first place the Communists."[62]

An Observer's article in *Pravda* of 3 April 1961, entitled "The Pukhtoon Problem Awaits Solution," referred to an earlier article—"The Pukhtoon and Politics"—in the same paper. It expressed the hope that the dispute between Pakistan and Afghanistan would be solved by peaceful means on the basis of respect for the rights of the Pakhtoon people to determine their destinies themselves. That statement, the Observer stated, was received with gratitude and great appreciation in Afghan political quarters and by the public at large. However, the official representatives of Pakistan expressed their dissatisfaction with it. Obviously, influential quarters in Pakistan, the Soviet commentator asserted, did not wish to abandon their plans of settling the Pakhtoon problem "through the forcible suppression of the just national aspirations of the Pukhtoons." In that connection, he recalled the despatch of regular Pakistani troops, supported by tanks and aeroplanes, to bomb peaceful Pakhtoon villages.

The Soviet writer expressed sympathy with Afghanistan's desire to rectify "the crying injustice committed by the colonialists" with regard to the Pakhtoons. He declared that Moscow could not remain indifferent to the situation emerging in direct proximity to its frontiers. The *Pravda* article then went on to observe :

> Clinging to the doomed attempts to impose their solution of the Pukhtoon question by force, the Pakistani ruling quarters only aggravate the conflict, whose consequences are dangerous as it is, and are increasing tension in this area of Asia. It is not excluded that this prospectless position is brought about by outside influences exerted by those aggressive forces that are interested in increasing tension in this area of Asia, in creating new seats of military conflicts.

The wisest way to achieve a peaceful settlement, the *Pravda* Observer pointed out, was the application of the principle of self-determination—a principle recognized by the UN Charter. Afghanistan's demand that the Pakhtoon people be given a chance to express their will through a free referendum and to decide whether they wished to remain within the bounds of

Pakistan, to form their own independent State or to reunite with Afghanistan, was considered fully justified.[63]

A broadcast in Bengali from Moscow Radio on 31 January 1962 doubted whether there was any other country save Pakistan in Asia so tied up with the United States through as many as 80 agreements in the military, political and economic fields. It warned Pakistan of "dangerous consequences" because of the "several difficult obligations" it assumed under "aggressive military pacts." These obligations, the Soviet broadcast added, had "completely mortgaged the foreign policy of Pakistan" which had been given the role of becoming a nuclear "graveyard in any possible future war" by its Western masters.[64]

The Soviet use of the veto in 1962 in the Security Council on the Kashmir question irked Pakistan. In vetoing the Irish-sponsored resolution calling upon India and Pakistan to resume negotiations, the Soviet representative observed that Moscow was not against direct bilateral negotiations. He said that Moscow was against negotiations "on the basis of the principles set forth in the outdated resolutions of the Security Council and UN Commission on Kashmir."[65] Similarly, the statement of the Soviet representative in the Security Council in February 1964 that "the question of Kashmir's belonging to India has already been decided by the Kashmiri people" and that "the India-Pakistan dispute should be settled directly by the parties concerned" hardly gave any consolation to Pakistan. Speaking in the National Assembly in 1964, Z.A. Bhutto described Pakistan's relations with the USSR as "subnormal."[66]

Although USSR-Pak relations were at a low ebb and remained so practically during the whole period of the Khrushchov leadership, Pakistan was not written off completely by the rulers of the Soviet Union. Even when Khrushchov extended support to India's stand on the Kashmir question, he, at the same time, expressed his desire to have friendly relations with Pakistan. He observed : "We shall persistently strive to improve these relations in the interest of peace."[67] Mikoyan subsequently stated : "Pacts or no pacts, the Soviet Union wanted cordial relations with Pakistan."[68] There was, however, no response from Karachi to Soviet offers of economic and technical assistance that were repeatedly and constantly made. As such, USSR-Pak relations in, the second half of the 1950s, remained bedevilled by Pakistan's close alliance with the Western Powers—heightened tension and bitter hostility being the main characteristic feature of their relations.

A combination of factors in the early 1960s, however, impelled both the USSR and Pakistan to come closer to each other. The U-2 incident induced both nations to realize the dangerous implications of geographical proximity to each other's borders. Mutual misunderstanding ought not to be permitted to run riot. With the coming into power of the Democrats under John F. Kennedy in Washington and the change in the US' attitude about India (the new US administration had adopted a benevolent and friendly attitude towards India and laid greater stress on economic assistance), a process of disenchantment or dissatisfaction towards Washington set in motion in the Pakistani mind.

The extension of military assistance to India by the USA in the wake of the Chinese aggression on India's northern borders further alienated Pakistan from the Western Powers. Islamabad viewed such assistance as an unfriendly act—upsetting the balance of power in the sub-continent to Pakistan's disadvantage.

The beginning of *detente* and cooperation between the East and the West after the Cuban missile crisis of 1962 also contributed to the creation of favourable conditions for the development of USSR-Pak relations. The US-Soviet *detente* encouraged Pakistan to look forward to improving its relations with Moscow without being misunderstood in the West. However, in the wake of its growing rift with Peking, Moscow could not but feel concerned about the possibility of Pakistan leaning heavily on the side of China. This was reflected in Suslov's report to the Central Committee of the CPSU in February 1964 in which he chided the Chinese leadership which allowed relations with non-aligned India to deteriorate and "has factually made an alliance with Pakistan, a member of the SEATO and the CENTO, which are threatening the peace and security of the Asian peoples."

The growing intimacy between China and Pakistan after the Sino-Indian Conflict caused strains in US-Pak relations. It was also a cause of serious concern to Moscow, which did not wish to see Islamabad come under the hostile influence of China. The Soviet Union seemed keen to profit by the developing fissures in US-Pak relations and endeavoured to move Pakistan out of the Western orbit. At the same time, Moscow thought of neutralizing the growing Chinese influence in Pakistan in view of the growing Sino-Soviet rift. Thus, Moscow realized the importance of cultivating relations with Islamabad, creating its presence and building its influence there in order to accomplish its dual task *vis-a-vis* its two rivals—the USA and China.

The Sino-Indian Conflict, observes S.M. Burke, a Pakistani writer, "furthered the process of Soviet-Pakistani rapprochement for a variety of reasons." Pakistani disaffection with the West in the wake of the Western Powers' arms aid to India and the necessity of preventing Pakistan from becoming too much dependent on China, or "a satellite" thereof has already been noted. Burke also thinks that Pakistani disaffection with the West was likely to influence "her fellow Muslim members of CENTO, Turkey and Iran, also to adopt a more independent foreign policy." He further refers to the Kremlin's anxiety about India being drawn into the American camp because of the massive economic aid rendered by the USA and the perceptible strength gathered by the Rightist forces in India. Along with military supplies from the West, he adds, New Delhi also allowed Western military teams to familiarize themselves "with the Indian military machine and with important frontier areas." Burke observes that "this was something the Russian military experts had never been able to achieve."[69]

Just as Moscow was trying to exploit fissures or strains in US-Pak relations in order to improve its relations with Islamabad, Washington, on its part, also sought to profit by the worsening Sino-Indian relations. The Kremlin's inability, for the time being, to move beyond a neutral posture in the Sino-Indian Conflict was made use of by the USA to further its interests in India. Soviet concern in the matter was reflected in the *New Times* allegation that the USA was trying to "inflate the border confiict" in order to encourage the pro-Western elements in India.[70] It was pointed out in the Soviet press that reactionary forces within India were using the conflict for pushing her off her neutral course and drawing her into the military-political blocs of the West. A Pakistani observer (Burke) went to the extent of asserting that, at the time, it looked to the Soviet Union as if India and Pakistan were changing places—that "India seemed to be coming under American domination while Pakistan was slipping out of it."[71]

In so far as the Indian military debacle in the Sino-Indian Conflict of 1962 demonstrated India's weakness and convinced the USSR that India could not possibly stand against China alone, Moscow might have begun to think that only after India and Pakistan were able to live together on friendly terms, and co-operate in various matters, could Chinese power be effectively checked, a proper balance of power established and stable conditions created in Asia. The achievement of that objective necessitated that not only should the Kremlin continue to maintain its friendly relations with India, but also try to broaden the base of its policy in the Indian sub-continent by establishing mutually beneficial and harmonious relations with Pakistan as well.

A beginning in that direction was made in March 1961 when Pakistan accepted a $30 million Soviet loan for the exploration of oil, thereby departing from its previous stand of depending almost exclusively on the Western Powers with regard to matters of aid. This was followed by another Soviet loan of £11 million and a barter deal in August 1963. A civil aviation pact (a Karachi-Moscow air route agreement) was signed in October 1963. Moreover, the oil and gas exploration agreement of 1961 was extended in 1963. In the words of I.M. Kompantsev, the Government of Pakistan, thus, "dropped its unreasonable positions" with respect to trade and Russian access to the country. A Pakistani-Soviet Cultural Association was also formed in the year 1963. It was for all these reasons that the author of the standard Russian history on the subject, *Pakistan i Sovetski Souiz* (1970), considered 1963 a "breakthrough" year in Soviet-Pakistan relations.[72] A further $11 million credit was given in June 1964, when an agreement on cultural and scientific exchange was also signed. Pakistan's Ambassador to the UN, Zafrullah Khan, stated in June 1963 that the impression he got from his talks in Moscow with Premier Khrushchov and Foreign Minister Gromyko was that the USSR would be "very responsive" to any move by Pakistan to establish closer relations not only in the economic but in other spheres as well.[73]

Pakistani observers came to notice a "perceptible Soviet shift,"[74] from their earlier position of unqualified support for India on Kashmir, in the remark of the Soviet delegate to the Security Council in May 1964 that the dispute between India and Pakistan should be settled by "the two interested parties" by peaceful means.[75] This was interpreted as a subtle change in the Soviet posture in so far as it amounted to Soviet recognition of the existence of a dispute over Kashmir, despite reaffirmation of the earlier Soviet position that the question to which country Kashmir belonged had already been settled by the people of Kashmir.

Even President Ayub's visit to the USSR, which took place in April 1965, was actually planned during Khrushchov's time. Again, in September 1964, when the Indian President, S. Radhakrishnan, visited Moscow, the Kremlin refrained from endorsing the Indian position over Kashmir in the joint communique. This departure from the earlier Soviet practice, an Indian researcher observes, was "perhaps motivated by a desire not to hurt Pakistani susceptibilities" and to preserve and consolidate its friendly presence in both India and Pakistan.[76]

4

Indo-Pakistan Conflict of 1965

THE tendency towards improvement in USSR-Pak relations, which was noticeable during the latter part of Khrushchov's leadership of the Soviet Union, became more marked after his exit in October 1964. In so far as Khrushchov's name was associated with close friendship with India and he was considered the chief architect of that policy, his exit created favourable conditions for the future of Soviet-Pakistani relations. Ayub could approach the new Soviet leadership with greater confidence and the latter was in a better position to modify the Soviet posture and adopt, more openly, a non-partisan or neutral attitude on Indo-Pakistan disputes. A few days after Khrushchov's ouster, the new government in the Kremlin renewed the invitation to Ayub, which had been extended to the Pakistani President during Khrushchov's time. Contacts at the highest level, thus, came to be established between the two countries.

After Khrushchov's exit, Moscow pursued a concerted and vigorous policy of cultivating friendship with its neighbours on its southern periphery. Pakistan's initiative in forging close relations with Turkey and Iran in the form of Regional Cooperation for Development in 1964 had not gone unnoticed in Moscow. In the following years, the Kremlin went to the extent of endorsing the Turkish position in Cyprus when it spoke of observing "the legitimate rights and interests of the Greek and Turkish national communities" in Cyprus.[1] Moscow was also seen extending a credit of $110 million to Iran for the purchase of Soviet arms and accepting repayment of the loan by constructing a 600-mile pipeline to take Iranian gas for use in the USSR as late as in the 1970s. Thus, Soviet policy in normalizing relations with Pakistan can be said to be in line with its policy of detaching Washington's old allies, *viz*. Turkey, Iran and Pakistan, utilizing, wherever possible, their disillusionment with US policies and actions—and befriending them by cultivating relations with them.

Direct contacts between Pakistan and the Soviet Union, at the highest level, were first established in April 1965 when President Ayub Khan visited the USSR. This was not, in any way, accidental. It was in consonance with the growing Pakistani posture of adopting an independent foreign policy. It was in Pakistan's interests to give the impression that, after giving up dependence on the United States, it was not becoming a satellite of China. The other motive in the Pakistani President's decision to visit Moscow was his desire to weaken Soviet sympathy for India. Moreover, it was in accordance with Pakistani tactics of playing one great Power against another with a view to securing the maximum benefit from both and exploring possibilities of economic co-operation and assistance for strengthening its economy.

President Ayub Khan had to engage in "a great deal of plain talk" at the Kremlin to discover that the Soviet leaders were "firm on their basic assumptions." He was unable to convince them that, by its participation in the Pacts his country was serving "as a moderating influence" or that India was not a non-aligned country. Whenever, in his discussions with Soviet leaders, he broached Indo-Pakistan problems posed by the Kashmir issue, or the "aggressive and expansionist policies" being pursued by India or "the Indian arms build-up," he was plainly advised to evolve "some mode of practical coexistence" with India and to resolve his country's problems through "direct negotiations." When Ayub referred to Soviet military aid to India and observed that "by a peculiar coincidence the policies of the USSR and the United States seemed to have coincided in India," Kosygin bluntly told him : "Only some enemy of ours could have told you that." According to Ayub Khan, Moscow justified its arms supplies to India on grounds of maintaining "the balance in Asia."

Inspite of the factors outlined above, Ayub got the impression that his frank discussions in the Kremlin resulted in "better appreciation" of Pakistan's position by Soviet leaders and that both sides recognized that there were "tremendous possibilities of cooperation" between Pakistan and the USSR.[2] This was certainly true in so far as economic and cultural relations were concerned. The joint communique stated that the two countries had signed a trade agreement on commodity exchange, a protocol on the delivery of Soviet machinery and equipment and an agreement on cultural exchange in the course of Ayub's visit to the Soviet Union. The Soviet Union also agreed to provide a credit of Rs. 150-250 million for the purchase of machinery[3] and to assist Pakistan in implementing 30 major development projects during the latter's Third Five-Year Plan period, including steel and power plants, radio communications, seaports and airfields.[4] In that connection, the Soviet Ambassador in Pakistan observed :

> In 1965 stagnation was done away with and a period of rapid growth of mutually beneficial trade set in; Soviet-Pakistan trade acquired a stable character. The two countries signed several long term agreements on commodity exchange and delivery of machinery and equipment on the instalment basis. This made it possible to establish firm business contacts between Soviet and Pakistani foreign trade agencies and allowed them to get a better idea of each other's requirements and possibilities.
> The results were not slow in coming. In 1966 Soviet purchases of Pakistani goods rose by more than 600 per cent. Simultaneously, the USSR greatly increased its deliveries to Pakistan. In subsequent years Soviet-Pakistan trade has remained on a higher level. When economists studied the results, it was found that in 1965-69, Soviet-Pakistan trade grew much in excess of the figure for all the 18 independent years of Pakistan. The range of export and import commodities has grown immeasurably.[5]

On political matters, the communique was quite vague and spoke of "useful and frank exchange of opinions." The two sides seemed to agree on the "great importance in the present stage" of preventing the proliferation of nuclear weapons and establishing nuclear-free zones in various areas of the world. However, they could not reach any agreement on the situation in South-East Asia, particularly on the events in Vietnam. The

communique merely recorded the exchange of respective viewpoints in the matter.[6]   On his return from the Soviet Union,
Ayub sought to derive much comfort from the reference made
in the joint communique to principles such as the right of the
peoples to determine their future and the honouring of
international agreements.   Those principles were said to have
"a direct relevance to many problems of this area,"[7] thereby
claiming Soviet support for Pakistan's stand on Kashmir.
There seemed little justification for such an assertion, particularly in the light of the revelations contained in his political
autobiography, *Friends Not Masters.*

That Ayub's visit to Moscow was not completely devoid of
results in the political field was amply proved by subsequent
events.   During the Rann of Kutch conflict between India and
Pakistan, Moscow adopted a non-partisan attitude.   On many
other issues also the USSR gave the impression that it would
like to continue its policy of improving relations with Pakistan.
Pakistan, on its part, also took certain steps from which Moscow could derive some satisfaction.   Thus Pakistan, along
with France, refused to toe the US line on Vietnam and had
its dissenting opinion recorded in the SEATO Council communique issued on 5 May 1965.   Pakistan's alignment with the
French rather than with "the American side" was taken note
of and welcomed in Moscow.[8]

Four days later, the Soviet Government appealed to both
India and Pakistan, which were engaged in hostilities in the
Rann of Kutch, to resolve their differences "through direct
negotiations, taking into account the interests of both sides."
Such a solution, it was pointed out, would benefit "not only
the peoples of India and Pakistan but also the cause of general
peace."[9]   The US Assistant Secretary of State, Phillips Talbot,
at that time, threatened a reappraisal of his country's aid programme for Pakistan and the World Bank consortium decided,
in July 1965, to postpone its meeting on providing economic
aid to Pakistan as pressure tactics.   That was labelled as
blackmail by *Izvestia.*[10] Considering it an opportune moment,
Moscow announced the supply of Rs. 1.5 crore worth of
machinery on credit for the construction of an airport in
Pakistan.[11]

The Soviet posture of goodwill and friendship towards Pakistan was also discernible in the 1965 May Day slogans, which, for the first time, included the people of Pakistan, along with those of Iran and Turkey, with whom the Soviet people desired friendly relations to "develop and grow stronger." The same attitude was reflected in the deletion of all references to Kashmir in the *Pravda* report (13 August 1965) on Aruna Asaf Ali's speech on the occasion of her acceptance of the Lenin Peace Prize. K. Mazurov, First Soviet Vice-Premier, observed in New Delhi that his country should not be expected to allow its relations with India and Pakistan to be governed by the mutual relations of those two countries.[12] Besides, *Pravda* omitted all references to Pakistani aggression in Kashmir, which were contained in the resolution passed by the National Council of the Communist Party of India.[13]

Soviet reporting of developments in the Indian sub-continent became quite restrained and Moscow seemed to adopt a non-committal attitude in the matter. No mention was made of Pakistani infiltration in Kashmir till 6 September 1965. Unlike Peking, Moscow did not take a one-sided view of the situation. Consequently, while quoting from Indian sources, Soviet news media did not forget to cite Pakistani versions of events and incidents, thereby presenting a balanced appraisal of the overall situation.

The Soviet representative, in his speech in the Security Council on 4 September 1965, emphasized that India and Pakistan themselves should find a way out to put "an immediate end to the bloodshed in Kashmir and to halt this conflict." He spoke of the two neighbouring countries resolving "the outstanding issues between them by peaceful means, *with due regard for their mutual interests*."[14]

The *Tass* statement of 7 September 1965 referred to violations of the cease-fire line in Kashmir and the involvement of large military units "in the military operations from both sides," without censuring either India or Pakistan for the armed conflict. Realizing the intricacy of the situation, the *Tass* statement appealed to the statesmen of both countries to display "realism, restraint and an understanding of the grave consequences of a development of the armed conflict" in order

to find a peaceful solution of the outstanding disputes. The
Soviet Government urged both sides to immediately halt all
military operations and effect a mutual withdrawal of troops.
Moscow reiterated its offer of good offices, if both sides deemed
that useful.[15]

Another *Tass* statement of 13 September 1965, viewed with
concern the widening of the conflict to new areas and the
alarming prospect of other States becoming involved therein.
It asked the Governments of both India and Pakistan not to
pay attention to the cause of the outbreak of hostilities. Once
more it urged them to show wisdom and take measures to stop
hostilities at once.[16] In a message to President Ayub Khan on
17 September 1965, Premier Kosygin further developed
his offer of good offices by suggesting that a meeting of the
leaders of India and Pakistan could be held either in Tashkent
or any other city in the Soviet Union, with his own participation therein, if both sides so desired.[17]

Since earlier Security Council resolutions had failed in
stopping hostilities, the Soviet Union did not hesitate to join
hands with the United States in "demanding" (a strong word
seldom used—amounting to a decision—the flouting of which
could invite sanctions under Chapter VII of the Charter)
an end to the bloodshed in the Indian sub-continent. After
the adoption of resolution 211 (1965) of 20 September
1965, the President of the Security Council observed that the
word "demand" was one that was not easily or readily used
in relation to sovereign nations and that it could only be justified in the interest of serving the cause of peace. In an attempt
to take care of the susceptibilities of Pakistan, the resolution
concerned itself not merely with a basis for the achievement of
a cease-fire. It also stated that the Security Council would
consider, as soon as the fighting had stopped, "what steps
could be taken to assist towards a settlement of the political
problem underlying the present conflict." India was unhappy
over this reference because it implied reactivation of Security
Council interference in the Kashmir problem. The Soviet
representative sought to assure India by stating, on 25 October
1965, that since the Council's decisions calling for a complete
cease-fire and the withdrawal of armed personnel had not been

fully implemented, it would hardly be in keeping with the spirit and letter of resolution 211 (1965) for it to consider other aspects of the problem. Accordingly, he urged the Council to discuss questions directly connected with the settlement of the armed conflict between India and Pakistan.[18] While welcoming the cessation of hostilities as a positive development, he stated that the main task was to consolidate the cease-fire, to ensure strict and scrupulous observance of the cease-fire agreement and "take the next step towards strengthening peace between India and Pakistan." Lest this "next step" might be construed by India as even vaguely referring to the Security Council consideration of the other aspects of the problem, the Soviet delegate, Fedorenko, hastened to observe that the withdrawal of troops and all armed personnel by both sides from the positions they occupied upto 5 August 1965, must proceed more rapidly.

In order not to be misunderstood in Pakistan, Fedorenko also stated that "these are the questions that must be settled *first*, these are the questions to which attention must be given in the situation that has now arisen." (Emphasis added.) Thus, he did not seem to rule out the possibility of the consideration, by the Security Council, of the political problem underlying the conflict at some future date. The resolutions adopted by the Security Council, he said, were an essential factor in the restoration of normal relations between India and Pakistan. The USSR has "constantly called for, and calls for, strict compliance with the Council's resolution."[19] Obviously, the use of cautious, calculated and measured phraseology indicated that Moscow was keen on preserving its neutral image and not jeopardizing its chances of playing a useful role as a mediator between India and Pakistan.

Moscow's motives in adopting the attitude it did during the Indo-Pakistan Conflict of 1965, can be gleaned from the *Pravda* statement of 24 August 1965, from the Soviet representative's statements in the UN Security Council and from Premier Kosygin's quiet and persuasive diplomacy at Tashkent. Evidently, Moscow could not but be concerned with the Conflict as it was taking place, as Kosygin put it, "in an area directly adjacent to the borders of the Soviet Union."[20] The *Pravda* statement of 24 August 1965 observed :

> Striving for the further development of its relations with Pakistan, the Soviet Union proceeds from the fact that neighbourliness between our States does not contradict our friendship with any third country. Strengthening the ties between the USSR and Pakistan must be regarded as a part of a general policy aimed at ensuring peace in Asia and throughout the world. We would like Soviet-Pakistani relations, like our traditional friendship with India, to be a stabilizing factor in the situation in Asia and to contribute to the normalization of relations between Pakistan and India.[21]

In the opinion of *Pravda*, the conflict in the sub-continent would have had an injurious effect on the weak economic condition of both India and Pakistan. The exacerbation of the conflict "would complicate even more" the situation in Asia—which was already suffering from instability because of the war in Vietnam. The *Pravda* statement acknowledged the existence of the Kashmir "dispute" but wanted both India and Pakistan to approach the disputed problems "realistically." In a way, it implied that each of them should give up resort to force for liberating the part occupied by the other and accept the *status quo*. That was also the import of the suggestion contained in the *Pravda* statement that India and Pakistan should settle "the disputes and unresolved questions existing between them by peaceful means, with mutual regard for each other's interests and without resorting to arms."[22]

The Soviet Union was quite aware of the existence of a *de facto* alliance between Pakistan and China and felt concerned about the involvement of Peking in the Indo-Pakistan Conflict. It realized the dangers inherent in that situation which continued to grow and threatened to develop into a larger military conflict. Kosygin, therefore, advised both the Pakistani President and the Indian Prime Minister to settle "all disputes, including the questions associated with Kashmir...by peaceful means alone." The extension of the Conflict, he said, would

> serve the purposes only of those external forces that seek to divide the States which have liberated themselves from the colonial yoke and to set one against the other, forces that are interested in weakening the unity of the Afro-Asian

countries. These forces are not averse to instigating Pakistan and India to increase the bloodshed for their own ends, which have nothing in common with the interests of the Indian and Pakistan peoples.[23]

The above-mentioned remarks of Kosygin were clearly directed against China. On 11 September 1965, Brezhnev warned against "third forces" that tried to benefit by the aggravation of Indo-Pak relations and "sometimes added fuel to the fire."[24] The *Tass* statement of 7 September also had Peking in mind when it spoke of "outside forces" that sought "to disunite and set at loggerheads the States that cast off the colonial yoke."[25] The statement of the Soviet representative in the UN Security Council on 18 September likewise asserted that the continuation of the conflict "benefits only the forces which are pursuing the criminal policy of dividing peoples so as to achieve their imperialist and expansionist aim."[26]

The *Tass* statement of 13 September 1965 was even more specific in criticizing China, though again without naming it. It blamed "the forces of imperialism and reaction" that were said to "benefit from spreading hostilities further." At the same time, it accused "those who facilitate the widening of the conflict by their provocative statements and policies." It desired that "all States, the whole world, should warn them that they were assuming a grave responsibility for this policy, for these actions." "No government has the right to throw fat in the fire," it asserted.[27] Operative Para 3 of the Security Council resolution of 20 September 1965 called on all States "to refrain from any action which might aggravate the situation in the area." For obvious reasons, the USA joined hands with the USSR in issuing such an emphatic warning to Peking. On 23 September 1965, *Pravda* criticized China for adopting a wholly partisan attitude as regards the Indo-Pakistan Conflict. The Soviet paper endorsed Indian Prime Minister Shastri's statement that Peking was attempting "to prolong the conflict between India and Pakistan and to expand its scale" by its threatening language and ultimatums. It expressed deep "concern" of the Soviet Union about reports of the movement and the concentration of Chinese armed forces on the borders with India.[28]

The neutral stance of the Soviet Union in the Indo-Pakistan Conflict of 1965 was clearly perceptible in the *Novosti* Press Agency (APN) commentary by N. Smetanin, released by the Press Information Department of the USSR Embassy in Karachi on 12 November 1965. The commentary stated that the cease-fire did not mean the elimination of the causes of conflict between the two peoples fraternal to the USSR. The Commentator spoke of taking into account the interests of both India and Pakistan. The elimination of the causes of conflict, he said, was a matter *abave all* for India and Pakistan and they should sit down at the conference table in order to settle "this old and dangerous issue," *i.e.* Kashmir. He then went on to add :

> Attempts are at times made to claim that the Soviet Union is allegedly not objective and is inclined to support one side at the expense of the other side. Such opinions are far from reality. The only thing desired by the Soviet Government is the establishment of a stable peace between Pakistan and India and, as far as this basic desire is concerned, the Soviet Government equally appeals to the leaders of Pakistan as well as to those of India with the call to display wisdom, restraint and patience. Soviet people are convinced that only under these conditions, not on the battlefield but at the round table of peaceful negotiations, can and should a final and stable agreement be reached between Pakistan and India on the Kshamir problem.[29]

Moscow's non-partisan attitude was necessary for it to establish its credibility with both India and Pakistan as regards mediation. However, this did not mean that the USSR overlooked the importance which India had for the Soviet Union. India's policy of non-alignment, her size, population, and the useful role she could play in maintaining a proper balance of power in Asia, particularly *vis-a-vis* China, could not obvioualy be ignored by Moscow. India provided greater scope in economic cooperation. Moreover, she had a strong base of leftist elements which made for greater possibilities of keeping her on friendly terms with the Soviet Union on a long-term basis. For all these reasons, New Delhi counted more than Pakistan in Soviet calculations. This preference for India was reflected in occasional references about Kashmir being an integral part of India and in the continuation of Soviet supplies of military hardware to New Delhi. Under an agreement concluded in September 1965 itself, Moscow agreed to sell several submarines to India. The Kremlin also rendered support to India in the United Nations as and when necessary. For instance, Moscow opposed the simultaneous consideration of the underlying political problems and rejected the Western Powers' proposal regarding the setting up of a four-Power Commission consisting of the Big Four. The Soviet proposal was primarily concerned with the consolidation of the cease-fire and the withdrawal of forces to positions of 5 August 1965. The political solution was relegated to a secondary place. It was considered a complex problem requiring meaningful talks between the parties in which Moscow was willing to assist, if the two sides so desired.

Although Soviet sympathies were largely with India, Moscow deemed it prudent not to support her openly or to criticize or condemn Pakistan. The Kremlin was primarily interested in the conclusion of a satisfactory and sensible peace settlement, which would ensure stable conditions on its southern flank and, at the same time, preserve its friendship with both the sides. Besides, Moscow desired to see a stable balance established in Asia. For that matter, the Soviet Union sought to guard against Pakistan drawing too close to either Peking or Washington. At the asme time, it could not afford to see India sliding towards the West or China. Moscow could not rule out these possibilities. In case the Soviet attitude failed to satisfy New Delhi and Peking was found strongly supporting Pakistan, India might be favourably inclined towards the West. And in case India came to the conclusion that both the super Powers were supporting Pakistan, she might be left with no alternative save that of patching up with Peking.

In these circumstances, it was, indeed, an exercise in tight-rope walking on the part of the Soviet Union. This was well reflected in the guarded statements of the Soviet representatives, in the cautious coverage of news and views in the Soviet press and in the skillful diplomacy of Soviet leaders. Soviet papers refrained from condemning either India or Pakistan. They simply reported suitably edited versions of the allegations of breaches of ceasefire by either side. The successful outcome of talks at Tashkent was, indeed, a remarkable feat of Soviet diplomacy. Tashkent enabled Moscow to acquire "a new leverage in the sub-continent's politics by giving both India and Pakistan a stake in her friendship."[30]

Before Ayub Khan agreed to the Tashkent meeting. under the auspices of the USSR, he had primarily depended on the United States. This was partly due to the fact that he was not fully convinced of the *bonafides* of Moscow, even though the Kremlin seemed to take a non-partisan attitude in the Indo-Pakistan Conflict. Here it is significant to recall that in the *Pravda* statement of 24 August 1965 and in the 4 September 1965 speech of the Soviet representative in the Security Council, Kashmir was described as "the Indian State of Jammu and Kashmir." Moreover, Moscow had opposed the proposal of constituting a four-Power Commission of the Security Council to resolve Indo-Pakistan problems. This proposal could be said to be the nearest to adopting Ayub's suggestion of instituting a self-executing arrangement for resolving the real cause of the Conflict, *viz*. the Kashmir dispute, under the aegis of the UN. For these reasons, Ayub appeared hestitant in accepting the Soviet offer of good offices initially. He accepted the Soviet proposal as regards mediation only "in principle." He wanted the necessary ground to be prepared first. He preferred the Conflict being resolved in the Security Council, where he counted on the strong support of Washington and London. He believed that Kosygin's proposal about a meeting at Tashkent "would not at present be fruitful." Instead, he suggested that Moscow should coordinate its efforts in the Security Council so that "a meaningful resolution that can lead to an honourable settlement of the Kashmir dispute" could be worked out there. It was only when Ayub failed to get the required satisfaction from the Security Council (where he could only get a fragile cease-fire) that the Foreign Minister of Pakistan announced his country's unconditional acceptance of the Soviet offer of good offices at Tashkent. He then also made a strong plea for Kosygin to take an active part in the meeting.

The presence of Indian troops on the outskirts of Lahore was particularly galling to Islamabad. It greatly damaged the prestige of the military rulers of Pakistan. The

withdrawal of Indian troops from Lahore, as also from certain
vantage points such as Haji Pir Pass, was an immediate
necessity for Pakistan. Secondly, the specific mention of the
Kashmir dispute in the Tashkent Declaration marked a distinct improvement over the vague reference in the Security
Council resolution of 20 September 1965—that the Council
would consider "the political problem underlying the present
conflict" at an appropriate time after the withdrawal of forces
had been completed. This afforded some satisfaction to
Pakistan as, after a lapse of many years, it seemed to revive
the Kashmir dispute on the international plane. Thus, what
Pakistan failed to achieve with the support of its powerful
allies, the USA and the UK, and with the ultimatums of
China, it was able to secure from the good offices of Moscow.
Ayub Khan was, therefore, especially grateful to the Soviet
Union for its role at Tashkent, which helped him in extricat-
ing himself from a difficult situation.

To sum up, although some initial steps in the direction of
an improvement of USSR-Pak relations could be said to have
been taken during Khrushchov's time, a real breakthrough in
their political relations was achieved subsequent to his ouster
and after Sino-Pakistan collusion became a patent fact. Ayub's
visit to Moscow in April 1965 was an important event in
USSR-Pak relations. That visit, the Soviet Ambassador to
Pakistan asserted, marked a "big and drastic change," in the
relations between the two countries.[31] Thereafter, a visible
shift towards "a more even-handed Soviet policy towards
India and Pakistan became noticeable."[32] This found reflec-
tion in the attitude adopted by Moscow during the Rann of
Kutch crisis in April-May 1965 and in the Indo-Pak Conflict of
September 1965. Thus, a parallelism in the policies of the
USA and the USSR towards the sub-continent was quite
apparent. Both the super Powers warned China against any
intervention in the affairs of the sub-continent. Guided by a
similar approach and with all the blessings of Washington,
Moscow assumed the role of a mediator at Tashkent. It was,
therefore, hardly surprising that while the USA warmly welcomed the Tashkent Declaration, Peking came to denounce it
in strong terms.[33]

Tashkent represented a great diplomatic victory for Moscow *vis-a-vis* both China and the USA, Peking in particular. It made the Soviet presence felt in the Indian sub-continent and confirmed the status of the USSR as an Asian Power. While the Chinese image was tarnished as one of a mischief-maker, that of the Soviet Union, as a peace-maker, received a boost. As a result, Soviet influence was greatly enhanced in the entire Indian sub-continent and Moscow was able to consolidate its ties with both India and Pakistan. In so far as it helped in effacing the "impression created by Khrushchov of Soviet partisanship for India,"[34] it greatly facilitated the improvement of USSR-Pak relations. Henceforth, Moscow began to extend large-scale economic assistance to Pakistan for a number of projects and trade relations came to be considerably strengthened.

5

After Tashkent

AFTER Tashkent, Moscow believed that the time was propitious to cultivate Pakistan in a big way. The Soviet Union extended large-scale economic assistance to Pakistan. Trade expanded and a number of visits were exchanged between the two countries during 1966. The Soviet Minister of Geology attended the Pakistan National Day Celebrations in Moscow on 24 March 1966 and K.T. Mazurov led a nine-member parliamentary delegation to Pakistan in May-June 1966. In June-July 1966, Air Marshal Nur Khan visited Moscow as the leader of a military delegation. On 25 September 1966, the Soviet Deputy Foreign Minister, N.P. Firyubin, paid a hurried visit to Pakistan. He brought with him a message from Prime Minister Kosygin which was said to have invoked the Tashkent spirit.[1] In November 1966, a Russian tennis star and a football team came on a goodwill visit to Pakistan. In the same month, Professor G. Sverglov of the Institute of World Economy and International Relations visited Pakistan. He was followed by a three-man Soviet trade union delegation led by G. Podelshikov.

While in the 1965 May Day slogans, Pakistan had been grouped together with Iran and Turkey, the 1966 May Day slogans contained separate greetings for Pakistan, in just the same way as for the UAR and India. It was stated : "May the friendly and good neighbourly relations between Pakistan and Soviet Union develop and grow." This was in consonance with Brezhnev's earlier remark that some improvement in relations with Pakistan had taken place.[2]

A barter agreement providing for the exchange of Pakistani rice for Russian vehicles and road-building and engineering machinery was concluded in January 1966. A contract with regard to the construction of a 110,000 kw thermal power station in Gorzala by the USSR was signed during the visit of the Soviet parliamentary delegation.[3] Under the important Soviet economic assistance agreement of September 1966, the Soviet Union undertook to render technical assistance in the construction of 21 projects in Pakistan. These included two plants for the production of electrical machinery and the Guddu Thermal Power Station on the Indus river—the biggest in Asia with a total capacity of 820,000 kilowatts. The Kremlin also agreed to build 15 broadcasting houses, a high-voltage transmission line, more than 1,000 km long, and a railway-cum-highway bridge across the Rupsa river. To finance these projects, the Soviet Government granted a long-term state credit of 20 million roubles and a commercial credit of Rs. 300 million at 2.5 per cent interest.[4]

By the end of 1966, the USSR had provided $176 million worth of economic aid to Pakistan for various purposes—$30 million in 1961 for oil exploration, $11 million in 1964 for the import of agricultural machinery, $50 million in 1965—the first general credit—and $85 million in 1966. The period of repayment of these credits ranged from 10 to 12 years and the rate of interest was also "favourable." According to M.M. Ahmad, the Deputy Chairman of the Pakistan Planning Commission, the other good features of these credits were the favourable prices of commodities and the acceptance of repayments in the shape of goods from Pakistan. In an interview in January 1968, M.M. Ahmad observed that while the cut in aid in the US Aid Bill had not affected the already committed $140 million of commodity assistance to Pakistan, it did affect project assistance. He was, therefore, constrained to remark : "There is remote chance of getting project assistance now from the United States."[5]

The total availability of project aid from Socialist countries upto March 1967 was enumerated by the *Pakistan Times* as—$134 million from the USSR, $30 million from China, $43.5 million from Czechoslovakia, $14 million from Poland and

$80.8 million from Yugoslavia.[6] There was also a sharp increase in USSR-Pakistan trade which rose from Rs. 3.7 million in 1956 to Rs. 42.8 million in 1962, to Rs. 65.0 million in 1964, to Rs. 81.4 million in 1965 and to as much as Rs. 326 million in 1966. A characteristic feature of this trade was a steady growth in the supply of Soviet machinery and equipment.[7]

An editorial in the *Pakistan Times* of 21 January 1967 entitled "Oil Horizons" criticized foreign private oil groups, whose chief consideration was to obtain one-sided "concessions." It spoke in favourable terms of the 120 Soviet experts engaged in a joint venture of oil exploration in Pakistan, the import of special Soviet equipment and technological methods, as also the utilization of the initial Soviet credit worth Rs. 14.5 crores. All this, it said, had been highly beneficial for Pakistan. The very fact that the Pakistan-Soviet oil agreement (signed six years earlier) had been extended for three years and the allocation for oil exploration under the Third Plan raised to Rs. 65 crores, clearly indicated that the prospects of striking oil in the days ahead were considered bright. (Till then no oil had been struck there.) The current visit of the Soviet Minister for Geology, Sidorenko, it added, had also indicated that his Government might be willing to undertake mineral exploration in Pakistan, thereby opening "new vistas of cooperation between the two countries."

As the Soviet Union was giving valuable assistance for certain key projects "designed to promote economic self-reliance," Moscow's solicitude for Pakistan's welfare was considered "genuine and growing." With the USSR becoming "the second largest donor State," and with more frequent contacts at the highest levels, Pakistan-Soviet ties were said to have "gone beyond the stage of normalisation and acquired new depth since President Ayub's epoch-making visit to Moscow in 1965." Following the lead given by the Soviet Union, other Socialist countries of Europe also began to extend economic and technical assistance to Pakistan. Commenting on it, the *Pakistan Times*, in an editorial, observed :

Emulating the Soviet Union's example, several Socialist States have lately stepped up their commercial, technical and cultural exchanges and come forward to participate in the implementation of the Third Plan in a big way. All this has made a visible impact on the socio-economic scene in Pakistan and given an enduring basis to its ties with the Socialist world.[8]

Ayub Khan was evidently quite impressed by the development of Pakistan's relations with the Soviet Union in 1966-67. He realized that while close alliance with the USA and China was important, friendship with USSR was no less desirable. Washington had helped Pakistan to modernize its armed forces. It had supplied huge amounts of military hardware and economic assistance in the past and could, in the future, be relied upon so far as economic aid, the supply of spares and support in the UN was concerned. However, Washington was found undependable as it had suspended military help during a crucial period, while Moscow had continued fulfilling its commitments to India. Thus, the USA could not be completely relied upon so far as confrontation with India was concerned. It was China which served that purpose. Though Peking was not in a position to render military or economic aid to Pakistan on the scale that the USA had done or the USSR could do in the future, it could, unlike the two super Powers, be depended upon in its hostility towards India. Moreover, the geographical proximity of China gave strength to the effectiveness and credibility about Chinese support against India. Pakistan, therefore, felt inclined to maintain close relations with Peking. At the same time, Ayub Khan believed that Pakistan stood to gain a great deal from developing friendship with the USSR—one of its three big neighbours. That enabled his country to procure much-needed economic and technical assistance from the latter, thereby ensuring the success of its development plans. Although the visit of a Pakistani military mission to Moscow in June 1966 did not bear fruit, Ayub did not lose hope of obtaining military aid from the Soviet Union. The negative gains of cultivating relations with the USSR were no less important. H.K. Burki observed :

The negative aspect, though never stated by either side, is nonetheless very important. Pakistan has been normalising and developing its ties with the Soviet Union to challenge India's monopoly on Soviet sympathy and, if possible, to neutralise Moscow's support for Delhi...the

Soviet Union, having helped in the conclusion of the Tashkent Declaration, was morally bound to take a neutral position and not to add to Pakistan's difficulties by pumping into India some of the most sophisticated weapons...If Russia desired to strengthen her ties with Pakistan then she had to take care that its vital interests, and nothing could be more vital than Pakistan's security, were not threatened.[9]

The advances in technology, especially the development of inter-continental ballistic missiles, diminished the utility of military bases. The growing rapprochement between the two super Powers further reduced the utility of Pakistan as a formal ally of the USA. For all the reasons mentioned above, Ayub realized that neither exclusive dependence on Washington nor a special relationship with China was the answer to Pakistan's requirements. He came to the conclusion that Islamabad should develop fruitful relations with all the three Powers— the USA, the USSR and China. Thus, the theory of "bilateral equations" or equi-distance from all the three Powers was evolved. It was, indeed, a well-thought-out policy. It sought to preserve the formal alliance structure with the West as well as the informal understandings with Peking, At the same time, Pakistan looked towards Moscow not only as regards the expansion of trade and the extension of economic assistance, but also for the supply of military equipment and political support. By this stratagem, Pakistan sought to derive maximum benefits in various fields from both Western and Communist sources. Moreover, its posture of pursuing an independent foreign policy enabled Pakistan to maintain its moorings in the Third World, the Afro-Asian community in particular. Commenting on the disadvantages arising out of total alignment with the West, Z.A. Bhutto (in his book *The Myth of Independence*) observed as follows :

She [Pakistan] had incurred the hostility of the Soviet Union, which openly supported Afghanistan and India against Pakistan. The policy of alignment also damaged Pakistan's image in the United Nations, strained her relations with neighbouring Islamic Arab States, and drove her towards isolation in the community of Asia and Africa.[10]

Ayub Khan described the policy of "bilateral equations" with the three great Powers in his autobiography (*Friends Not Masters*, published in 1967) in the following words :

We should endeavour to set up bilateral equations with
each one of them, with the clear understanding that the
nature and complexion of the equation should be such as to
promote our mutual interests without adversely affecting the
legitimate interests of third parties...No bilateral equation
could be established in isolation; other equations would
influence its level. In the end each equation would be
determined by the limits of tolerance of third parties. So
each equation would have to be acceptable to third parties
with whom we might be able to establish bilateral relations
of mutual benefit. That is where all the complications and
difficulties would arise. It would be like walking on a trian-
gular tightrope.[11]

Z.A. Bhutto, who was Ayub's main adviser on international
affairs till 1966 but subsequently became a bitter opponent of
his former master, likewise, believed in a similar policy, which he
called "normal bilateral relations" with the three Global Powers.
There was, however, a difference. He considered that policy
applicable not only to Pakistan but to all the small countries of
Asia, Africa and Latin America as well. Moreover, of the three
Global Powers, he attached greater importance to his country's
relations with China, with which its basic interests were said to
"conform."[12] Accordingly, he advocated "normal but qualified" relations with the USA and the USSR and "normal and
unqualified" relations with Peking.

This marked perference for China in Bhutto's scheme of
things did not suit Ayub, particularly at a time when he was
trying to repair the damage caused to US-Pak relations and
evolve "a better understanding" with Washington by reducing
"irritants." The dismissal of Bhutto from office was part of that
policy. To the author of The Myth of Independence, however,
that seemed to be "a measure of her penance" vis-a-vis the
USA and leading to the revival of a "special relationship" with
the United States "which had been shattered in the aftermath
of the 1965 war."[13] Bhutto had been the indefatigable champion of confrontation with India and a firm believer in a special
relationship with China, which he always regarded "a plus-
factor for coping with India."[14] His dismissal, therefore, offered
much relief to both Moscow and Washington.

Speaking on 15 February 1967, the Information Minister of
Pakistan, Khwaja Shahabuddin, observed that Soviet influence

in the region should be of "considerable assistance" to both India and Pakistan in resolving their outstanding disputes, especially the dispute relating to the State of Jammu and Kashmir. Pakistan's friendship with the Soviet Union, he said, was "entirely consistent with maintenance of good relations with the West and development of strong friendly ties with People's Republic of China." He regretted that the former Foreign Minister, Z.A. Bhutto, had adopted an "equivocal attitude" as regards the Tashkent Declaration on his return to Pakistan. He appreciated the "initiative" of the Soviet Union—unprecedented in Soviet history—in facilitating a settlement between India and Pakistan. The pressure exerted by Soviet leaders, he said, was only of a "moral character" as their sole anxiety was to promote understanding and peace in this region. The Soviet attitude throughout the long period of difficult deliberations, he added, was "dispassionate, neutral and constructive." He considered it "fortunate" that, inspite of what Bhutto had been saying and doing, relations between Pakistan and the Soviet Union had continued to grow along friendly lines and added : "We are now looking forward to the visit of the Soviet Prime Minister."[15]

In the beginning of 1967, numerous steps were taken to cement the ties of friendship between Pakistan and the USSR. In February 1967, a trade agreement was concluded. It laid a firmer economic base for building closer relations. A commercial section was opened in the Pakistani Embassy in Moscow to look after the expanding trade. A new Soviet magazine called *Tulu*, devoted to Pakistan, made its appearance and was reported to have been well received in Pakistan. The first Pakistani publication on the Soviet Union entitled *The Modernisation of Soviet Central Asia* also came out in February 1967. The establishment of an exchange between the Soviet Press Agency (APN) and the United Press of Pakistan was announced a month later. About the same time, the first ship of more than 12,000 deadweight tons, constructed in the USSR for Pakistan, was launched at a Soviet shipyard near the Black Sea. Thus, Soviet-Pak relations began to develop in all directions, particularly in the fields of trade and culture.

The year 1966 was a high watermark in the relations of

Pakistan and the Soviet Union. After 1966, exchange of visits at the level of heads of State or government became almost a regular feature and periodic mutual consultations commenced between the two countries. However, the unabated Russian supplies of arms to India, at a time when the delivery of US military hardware to Pakistan remained suspended, remained an eye-sore for Islamabad. It is said that Soviet economic aid commitments to India totalled more than $1 billion. $300 million worth of credit was also reported to have been provided by the USSR for India's defence requirements.[16] Soviet military assistance to India was stated to have increased considerably after 1964. Another estimate, said to be based on both Indian and foreign sources, put the value of Russian arms supply to India in the range of Rs. 750 to Rs. 900 crores.[17]

Islamabad must have raised the question of Soviet arms assistance to India in the course of exchanges with Soviet leaders, particularly during the visit of the Pakistani military delegation, led by Air Marshal Nur Khan, to Moscow in June-July 1966. Pakistan must have argued strongly against the augmentation of India's might, which was said to give New Delhi an edge over Pakistan and disturb the military balance of power in the subcontinent to Islamabad's disadvantage. Nur Khan must have argued that either Moscow put an embargo on or stop the supply of arms to India, or as an alternative, start giving arms to Pakistan. A Pakistani writer, Mohsin Ali, referred to "a grave imbalance in the arms potentials of India and Pakistan" due to the "unrestricted supply of Soviet arms to India." He then observed :

> The sub-continent's peace—and Soviet friendship for Pakistan— demand that Moscow halt the supply of arms to New Delhi or at any rate reduce its volume to the level of spares for weapons already supplied or else arm Pakistan also.[18]

During his second visit to Moscow in September-October 1967, Ayub Khan must have impressed upon Soviet leaders the necessity of doing something about the military imbalance in the subcontinent, conveniently ignoring or overlooking the military assistance received by Pakistan from China. His expectations from the Soviet Union were reflected in the speech delivered by him at a banquet in the Kremlin. In that speech, he dwelt on the similarity of views between Pakistan and the USSR on the conclusion of a treaty on the non-proliferation of nuclear weapons "without further delay" so as to prevent "under all circumstances the emergence of a sixth nuclear power." Ayub Khan also referred to the dispute over Jammu and Kashmir as "a source of serious tension in South Asia, the main stumbling block in the way of good-neighbourly relations between Pakistan and India," thereby imploring Soviet leaders to exert themselves with a view to securing a favourable solution for Pakistan in the matter.

Ayub Khan then drew Moscow's attention to the urgent problem of "the indiscriminate increases in armaments and the growing military imbalance in the subcontinent" which he considered "a danger to peace."[19] Obviously, he wanted Soviet leaders to supply arms, even though on a limited scale, to Pakistan, if the discontinuance of military assistance to India was not acceptable to Moscow. That this was the uppermost problem in Ayub's mind was also evident from his dinner speech in Moscow (in which he expressed concern about "our security" and highlighted "the need for maintenance of proper balance in areas of tension"[20]) and his broadcast to the nation, on his return from the Soviet Union. Speaking over Pakistan Radio on 5 October 1967, Ayub observed :

> When world powers say that they desire to establish peace and security in the subcontinent, it is their duty to remove the imbalance that is being created by the Indian arms build-up.[21]

Ayub also requested "further economic assistance," in the form of greater Soviet participation in Pakistan's Third Five-Year Plan.

Apart from promises of liberal economic assistance and recognition of the importance of maintaining personal contacts between the statesmen and representatives of the two countries at different levels, Ayub, it seems, could not cut much ice with Soviet leaders, particularly as regards Pakistan's outstanding problems with India. In his speech, Kosygin drew Ayub's attention to the fact that "roads to the solution of existing differences can and must be patiently sought." He stressed that "the profound community of the interests of the peoples" should always be rated higher than "the differences and contradictions." He advised Ayub to seek a peaceful solution of his country's problems with India, to improve relations with her and learn to "live and work in conditions of good neighbourhood and peace." He assured him of the willingness of the Soviet leaders to "facilitate in every way" the creation of stable conditions of peace in the region.[22]

That the Soviet Union rejected Ayub Khan's arguments in regard to the so-called military imbalance in the sub-continent, restoration of power-parity or balance of power *vis-a-vis* India is quite obvious from the reported Soviet decision (in early 1968) to supply about a hundred supersonic SU-7 fighter-bombers to India. Pakistan's Foreign Minister deprecated the Russian move as further widening "the military imbalance between India and Pakistan," and contributing to the arms race, thereby hindering their economic development.[23] The *Pakistan Times* blamed Soviet leaders for the step that was "contrary to their professions of friendship with Pakistan" and went against the latter's security interests.[24]

The joint communique issued on Ayub's visit on 4 October 1967 recorded a similarity of views on the Middle East (co-demning Israel's acts of aggression and calling for the immediate withdrawal of its troops from Arab territories) and "the urgent conclusion of an international treaty on non-proliferation of nuclear weapons." However, it contained only vague references to Vietnam (belief in the need for immediate cessation of war on the basis of recognizing the Vietnamese peoples' right to decide their fate without outside interference as envisaged in the 1954 Geneva Agreements) and Indo-Pak relations. Ayub was allowed to express his keen desire "for an early settlement of the disputes between India and Pakistan and for the establishment of normal good neighbourly relations between them" without the Soviet side expressing any views in the matter. That no reference was made in the communique to the Tashkent Declaration might have been due to Pakistan's insistence.

The main achievement of Ayub's visit to the USSR may be said to be in the economic and cultural fields. The two sides agreed "to further strengthen the existing ties and to enlarge the areas of cooperation in political, economic, cultural and other spheres." They also agreed "to work out a plan for further substantial increase in economic cooperation and trade extending up to 1975" through the experts of their Governments in the near future. The communique further added that the two sides expressed their intention to widen Soviet-Pakistan ties in the sphere of science and technology. The Soviet Union expressed its readiness to provide "friendly assistance" to Pakistan in the preparation of national cadres of trained teachers, physicians, scientists and specialists in other fields.[25]

The supply of Soviet arms to India, particularly the latest SU-7 supersonic fighter-bombers, irked Pakistan, just as the presence of hostile bases on the soil of Pakistan, in close proximity to Soviet borders, was disliked by Moscow. When Moscow submitted a draft resolution in the United Nations on the immediate dismantling of all American and other Western military bases in Asia, Africa and Latin America, a *Dawn* correspondent readily sensed Soviet susceptibilities in regard to the presence of US intelligence installations near Peshawar. He observed :

Though the Soviet delegate did not actually spell it out, the USSR is also said to be for eliminating some American bases which go under the name of Communication Centres. Equipped with ultra-modern electronic devices, they are used for listening into strategic areas of 'potential enemy territory'. One such base, the Russians hold, exists on the eastern side of the Khyber Pass where some 2,000 Americans are said to be manning a gigantic network of listening posts directed at strategic parts of the Soviet Union and China.[26]

Before meeting Pakistan's wishes about the supply of Soviet arms, even to a limited extent, Moscow evidently wanted a *quid-pro-quo* from Islamabad in the form of the removal of US bases near its borders. In 1966, the Kremlin had agreed to supply some helicopters and other equipment, such as jeeps, etc. Though they could be utilized for military purposes, they did not come in the category of lethal weapons. Thus, in a subtle way, Moscow sought to kindle hopes in the minds of Pakistani leaders, provided Islamabad also took steps in the direction of meeting Russian wishes in a matter concerning their security. Premier Kosygin must have received some assurances on the part of Pakistan, in that regard, before he visited Pakistan in April 1968. In a despatch from Rawalpindi, a Russian journalist recalled the refusal of Islamabad, in the last few years, "to take part in exercises within the framework of military blocs." He also referred to the recall of the Pakistani representative from the SEATO Military Advisers Group and his participation in the April session of the SEATO Council in London only as "an observer" as instances of Pakistan taking a generally independent line in its foreign policy. He then hastened to remark : "There is still an American base in the country, although the *Pakistani press has hinted it may soon be closed down.*"[27] Moscow could hardly derive much comfort from Pakistan's non-conformist posture in the SEATO. Such an attitude was actually more beneficial to China. Although the closure of the US Military Assistance Advisory Group in Pakistan was announced on 12 April 1967, the US intelligence bases near Soviet borders continued to exist and these directly affected Soviet security interests.

Before Kosygin set his foot on Pakistani soil on 17 April 1968, Islamabad served notice on Washington under paragraph 12 of the 18 July 1959 US-Pakistan agreement relating to the establishment and operation of the communications unit (intelligence base) at Badaber near Peshawar. It was stated that Pakistan would not be interested in the renewal of the agreement for "a second period of ten years."[28] Though this did not foreclose the possibility of year-to-year renewal, it was considered unlikely that the USA would be much interested in such an arrangement, particularly when it had other sources, *e.g.* satellites, to gather similar intelligence. This significant gesture of goodwill towards Moscow created a favourable atmosphere for Kosygin's five-day official visit, which was arranged at short notice and announced only a fortnight before it was scheduled to take place.

Under these circumstances, Ayub Khan was more hopeful of getting a satisfactory response from Moscow with regard to the supply of military hardware, as also on the Kashmir dispute with India. Speaking at a banquet given in honour of Premier Kosygin, he observed :

Pakistan prizes peace and friendship but it must at the same time be assured of security. It is only when this comes that confidence returns and the path towards reconciliation and cooperation can broaden. This is very simply why we in Pakistan are naturally concerned at anything which may tend to increase what we consider to be risks to ourselves.

As students of history we have learnt that when nations become too strong, too confident, too arrogant, they threaten peace....May I entertain the hope that a just and honourable settlement of the basic dispute of Jammu and Kashmir will be found and the main obstacle to the establishment of good neighbourly relations between the two countries [India and Pakistan] removed.[29]

Premier Kosygin's was the first visit by a Soviet dignitary at that level. He agreed to render technical and economic assistance in the construction of the $100 million steel plant at Kalabagh in West Pakistan, a nuclear power station at Roopur in East Pakistan, a radio link between Karachi and Moscow and a fishery development project. This was "much more than the economic aid" the Russians had till then extended to Pakistan.[30] However, it was not that easy for the Soviet leader to concede Ayub's demands on arms aid or on Kashmir without taking into account Moscow's relationship with India which was considered more important. In his speech, Kosygin stated : "Pakistan, as other countries of Asia, indeed needs a situation of peace and cooperation and not that of tension and conflict." He advocated a "step by step" approach in settling existing problems between India and Pakistan, thereby laying a "firm foundation of good relations between both countries for many years to come."[31]

Commenting on the Soviet promise of help for the nuclear power plant at Roopur, a project on which the United States had backed out for the "technical" reasons in 1967, an Indian author remarked :

The agreement on the nuclear plant in East Pakistan was an extremely shrewd move. Rawalpindi's decision to postpone the project, following the withdrawal of American backing, had led to vociferous protests in East Pakistan. Kosygin was able to strengthen the Soviet image in an area where the appeal of China was believed to be strong; he was able to take some pressure off Ayub Khan in a very sensitive part of his country.[32]

The joint communique, issued at the end of Kosygin's visit, revealed a similarity of views as regards condemnation of Israel with support for the Security Council resolution of 22 November 1967; the importance and urgent necessity of an early conclusion of a treaty on the non-proliferation of nuclear weapons by declaring that "any further increase in the number of nuclear powers" would be detrimental to world peace; the holding of "periodic consultations" between the official representatives of both States, in particular between the Ministers of Foreign Affairs; and a political settlement in Vietnam on the basis of the right of the Vietnamese people to decide their destiny "without foreign interference."

As regards the situation in the Indian sub-continent Ayub Khan was allowed to explain Pakistan's position "on all problems and disputes which were affecting peace and stability in the sub-continent." However, Premier Kosygin went only to the extent of expressing his satisfaction at the "steps that have been taken so far towards the settlement of some Indo-Pakistan issues." He expressed the hope that "the two countries would resolve their outstanding disputes in the spirit of the Tashkent Declaration."[33] By such a formulation, Kosygin seemed to give a good chit to Pakistan in so far as the implementation of the Tashkent Declaration was concerned. However, the mention of the Tashkent Declaration was a distinct improvement, from India's viewpoint, over the 1967 communique, which had omitted such reference.

The communique was silent about the supply of arms to Pakistan. However, it seemed that, in the course of the exchange of views with Kosygin, Ayub had succeeded in extracting a promise of Soviet military aid, however limited. It was "believed in knowledgeable quarters," the *Pakistan Observer*'s political commentator remarked, in an article appearing in that paper on 14 July 1968, that "an agreement in principle on delivery of arms to Pakistan must have been reached" during Kosygin's visit. In July 1968, Ayub despatched to Moscow a high-powered military delegation, led by General Yahya Khan, Commander-in-Chief of the Pakistani armed forces. At the end of Yahya Khan's 12-day visit, it was announced that Moscow had agreed to sell arms to Pakistan. According to Ayub, that aid was not very spectacular as it only helped "to fill some gaps here and there" in Pakistan's defence requirements.[34] The Soviet decision to supply arms to Pakistan evoked strong criticism in India. People began to talk of Soviet betrayal and the Opposition parties sought to exploit the situation to their advantage. Thus, the Jan Sangh Party spoke of the USSR stabbing India in the back while the anti-Communist Bombay weekly, *Current*, observed : "Once again, a Communist country has betrayed our friendship. It was China in 1962. It is Russia in 1968."

Before arriving at their decision to supply arms to Pakistan, Soviet leaders must have taken the susceptibilities and the apprehensions of India into consideration. This was evident from Kosygin's brief visit to New Delhi on his way from Rawalpindi to Moscow and the assurance given to India that the Soviet Government's decision to sell a very limited quantity of arms—that too of a defensive nature, such as helicopters, spare parts for aircraft, some medium tanks and field guns— "would not, in any way, affect their relations with us, their friendship with us, nor would it injure our interests," as Indian Prime Minister Indira Gandhi disclosed in the *Rajya Sabha* on 24 July 1968.[35] Sophisticated weapons like supersonic fighter bombers, etc., were not supplied to Pakistan. The amount of Soviet military aid to Pakistan was estimated to be between $5 to $10 million only as compared with $600 to $700 million worth of military assistance rendered to India. Even Iran and Afghanistan were said to have received as much as $100 million and $260 million respectively in Soviet arms assistance.[36]

The Pakistani press considered Soviet arms aid as "symbolic" and no more than a "gesture." It had only a very limited value. The "small supply of minor weapons" to Pakistan was "more than counterbalanced by the arms aid to India." Moreover, it was subject to the condition that it would not be used "against the likeliest aggressor," *i.e.* India. Nevertheless, the "friendly gesture" on the part of the Soviet Union was welcomed. It was said to mark "the beginning of realisation that power politics provides no enduring base for peace with justice and that not even a Super Power can continue to harbour a glaring inequity indefinitely."[37] Another Pakistani writer saw a

significant shift in the Soviet arms policy in Moscow's decision
to supply arms to Pakistan, in the face of "loud protest and
opposition" from the Indian Government. According to him,
the decision came "as a logical sequel to the latest trends in
Russian policy towards South Asia."[38]

About the same time, Premier Kosygin was reported to have
suggested that India and Pakistan settle their dispute over the
Farakka Barrage on the lines of the Indus Waters
Treaty. That suggestion was said to have been rejected by
India. On 17 July 1968, *Dawn* described the feelings of "politi-
cal circles" in Rawalpindi in the matter in the following words :
"The mere fact that the Soviet Premier has found the dispute
worth his direct interest was very significant for Pakistan." In
November 1968, the visit of a Soviet naval squadron to Karachi
took place.

Soviet leaders assured India that they would stand by their
agreements and fufil all their commitments to her. In selling
arms to Pakistan, they took into account the intense pressure
mounted by Pakistan during the preceding two years concerning
the arms deal, however symbolic or minimal it might be. The
decision to supply arms to Pakistan was based on the realization that no amount of economic assistance would be as effective as a token supply of arms in creating an impression on the
Pakistani mind. In July 1968, Moscow extended a $66 million
credit to Pakistan for the purchase of capital goods. However,
Soviet assistance was no match to the assistance rendered by the
USA. Washington committed approximately $300 million—
nearly 10 times the Russian assistance to Pakistan in 1967.[39]

Pakistani expectations from the USSR seemed to be running
high at that moment. The diplomatic correspondent of the
Pakistan Times, H.K. Burki, considered the sale of Russian
weapons to Pakistan, in the face of "Indian hullabaloo," an acid
"test" for Moscow's stated policy that it would not
develop its relations with India at the cost of its ties with
Pakistan and *vice versa*. He added :

> If after two years of secret and not so-secret exchanges bet-
> ween Pakistan and Russia a sale does not take place now,
> only one conclusion would have to be drawn. Indian
> efforts at blocking the transaction had succeeded....

The Soviets are now well aware of Pakistan's apprehensions. What is more important, they bear a heavy responsibility for creating a frightening military imbalance in the sub-continent. After all, by providing or making commitments to supply weapons and production facilities amounting to almost a billion dollars, Moscow has become the most important factor in India's military might.[40]

Moscow had often stressed that its sale of arms to Pakistan was purely symbolic—a very small percentage of their huge supplies to India. It was stated that this aid was given in order to wean Pakistan away from China and to influence Islamabad so as to promote peace in the sub-continent. Thus, it was asserted in a commentary by P. Unnikrishnan, in the pro-Soviet Indian paper, *Patriot*, on 25 July 1968, that Soviet arms supply to Pakistan was meant to forestall the Chinese design in the Indian subcontinent. "What would appear to have influenced Soviet policy makers most and speeded the decision to supply arms to Pakistan," he said, were intelligence reports, that became available to the Soviets, about "a major plan of Chinese-Pakistani collusion." Accordingly, it was believed that, after Yahya's probing mission to Moscow, a high-powered Pakistani delegation, led by Foreign Minister Arshad Hussain, was to go to Peking where a plan "of large-scale supplies of varied equipment and of closer coordination of moves against India" was to be unfolded. In that connection, it was stated that Arshad Hussain's claim that Pakistan regarded China as its most reliable ally "was apparently not mere rhetoric."

According to the commentary in the *Patriot*, Soviet leaders thought that, by their stepping in nominally, they would introduce a new element into the picture which they hoped would be a factor in favour of peace and stability. Soviet military interest in Pakistan, it was asserted, would act "as a deterrent against China as well as the West" and that it would help "to foil any dramatic bid, joint or several, to upset the balance of power in the Indian sub-continent." Furthermore, it was pointed out that it remained Moscow's aim "to use its increasing influence in Pakistan to make the Tashkent Declaration the decisive factor in Indo-Pakistan relations." The USSR, it added, would also promote brotherly relations and strengthen the

economies of both against outside forces which had so far pro-
fited from conflicts and which "search for newer and subtler
ways of deepening existing animosities." It was stated that Soviet
supplies to Pakistan would be on a meagre scale. It was pointed
out that "the Soviets had secured from Pakistan an assurance
of virtual non-aggression against India." There was also the
commitment that Soviet arms would not be used against India,
and that in the event of aggression, Moscow would take the side
of the victim and not remain neutral. All these arguments were
advanced to allay the apprehensions and misgivings in the Indian
mind which were quite widespread. The *Patriot* admitted that
even Prime Minister Indira Gandhi's stand and that of other
democratic and progressive forces, though "one of dignified
restraint and understanding," was "tinged with a sense of
anxiety."

A close examination of the reasons given in the above-mentioned commentary in the pro-Soviet Indian newspaper, however, left many questions unanswered. For instance, if Soviet
arms supply to Pakistan had to be very meagre, how could it
possibly succeed in preventing the unfolding or materializa-
tion of the "master plan" between China and Pakistan? How
could an insignificant Soviet military interest in Pakistan act
as a deterrent against both China and the West and foil any
attempt at upsetting the balance of power in the sub-continent,
if the other two Powers were determined to upset it? How was
it possible for the Soviet Union to obtain an assurance of
"virtual non-aggression against India" from Pakistan by agreeing to make a token supply of arms when Washington could
not do so even after providing massive military assistance to a
country which had all along nursed intense hostility towards
India? What guarantee was there that, when the USA had
failed in preventing the use of weapons that it had supplied
against India, the Kremlin would succeed? How could Moscow,
with an insignificant arms supply, gain such a great amount of
influence in Islamabad that it would be able to persuade Pakistan
to patch up with India, to honour the Tashkent Declaration
and to arrive at an amicable settlement of all its disputes with
India? P. Unnikrishnan had asserted that there was no change
in the Soviet stand on Kashmir, that Indo-Soviet friendship

remained intact and that Moscow would continue to render and even expand its large-scale military assistance to India. In these circumstances, how could the supply of a small quantity of arms to Pakistan carry conviction with the authorities in Islamabad to induce them to shelve their "master plan" with China, to give a no-war assurance against India and suffer any weakening of their relations with the USA and China?

Unlike Pakistani leaders, Soviet authorities had not justified their arms deliveries to Pakistan in terms of the balance-of-power theory. However, in March 1969, Marshal A.A. Grechko, Defence Minister of the USSR, who paid a six-day official visit to Pakistan, was not very far from endorsing that theory. He stated that Moscow believed that Pakistan was a peace-loving country and that it wanted to live in peace with all its neighbours. Marshal Grechko then observed : "To maintain peace, one must be strong so that the enemies may not get any pretext to reach one's borders."[41] Speaking earlier at the dinner given in honour of the Soviet Defence Minister, Pakistan's Defence Minister, A.R. Khan, had declared that it was imperative that the military balance in the sub-continent, which already "weighs heavily against us, is not allowed to tilt any further to our disadvantage." Pakistan, he said, desired peace. However, it needed the necessary strength and capability to maintain it against aggression.[42]

The statement of the Pakistani Ministry of Defence, issued at the end of Marshal Grechko's visit on 15 March 1969, referred to the Soviet Minister being received by President Ayub Khan. It was stated that views were exchanged between the Defence Ministers of the two countries "on some international problems." Pakistan-Soviet relations were also discussed. The statement then noted that friendly cooperation between the two countries "in numerous fields was developing satisfactorily." It stressed that "mutual contacts between the two States and military leaders" of the two countries would help "further improve Pakistan-Soviet relations."[43]

Moscow, indeed, went a long way in propping up the Ayub regime in Pakistan during 1966-69 in every manner possible, including arms supplies. This was because the Kremlin came to identify President Ayub Khan—the powerful dictator of Pakistan since 1958—with the creation of stable conditions in his country. The USSR, obviously enough, had a stake in the establishment of such conditions. The reasons why Moscow ventured to supply arms to Pakistan were, indeed, very subtle. The move had to be seen partly as a continuation of the Kremlin's post-Tashkent policy towards Pakistan—a policy of befriending Islamabad by providing large-scale economic and technical assistance in order to wean it away from China and obtain the termination of Western bases on Pakistani territory. It seemed to fulfil Moscow's desire to insure its southern flank by cultivating its neighbours, *viz*. Turkey, Pakistan and Iran—the last of which was given highly sophisticated weapons, including missiles worth $110 million. The USSR was quite conscious of the excesses of the Chinese Cultural Revolution and Peking's inability to take any initiative in regard to Sino-Indian rapprochement. Through its supply of arms to Pakistan and its diplomatic posture of not taking sides between India and Pakistan, the Kremlin sought to make India realize that it would be better for her to come to an amicable settlement of her problems with Pakistan. Moscow also seemed to be keen on impressing upon New Delhi that it would gain nothing by leaning more towards the West for necessary support in the wake of her food problem and foreign exchange difficulties—that had led to the devaluation of the Indian rupee.

In raising Pakistani expectations, by way of arms supplies and by its detachment *vis-a-vis* India, the Kremlin sought to loosen Pakistan's ties with the West as also China and to strengthen Russian influence in Islamabad. Moscow endeavoured to make Ayub realize that he would have to reciprocate the Soviet gesture by doing something concrete towards subserving Soviet interests. It is significant to note that although Soviet arms were pledged or promised in the middle of 1968, their actual delivery was effected only in 1969. In this way, Moscow tried to make sure that Islamabad would not renew the lease of the Peshawar base. Thus, the Soviet *demarche* in supplying arms to Pakistan was a well-calculated move, taken after careful consideration. It was meant to serve Soviet national interests *vis-a-vis* a number of countries—Pakis-

tan, India, the Western Powers and China. It was also designed to further secure its southern flank.

The prospect of pro-Peking elements, such as those represented by Maulana Bhashani or Z.A. Bhutto, or of the
extreme rightist forces, like the Jamaat-i-Islami, coming into
power, in the wake of unstable conditions, was far from appealing to Moscow, particularly as the election year (1969) was fast
approaching. During the political turmoil in Pakistan following November 1968, when Bhutto was arrested, the controlled
press of the Soviet Union came out in support of the establishment headed by Ayub Khan. It criticized Opposition parties
either for their being reactionary or for following a pro-Peking
line. China, on the other hand, maintained studied silence
throughout the period of turmoil, as also for about a month
after Yahya Khan took over in March 1969. A democratic set-
up in Pakistan, Moscow feared, might lean more towards
either China or the USA or both while the secession of East
Pakistan, as a result of internal turmoil and discontent, might
result in its becoming a satellite of Peking.

Like Tashkent, the decision to supply arms to Pakistan in
mid-1968 was an important move on the part of the USSR.
It was designed to consolidate the Soviet position in Pakistan
with a view to prevent Islamabad from looking too much to
Peking for support and to create conditions of peace and stability in the Indian sub-continent and in the whole of Asia. The
success of Moscow's attempt in weaning Islamabad away from
Peking or in softening the rigidity of the Pakistani rulers'
attitude towards India was, indeed, doubtful. Because of its
hostility towards India and its geographical proximity to
the Indian sub-continent, China was in a better position, than
either of the two super Powers, to exert direct military pressure
on India when the need arose. This was an important consideration for Pakistan. For that matter, the Chinese capacity to
influence Pakistan was undoubtedly greater than that of either
of the two super Powers.

Likewise, it was doubtful if the increase of Soviet influence
in Pakistan would have induced Islamabad to mellow down
its hostility towards India and to normalize its relations with

her. Prime Minister Indira Gandhi's offer of a "no-war pact" to
Pakistan was summarily rejected by Ayub Khan, in his first
of the month broadcast on September 1968, as "mere propaganda." Moreover, from 1968 onwards, Pakistan came to
insist that, apart from Kashmir, its demand on the Ganga
waters should also be met by India before Islamabad could
agree to give thought to a "no-war pact" with India or have
normal relations with her.

India's cooperative and peaceful approach towards Pakistan
was reflected in Prime Minister Indira Gandhi's letter of 22
June 1969 to President Yahya Khan. In that letter, she
suggested normalization of relations by easing regulations
for travel between the two countries, encouraging greater
cultural contacts, trade, resumption of shipping and air
services, etc. These measures would have been conducive in
removing misunderstandings between the two countries. The
suggestion of a "no-war pact" was also repeated. In his reply,
President Yahya Khan asserted that mutual trust could not
be brought about by eliminating minor problems or dealing
with peripheral issues. According to him, friendship between
India and Pakistan was not possible unless the two outstanding disputes regarding Jammu and Kashmir and the Ganges
waters were resolved, obviously to the satisfaction of Pakistan.
While India took a series of unilateral initiatives with regard
to resumption of trade, civil air flights, opening of all border
checkposts, return of seized cargoes and properties, cultural
exchanges, liberalization of *visa* procedure, etc., there was no
satisfactory response from Pakistan.

When Yahya Khan assumed the reins of Government from
Ayub's hands in March 1969, Moscow remembered him
for successfully negotiating an arms deal with the USSR. He
was, therefore, regarded as pro-Soviet by the Kremlin. About
the time Yahya took over, Soviet arms deliveries began to
arrive in Pakistan. Moscow had also extended its support to
the new establishment in Pakistan while Peking had maintained silence. All this was construed by the Soviet Union as
weakening of the Chinese hold in Pakistan.

It was in these circumstances that soon after Yahya Khan

suceeded Ayub Khan, Premier Kosygin sent a message assuring him that Pakistani leaders could "always count on the friendly understanding and support of the Soviet Union." Referring to the positive development of friendly ties between the two countries during the last several years "in political, economic and other fields," Kosygin noted President Ayub Khan's "great contribution" to that noble cause. He shared his confidence with Yahya about friendly relations between the two countries not only being preserved but also developing further. He, in fact, saw favourable conditions for the "further broadening and deepening" of their friendship and comprehensive cooperation.[44]

Not long after that message, Kosygin himself made a dash to Rawalpindi in May 1969. He tried to secure Pakistan's support in favour of regional economic cooperation in South Asia among Afghanistan, Pakistan and India. As Soviet relations with China were continuously deteriorating, in the wake of armed clashes on the banks of the Ussuri, Moscow seemed quite keen to cultivate Yahya, particularly *vis-a-vis* Peking. The joint statement, issued at the end of Kosygin's visit on 31 May 1969, said nothing new either on the Middle East or Vietnam, compared to what was stated in the 1968 communique. It merely spoke of "their views" having coincided on a number of important international issues. As regards the situation in the sub-continent, President Yahya Khan explained his country's continued efforts to settle all its outstanding disputes with India in a peaceful manner. Kosygin reaffirmed his conviction that an early solution of Indo-Pak disputes would be in the interest of the peoples of the sub-continent.

President Yahya Khan expressed his confidence that Pakistan's friendly relations with the USSR would "continue to grow in strength." Kosygin, on his part, assured him that the Soviet Union would "continue to work for the consolidation of friendly ties with Pakistan." Both sides reaffirmed their desire "to expand areas of cooperation between the two countries in the economic, cultural and other fields." It was stated that such cooperation served the interests of the peoples of both countries, the interests of the consolidation of peace in Asia and the world and was "not directed against any third state."[45]   The last phrase was presumably included in the joint statement at the instance of Yahya who probably wanted to avoid giving the impression to Peking that he was leaning too heavily on the side of Moscow.   Yahya thereby sought to strike a balance in Pakistan's relations with the three major Powers—the US, the USSR and China.   The phrase also suited Kosygin for it enabled Moscow to convey a similar assurance to India.

Kosygin, it seems, failed to secure Yahya's support to the regional economic cooperation scheme, which occupied a high place in Soviet thinking.   Here, it is significant to recall that the Moscow-Karachi air service was inaugurated as early as July 1964. It put USSR markets within easy reach of Pakistani businessmen.   Soviet completion of the construction of its highways right up to the Oxus river ports linked it with the road system of Afghanistan.   This meant the opening of a direct overland trade route between the USSR and Pakistan, which was much cheaper than the seaborne route through which all their trade was being conducted.   Commenting on it, Foreign Minister Z.A. Bhutto observed in the Pakistan National Assembly on 14 March 1966 :

> With our great and powerful neighbour to the north, the USSR, Pakistan's bilateral relations have been growing in all fields.   Recently a trade agreement was signed and soon, we expect, goods and traffic between the two countries would begin to flow along the new road which links the Khyber pass with the Oxus river, passing through Afghanistan.   This new and constructive development will prove beneficial to all the three countries and open a new and positive chapter in their relations with one another.[46]

Expansion of trade and economic co-operation between the two countries, as also the closure of the Suez Canal from the middle of 1967, added greater urgency to the scheme of constructing an overland route through Afghanistan.   Islamabad's anxiety in the matter was reflected in the editorial entitled "Trade with USSR" in the *Pakistan Times* of 17 December 1967.   It remarked :

The Government of Pakistan has also forwarded proposals

to the Soviet Union for opening up a new trade route through Afghanistan. It is hoped that with the completion of formalities in this connection the transportation of goods will be much cheaper and lead to further expansion in Pakistan-Soviet trade.[47]

Speaking in Peshawar on 6 March 1968, the Commerce Minister of Pakistan, Nawabzada Abdul Ghafoor, stated that Soviet-Pakistan trade *via* the land route through Afghanistan might be "immediately started, when the approval of the Governments of the Soviet Union and Afghanistan was available." Pakistan, he added, was "waiting for these approvals." Replying to questions, he disclosed :

> There was also some hitch due to the *reluctance of* Afghanistan which is not prepared to allow our trucks to pass through Afghanistan up to Sher-Bandar, the northern port on the Oxus in Afghanistan.[48]

After Premier Kosygin's visit to India and Pakistan in 1968, Indian officials were stated to be studying the possibility of laying an overland trade route to the Soviet Union through Pakistan and Afghanistan to mitigate the effects of the closure of the Suez Canal. In a report, datelined New Delhi, 31 May 1968, the *Pakistan Times* observed as follows :

> Once the proposed route is accepted by India, Pakistan and Afghanistan, it would not be difficult to implement it, as Asian Highway roads already pass through northern India and West Pakistan to Kabul. The 300-kilometre stretch from Kabul to Tashkergan in northern Afghanistan is due to be completed in 1970, and the only remaining stretch to be built would run about 160 kilometers from Tashkergan to the railhead of Khwaja Yabu in the Soviet Union. Officials said the proposed trade route would be welcomed by India as a means of avoiding the long sea route to the Soviet Union round the Cape of Good Hope but the idea was still in its preliminary stages. Official sources in Islamabad declined to comment on this report and said they had no knowledge about it.[49]

The idea of Pakistan, Afghanistan, India and other States of the region developing "mutual relations of friendship and constructive cooperation" was put forward by Kosygin in 1968. Thereafter, the proposal of regional economic cooperation began to be vigorously canvassed. While the Indian Prime Minister welcomed the proposal by stating that it had always been India's policy "to promote regional cooperation especially in trade and economic relations,"[50] Pakistan seemed reluctant in the matter. As a result, the contemplated initiative of the Afghanistan Government about inviting India, Pakistan, Nepal, the USSR, Iran and Turkey to a conference table in Kabul to discuss regional economic cooperation did not materialize and no invitations were issued. Apart from Pakistan, the other RCD partners, Iran and Turkey, it appeared, were also not favourably disposed towards the idea. However, since Pakistan was having very friendly relations with the Soviet Union during 1966-68, Islamabad could not summarily reject Kosygin's proposal. At first, Islamabad was somewhat evasive in the matter and seemed doubtful about its economic advantages for Pakistan. It was stated that Pakistan's attitude would depend on "what proposals and conditions it contained and whether it would be of interest to Pakistan."[51] The pressure of domestic public opinion created by Bhutto, with his policy of confrontation with India, and Peking's influence subsequently led Islamabad to oppose the Soviet proposal.

Strongly criticizing Kosygin's proposal, Bhutto observed in April 1968 :

> An overland link through Pakistan would give India access to the frontiers of the Soviet Union and undermine the strategic importance of this country. No better evidence of reconciliation need to be sought if Pakistan submitted to such a proposal. This proposal has not been born out of the closure of the Suez Canal. It was made two years ago for the flow of transit traffic between Pakistan, Afghanistan and the Soviet Union. At that time the Government of Pakistan refused to permit India the benefits from the arrangement.

Bringing China in the picture, Bhutto asked : "If Pakistan opens its frontiers to India to promote regional commerce, would India allow Chinese convoys to use the Tibet-Nepal Highway to reach East Pakistan, Burma and Ceylon through the length and breadth of Indian territory?"[52] It appears from Bhutto's remarks that ever since its Tashkent *demarche*,

Moscow had been active in canvassing support for an overland link through Pakistan and for promoting regional cooperation on its southern periphery in the direction of the Indian sub-continent. Moscow thereby sought to stabilize its southern flank and serve its economic interests by facilitating trade with Iran as also with the whole of South Asia. There also seemed to be obvious strategic reasons in which China and the road systems linking China and Pakistan through Gilgit in Pakistani-occupied Kashmir played quite a significant part. Bhutto's remarks indicated that the Pakistani Government's opposition in 1966 to the idea of an overland trade route linking India and the Soviet Union mainly sprang from considerations of Islamabad's hostility towards India. Bhutto, at that time, was an influential member in the Pakistani administration and, therefore, might have been instrumental in Islamabad's rejection of the Soviet proposal. It fitted well in his policy of confrontation with India. New Delhi was included both in the scheme of the overland trade route as also in the Soviet proposal about regional economic cooperation, which was frowned upon by Peking and rejected by Islamabad. Air Marshal Nur Khan's open opposition in Peking to the Soviet proposal of regional economic cooperation in July 1969[53] signified that steps which were conducive to Indo-Pak reconciliation and to peace and prosperity in the region were sacrificed at the altar of Sino-Pakistan collusion and Islamabad's anti-Indian posture.

It seemed that Pakistan assigned greater priority to its relations with China than with the USSR. However, Islamabad deemed it necessary to publicly take a posture of equi-distance between the three Powers, *viz.* the USA, the USSR and China. Hence, Yahya was seen reiterating his faith in the "policy of bilateralism" and taking pride in Pakistan having "friendly and cordial relations with all the three major Powers" of the world. In his speech before the joint session of the Iranian Senate and Majlis on 30 October 1969, he spoke of his country as having "settled down" to such a policy, which, in essence, meant that Pakistan wanted to conduct its relations with other countries "on the basis of mutuality of interest, independent of their relations with third countries" and avoid "over-commitment to any one power." After describing China as "a good friend of Pakistan" which "has been very correct in its dealings with us" and "has given us economic and military aid and political support on some issues of vital interest to us," President Yahya Khan spoke eloquently of the Soviet Union in the following words :

> With the Soviet Union, our relations in the 50's were under strain because of our membership of defence alliances which they regarded as directed against them. Pakistan's position is now better understood and our relations with the Soviet Union have steadily grown in depth from the mid-50's. Today our collaboration ranges over diverse fields. The Soviet Union has extended considerable credits to Pakistan and is assisting us in the execution of major projects. It has also started giving us some military hardware to enable us to build up our defence potential.[54]

On 9 December 1969, Pakistan and the Soviet Union concluded a trade agreement providing for the exchange of goods valued at Rs. 110 million each way during 1970.[55] Moscow supplied Pakistan a large number of tractors and cars and road building and agricultural machinery in 1970. On 20 May 1970, a ten-year agreement on collaboration in the peaceful uses of atomic energy was signed under which Moscow agreed to assist Pakistan with equipment, machinery and nuclear instruments and material required for the purpose.[56]

President Yahya Khan visited the Soviet Union for five days in June 1970, at the end of which a joint communique was issued. The visit was unsuccessful in so far as the augmentation of Yahya's war machine was concerned. The communique reaffirmed the desire of the two sides "to strengthen further the existing contacts" and recorded the utility of periodical consultations "along the lines of Foreign Ministries." It referred to the determination of both Pakistan and the USSR to continue their efforts to bring about a just and lasting peace in West Asia and to render support to the Arab nations. It also called for the unconditional withdrawal of foreign troops from Indo-China. The USSR played a helpful role in Pakistan's admission to the Committee on Disarmament in August 1969. Islamadad, on its part, strongly supported the joint US-USSR draft sea-bed treaty. The treaty was described in the June

1970 Pak-Soviet communique and in the Pakistani representative's statement before the Disarmament Committee, on 9 July 1970, as corresponding to the interests of all countries of the world and fit for submission to the 25th session of the United Nations General Assembly for its approval.

As regards Indo-Pak relations, the communique expressed Moscow's firm belief that a settlement of "disputable questions" by means of bilateral negotiations in the spirit of the Tashkent Declaration would accord with the vital interests of the peoples of Pakistan and India as well as the interests of peace in the region as a whole.[57] Mention of the Tashkent Declaration, which was missing in the May 1969 Pakistan-Soviet joint communique, as also stress on bilateral negotiations as a means of settling disputes, may be said to have been favourable to India.

The main achievement of Yahya's visit to Moscow was in the economic sphere. The Soviet Union agreed to provide $200 million for financing the cost of machinery and equipment for the Karachi Steel Mill, with a capacity of one million tons of steel annually. Moscow also agreed to closely study the list of other projects on which Pakistan desired economic and technical assistance from the USSR during its Fourth Five-Year Plan.[58] The two sides also agreed to conclude a long-term trade agreement for 1971-75 (signed in December 1970) providing for considerable growth in the volume of trade. The Soviet Ambassador in Pakistan stated :

> This long term agreement, the first in the history of Soviet-Pakistani trade relations, will promote the development of trade between our countries. Under the agreement trade between the two countries will grow by 6-7 per cent annually. The USSR will increase its purchase of Pakistani manufactured goods which will account for 60-65 per cent of the total volume of Pakistani exports to the Soviet Union.[59]

Soviet commentator Kondrashov, writing in *Izvestia* about the growing economic contacts between Pakistan and the USSR, had earlier observed :

> Ships flying the Soviet flags are now constant guests in Pakistan's principal ports, Karachi and Chittagong. They

carry from the Soviet Union, tractors, bulldozers, road-
making machinery, pig iron, various mechanisms, equipment, etc. Soviet machinery, durable and dependable
in exploitation, is in great demand. It is not without
reason that the Soviet-Pakistan trade has increased more
than ten-fold since 1957.[60]

By providing substantial financial assistance in the post-
Tashkent period for the development of Pakistan's key projects and basic industries (such as the Kalabagh steel project
and the Roopur atomic power station) Moscow sought to
reduce Pakistan's dependence on the West, thereby allowing
greater political manoeuvrability to Pakistan. At the same time,
Soviet influence in Islamabad was considerably enhanced. In
these circumstances, Pakistan began to lay greater emphasis on
the diversification of its economic and trade relations. "The low
demand for Pakistani goods in the European markets and
the 'ominous implications' of the ECM were the main factors
compelling Pakistan to explore new markets," Pakistan's
Commerce Minister pointed out.[61] This situation facilitated
the expansion of USSR-Pak trade relations.

Arms supply to Pakistan, even though on a modest scale,
marked a significant shift in the Soviet arms policy towards
the Indian sub-continent. It was meant to bolster Soviet
influence in Pakistan and thereby keep its southern flank free
from hostile influences. For that matter, the USSR did not
mind ignoring Pakistani violations of the Tashkent Agreement. Guided by its national interests and strategic requirements, the Kremlin seemed to be making determined attempts
to woo Pakistan in order to detach Islamabad from the
embrace of both Peking and Washington. In particular, the
growing influence of China in Pakistan continued to be the
cause of serious concern for Moscow.

6

The Bangladesh Crisis and the Indo-Pakistan War of 1971

THE Lahore Resolution of 1940 (generally known as the Pakistan Resolution), adopted by the All-India Muslim League at its 22nd annual session at Lahore on 23 March 1940, envisaged a federal structure for the two wings of Pakistan—the western and the eastern. According to that resolution, the two wings, geographically separated by more than 1,000 miles of Indian territory, were to be grouped "to constitute 'Independent States' in which the constituent units shall be autonomous and sovereign." The two regions were to have "all powers such as defence, external affairs, communications, customs and such other matters as may be necessary."[1]

There was nothing common between the people of the two wings of Pakistan except religion. "Ethnically, culturally, in their thought, language, way of life—in every way they were two nations."[2] When the eastern wing of Pakistan which was, in fact, more populous than the western, came to be dominated politically and exploited economically by a unitary form of government, it naturally began to think of resistance and the assertion of its basic rights.

The July 1970 official report, prepared by a panel of experts to the Planning Commission of the Government of Pakistan, cited examples of economic disparities in the two regions. It stated that the per capita income in West Pakistan, which was 32% higher than in the East in 1959-60, became 61% higher, almost double, in 1969-70 because the rate of annual growth of income was 6.2% in West Pakistan as compared to 4.2% in East Pakistan. With 60% of the total population, East Pakistan's share of the Central development expenditure had been as low as 20% during 1950/51-1954/55, attaining a peak of 36% during the Third Five-Year Plan period 1965/66-1969/70. East Pakistan's share of private investment was even smaller—less than 25%. According to official statistics of Pakistan, while the eastern wing's share of total Pakistani export earnings had varied between 50% and 70%, its share of imports had been in the range of 25% to 30%. As much as $2.6 billion worth of resources were transferred from East to West Pakistan over the period 1948-69.[3] About 94% of the total revenue of Pakistan—62% spent on the armed forces and 32% spent on the Central Administration—had been annually spent in West Pakistan. Thus, the western wing was becoming rich at the expense of the eastern wing.[4] Sheikh Mujibur Rahman criticized West Pakistan, which had a population of only 58 million, for taking 70% of the nation's foreign aid and 70% of its imports and for monopolising 85% of the central bureaucracy and 90% of the armed forces. In contrast, East Pakistan, having a population of 72 million, remained not only one of the world's most densely populated regions—1,400 per sq. mile—but also one of the poorest with an annual per capita income of $50. The economic disparity between the two wings is highlighted in the following words :

In 1949-50, the per capita income of West Pakistan exceeded that of East Pakistan by only 9 per cent. The figure rose to 30 per cent by 1959-60, 40 per cent by 1964-65 and 60 per cent by 1969-70. In the first 17 years of independence the per capita gross financial product in East Bengal recorded an annual rise of 3 per cent whereas West Pakistan recorded a growth rate five times faster than that in the eastern wing. In the twenty years preceding the 1970 elections in Pakistan, East Bengal had only one-third of the total development expenditure incurred by the Central Government. Over 80 per cent of the foreign aid was spent in West Pakistan. That wing had also the lion's share of the imports into the country whereas the foreign exchange earnings were mostly on account of the products of East Bengal. Over 20 years, West Pakistan had imported goods worth more than Rs. 3,000 crores as against its own foreign exchange earnings of barely Rs.1,300 crores.[5]

The economic domination and exploitation of the eastern wing was greatly facilitated by West Pakistani dominance of the Central Government. After 21 years of Pakistan's creation, Bengalis accounted for barely 15% in the Central Government Services and for less than 10% in the Defence services. All important, high and lucrative offices, in both the military and civil fields, were held by West Pakistanis, Punjabis in particular. All senior military officers hailed from the western wing. Of the senior officers in the Central Civil Services, 87% were West Pakistanis in 1960 and that proportion had not changed much in 1970. The Deputy Chairman of the Planning Commission and the Central Finance Minister—key individuals in the allocation of resources and funds—had always been West Pakistanis.[6] Similarly, all high offices such as Governorships, Chairmanships of Cotton Boards, P.I.D.C., Railway Board, P.C.S., Port Trust and WAPDA, etc., had always been in the hands of West Pakistanis.[7] The concentration of industry and the entrepreneurial class in West Pakistan was greatly encouraged by the location of the seat of the Central Government therein.

Whenever East Pakistanis put forward their demands, such as making Bengali one of the State languages of Pakistan, or asked for a joint electorate or regional autonomy, they were condemned by West Pakistani rulers as initiating moves aimed at undoing Pakistan or moves inspired by India. According to the 1951 Census, Bengali-speaking people accounted for 54.6% of the total population as compared with 28.4% for Punjabi, 7.2% Urdu, 7.1% Pushtu, 5.8% Sindhi and 1.8% English. Therefore, if Bengali could not be made the only *lingua franca* of Pakistan, it, at least, deserved to be made one of the two state languages. To Jinnah, however, there could be only one *lingua franca* and that language "must obviously be Urdu." For him, Urdu embodied the best in Islamic culture and Muslim tradition and was nearest to the language used in other Muslim countries. He believed that the language controversy was the product of "provincialism." Prime Minister Liaquat Ali Khan swore to obliterate that "provincialism for all times." It was only in 1954, and that too after many protests, demonstrations, arrests and much agitation, that the demand of making Bengali also a State language was finally conceded.

The rulers of Pakistan, however, refused to concede the the main demand, *viz.* regional autonomy. That demand was initially expressed in the 21-demands formulated by the All Parties Convention which met in Dacca in 1953. The Constituent Assembly of Pakistan, at the time, was debating on the Basic Principles to be adopted for the new Constitution. Later on, in early 1966, it was crystallized in the six-point programme put forward by the President of the Awami League—Sheikh Mujibur Rahman. In a resolution adopted by the Awami League Council in February 1957, the demand for full regional autonomy on the basis of the 21 points was reiterated. Maulana Bhashani warned that, if that demand was not conceded, a time may come when East Pakistan may have to split up. In April 1957, the Provincial Assembly adopted, by acclamation with only two negative votes, the resolution on regional autonomy for East Pakistan. It gave only three subjects to the Centre, *viz.* defence, foreign affairs and currency.

The people of East Pakistan continued to clamour against the injustices meted out to them by the West Pakistanis. Thus, as early as 25 February 1948, Begum Ikramullah, while speaking in the Constituent Assembly, referred to the growing feelings among East Pakistanis of "being neglected and treated as a 'colony of West Pakistan'." On 7 September 1955, Ataur Rahman Khan accused the leaders of the Muslim League of regarding East Pakistanis as "a subject race." Speaking in the National Assembly on 1 March 1958, Abdul Latif Biswas warned that a Government which treated the East Pakistanis merely as "hewers of wood and drawers of water" would face disastrous consequences.

Neither the 1956 nor the 1962 Constitution made a serious attempt to tackle the problem of autonomy for East Pakistan. The imposition of Martial Law in 1958 was a retrograde step in this regard as power came to be concentrated in the hands of a few military leaders of Pakistan—none of whom was a Bengali. Even when, under the pressure of a huge popular upsurge in 1968-69, the military *junta* was forced to concede many popular demands (such as direct election on universal and adult franchise, the restoration of parliamentary democracy, representation on the basis of population, the break-up of one unit in West Pakistan, the making of a new constitution, etc.) it side-tracked and ignored the issue of regional autonomy. In fact, when Martial Law was imposed in March 1969, its primary purpose seemed to be to stifle the demand of regional autonomy in East Pakistan.

During the ten-year period of Ayub's military dictatorship, some progress was no doubt made towards the creation of stable conditions and economic recovery. However, he miserably failed in removing disparity between the two wings and in suppressing the movement for regional autonomy. Bengali leaders like Sheikh Mujibur Rahman, the General Secretary of the Awami League, and Maulana Abdul Hamid Khan Bhashani and the Pathan leader, Khan Abdul Ghaffar Khan in NWFP, were arrested. Hundreds of agitating students were put behind bars. When Mujib demanded maximum regional autonomy based on his six-points in the second half of the 1960s, he was again arrested. He was implicated in the false Agartala Conspiracy Case in January 1968. Charges of conspiring to topple the Government and to turn East Bengal into an independent country with the active help of India were levelled against him. Earlier, H.S. Suhrawardy and A.K. Fazlul Huq had been described as "Indian agents." The nefarious design to discredit Sheikh Mujib was a clear attempt to stifle the movement for autonomy in East Pakistan and malign India in the eyes of the world. Writing in the *Pakistan Times* on 3 November 1968, Z.A. Suleri—the spokesman for the Establishment—used the well-known arguments of "foreign inspiration" and "the poison of provincialism" while speaking of Mujib's Awami League, Wali Khan's NAP, the Jamaat-i-Islami and G.M. Syed's followers.

During Ayub's military dictatorship, the West Pakistani bureaucracy and military oligarchy endeavoured to dominate over and exploit the majority of the people in the eastern wing. The ruthless suppression of the people of East Pakistan made them more determined than ever before in their struggle for political rights. They could not hope to obtain regional auto-

nomy until there existed a democratic and representative
government in Pakistan. The wave of resentment, which manifested itself in strikes and *bandhs* in Dacca and other towns of
East Pakistan towards the end of 1968, led to arrests on a mass
scale, numerous firings and deaths. The mighty agitation of the
people compelled the military rulers of Pakistan to free Sheikh
Mujib. The so-called Agartala Conspiracy Case was withdrawn and, in March 1969, a Round Table Conference of all
Parties was convened to which the Sheikh was also invited.
Ultimately, Ayub came to be replaced by Yahya Khan.

It might be recalled here that the presentation of the six
point programme in early 1966 was not quite unconnected with
the Indo-Pakistan War of 1965. During the conflict, the
people of East Pakistan had to suffer great hardships. They
came to realize that their very existence was being jeopardized
for the sake of Kashmir—an issue which had never been a live
one so far as the East Pakistanis were concerned. While tobacco
continued to be imported by West Pakistan from India, its
import into East Pakistan was banned, with the result that
many cigarette factories in Dacca were closed down. The imposition of a ban on the import of *Tendu* leaves from West
Bengal resulted in the unemployment of 1.5 million *bidi* workers
in East Pakistan. Likewise, a substantial number of seamen
from Noakhali and Sylhet were rendered jobless, as they could
not be employed in India. Jute began to sell at half the cost
of production while the price of rice ranged between Rs. 100
($21) and Rs. 150 ($31.5) a maund, mustard oil sold at Rs. 15
per seer and salt nearly at Rs. 8. Kerosene oil practically disappeared from the open market, petrol was drastically rationed
and coal became scarcer. During the 23 days of the armed
conflict, East Pakistan was almost completely cut off from
West Pakistan. There was little or no communication.

The imposition of a ban on the songs and poems of Rabin-
dranath Tagore greatly hurt the feelings of the people of East
Pakistan. East Pakistanis continued to suffer even after the Tashkent Declaration because the Ayub regime selectively implemented that agreement with India. Thus, while Islamabad was
keen to resume PIA flights and open tele-communications links,
it showed little interest in resuming river steamer traffic through

East Pakistan. In many respects, Islamabad refused to restore its pre-1965 relations with India. It did not favourably respond to India's offers as regards the restoration of mutual contacts, the full re-establishment of severed communications and the re-activization of trade and commerce, which would have benefitted millions of people in both countries. In these circumstances, it was hardly surprising that the East Pakistani reaction to the Tashkent Declaration was fundamentally different from that (of hostility) in West Pakistan.[8]

The neglect of East Pakistan's defence by the rulers of West Pakistan led the people of the former wing to conclude that they must have a greater say in managing their own affairs for the purpose of self-preservation, if for nothing else. East Pakistanis were heard asking what was the point "in remaining with West Pakistan if we are to be defended by China."[9] Voicing the feelings of their people in the National Assembly, East Pakistani members expressed concern about the fact that there was hardly one division to protect 1,500 miles of East Pakistan's border with India. They pointed out that East Pakistan's contribution to the national exchequer had been of the order of Rs. 2,000 crores during the last 17 or 18 years. However, when the time came, it was found that even a district headquarter, surrounded by India, had no money to buy petrol for the deployment of soldiers. It was cryptically remarked :

> The foreign policy which endangers the lives of 17 crores of Muslims for only 40 lacs of people is not at all justified. The lives of 7 crores of Muslims of India and of 10 crores of those of Pakistan were endangered for only 40 lacs of Muslims of Kashmir.[10]

The feeling of insecurity coupled with economic hardships and injustices strengthened the resolve of the people of East Pakistan to fight for their rights. It added a new urgency to their just struggle. This was reflected in the formulation and presentation of the six-point programme in February 1966. Commenting on the hijacking of an Indian plane and the subsequent banning of overflights by India of all aircraft between West and East Pakistan over Indian territory, the President of the National Awami Party, Maulana Bhashani, stated, on 16 February 1971, that, as a direct result of that ban, prices of various items of daily necessities had shot up. He considered it just another example like the last Indo-Pak War and observed that, in the event of an abnormal situation, West Pakistan would not come to the assistance of East Pakistan.[11]

The six-point programme called "Our Right to Live" was presented before his countrymen by Sheikh Mujibur Rahman in 1966 as "basic principles of a firm solution of the country's inter-wing political and economic problem." They were, in fact, the "long-standing demands of the people and pledges of their leaders awaiting fulfilment for decades." In short, they were, in the Sheikh's words, "the national demand of the people, particularly the people of East Pakistan." Thus, the East Pakistani people's hopes found their articulation through Mujib. To Ayub, however, the six-point programme of the Opposition appeared as directed towards achieving their "horrid dream" of "greater sovereign Bengal." The fulfilment of that "dream," he warned, would "spell disaster for the country and turn the people of East Pakistan into slaves." Addressing the Round Table Conference in March 1969, Sheikh Mujibur Rahman described the adoption of the Federal Scheme, presented in the six-point programme, as "an essential pre-requisite for the achievement of a political solution for the problems" of Pakistan. He visualized Pakistan as "one single united nation of one hundred and twenty million people,"[12] thereby refuting any suggestion that the demand for regional autonomy, based on the six-points, was a secessionist move.

Even after his landslide victory in the December 1970 elections, Mujib did not entertain any idea whatsoever of separation from Pakistan or of an "independent East Bengal" although persistent oppression and the suppression of democracy in the eastern wing had "already created a sentiment for 'Independent East Bengal' in a section of the people, especially after their experience of the struggle for the six-point and 11-point programmes (1966 and 1969)."[13] It was only after a calculated genocide and brutal atrocities came to be perpetrated on the people of East Bengal that its leaders became fully convinced that there was not the slightest possibility of their having democracy or autonomy by remaining an integral part of Pakistan. Consequently, they decided to declare their independence, repudiate their association with Pakistan and to work assiduously "to secure its right of self-determination through a national struggle."[14]

The Election Manifesto of the Awami League declared its faith in democracy, secularism and socialism. It sought to see Pakistan as a federation granting full autonomy on the basis of the six-point formula to each of the federating units. On the international plane, "an independent non-aligned foreign policy" with immediate withdrawal from the SEATO, the CENTO and other military pacts was considered ideal for "the basic interests" of Pakistan. It assigned high priority to the settlement of the Kashmir dispute on the basis of UN resolutions and voiced support to the rightful struggle of the people of Jammu and Kashmir for the realization of "their fundamental right of self-determination." It laid stress on living in peaceful co-existence with all countries, "including our neighbours," from which India was probably not excluded. As regards the Farakka Barrage issue, the Manifesto charged the earlier Governments of Pakistan of "criminal neglect" in allowing it to become a *fait accompli*. It merely spoke of "a just solution" of the problem without, in any way, accusing India in the matter.[15] On 8 August 1969, Sheikh Mujib observed :

> Out of Pakistan's total borrowing of Rs. 2,000 crores, East Pakistan's share was just around Rs. 500 crores and whereas solution for distribution of Indus waters was found no real effort was made to solve the problem of flood control of East Pakistan which caused annual loss of Rs. 50 to 100 crores. The excuse that dispute with India made its solution difficult was not tenable.

Thus, it was clear that Mujib disagreed with the policy of the ruling military *junta* of building up a confrontation with India over the Farakka Barrage issue. Islamabad sought to utilize the issue to divert the attention of East Pakistanis from their just demand for autonomy and to redirect their energies against India. At the same time, Islamabad seemed to be trying to involve Washington or the World Bank in some sort of an arrangement like the Indus Water Treaty that would have enabled Pakistan to secure economic assistance on a large-scale.

Since the Awami League considered the elections a referendum on regional autonomy, it was but natural that after it secured an absolute majority of seats in the National Assembly (167 out of 169 seats alloted to East Bengal out of a total strength of 313) its Working Committee reiterated its determination to frame the Constitution on the basis of the six-point programme. That programme *inter alia* included direct elections to the legislatures on the basis of adult franchise ; the transfer of all subjects except defence and foreign affairs to the federating units ; the introduction of separate, freely convertible currencies for the two wings ; abdication by the Central Government of its power to tax and collect revenue ; the maintenance of separate accounts of foreign exchange earnings of each wing and the setting up of a separate *militia* or a para-military force for East Pakistan "in order to contribute effectively towards national security."

Even when the Secretary-General of Bhutto's People's Party admitted the "hard economic and political fact" of East Pakistan being "indeed a colony," that Party continued to object to the six-point formula, particularly as regards foreign trade and aid. This was said to be the main stumbling block towards an early transfer of power to the Prime Minister-designate. (Yahya stated on 14 January 1971 that Mujib was going to be the future Prime Minister of the country.) Mujib deemed it necessary to explain the position in the following words :

Yet some of the basic objections now being raised to the Six-Point Programme, when carefully examined, appear to be nothing but calculated measures to perpetuate the colonial status of 'Bangladesh.' The colonial exploitation of the 70 million people of 'Bangladesh' and the transfer of its resources for the benefit of vested interests of the other wing has been done principally through the control of foreign trade, foreign aid and foreign exchange by the Centre. Thus over 80 per cent of all foreign aid obtained has been utilized for the benefit of vested interests of West Pakistan. Over two-thirds of all imports made over the last twenty-three years has been into West Pakistan. Foreign exchange earnings of 'Bangladesh' to the extent of over Rs. 500 crores has been utilised in West Pakistan. 'Bangladesh' has been used as a protected market of 70 million for the benefit of a handful of industrialists of

West Pakistan, who have been enabled to make gigantic profits. As a result of such ruthless exploitation, the economy of 'Bangladesh' is in a state of imminent collapse. Haunted by the spectre of famine and denied the bare means of subsistence, the people of 'Bangladesh' have been reduced to a state of total destitution. We can on no account allow this state of affairs to continue.

Such exploitation would not have been possible unless foreign trade and aid have been with the Centre.[16]

The foreign policy of the Awami League chief, Sheikh Mujibur Rahman, consisted of "non-alignment combined with active friendship with all nations of the world." That this included India was quite evident from his remarks to a correspondent of the *Keyhan* (Tehran daily). In February 1971, he told that correspondent that he would like to have "the best of relations with India....We share a sub-continent and whether we like it or not we have to live and trade together." Mujib was in favour of the solution of all disputes through peaceful means. He accused "the military caste" and "the capitalists" in Pakistan of exploiting the Kashmir dispute for maintaining their dictatorship and for heavy expenditure on armaments. To Mujib, friendship with China was dictated by the facts of "geography and policies." However, that did not mean, he said, that "we would change our system or outlook ; we are a Muslim nation and shall never accept Communism."[17]

The Communist Party of East Pakistan (Bangladesh) always regarded itself as "a part and parcel of the World Communist movement" and was a signatory to the documents issued by the World Communist Conference held in Moscow in 1969. In a letter, addressed through its Central Committee on 3 May 1971, it requested Fraternal Communist and Workers Parties in the world to render their support to "the liberation struggle against a ruthless and barbarous enemy armed to the teeth by the imperialists and having the support of the Maoists of China." It appreciated Soviet condemnation, "in unequivocal terms," of the genocide in Bangladesh and its emphasis on the political solution of outstanding problems. It expressed "disgust" at the attitude of "the British imperialists and Maoist leaders" of China in "openly supporting the reactionary ruling military junta of Pakistan," thereby condoning the genocide in Bangladesh. It described as "dire falsehood" the propaganda by "some pro-Peking groups that this liberation struggle is inspired by the imperialists."[18] The various pro-Chinese Communist groups decided to break with Peking after the surrender of the Pakistani troops. They formed a Central Communist Coordination Committee, which characterized Bangladesh's freedom struggle as a "People's Democratic Revolution." In their struggle against the Bengali bourgeoisie, they began to concentrate on the economic demands and aspirations of the people.

The Soviet Union exerted its efforts in urging moderation on Yahya Khan, with a view to facilitate a political solution within Pakistan and prevent an armed conflict between India and Pakistan. The Chinese attitude was, however, making its task quite difficult. Peking's partisan stand of condemning India and extending support to the "most-aggressive and anti-popular forces in Pakistan who stake not on a political settlement but on mass reprisals," as the *Novosti* Press Commentator, Vladimir Simonov, put it,[19] ran counter to all that Moscow was trying to achieve. It was, therefore, considered as "basically not in line with the interests of a peaceful settlement."[20]

Even at the beginning of 1971, a *Pravda* commentary on the anniversary of the Tashkent Declaration referred to "certain quarters," beyond the confines of India and Pakistan, which spared no effort "to whip up enmity and hatred between them, to aggravate Indo-Pakistan relations in pursuit of their selfish aims," and which regarded the Tashkent Declaration "a serious obstacle to spreading their subversive and provocative activities." For that reason, they resorted to all sorts of speculations and tried to prove that the Declaration had "allegedly, lost its significance, that it is hindering certain people from realising their aims."[21] A little later, the same *Pravda* commentator spoke of tensions in Asia playing into the hands of quarters "which seek to exploit the Indo-Pakistan conflict for their own purpose."[22]

Moscow was also painfully aware that if a political solution of the "serious internal political crisis"[23] was delayed and a protracted liberation struggle of the people of East Pakistan ensued, the moderate Awami League leadership was likely to give way to the militant and leftist forces in East Pakistan. It would also have enabled extremist elements in West Pakistan to have a major say in Islamabad. Thus Peking could exercise considerable influence in both wings of Pakistan, to the extent of creating, at some future date, an independent Bangladesh under its auspices. It was against such a background that Podgorny viewed with "great alarm" the "resort to extreme measures"—the use of the armed forces against the population of East Pakistan by the Military Administration. The Soviet President expressed his concern at "the arrest and persecution of M. Rahman and other politicians who had received such convincing support by the overwhelming majority of the people of East Pakistan at the recent general elections." His "insistent appeal" to Yahya (2 April 1971) for the adoption of "the most urgent measures to stop the bloodshed and repression against the population in East Pakistan and for turning to methods of a peaceful political settlement" must also be seen against that background.

The continuation of repressive measures and bloodshed, Podgorny said, would undoubtedly make the solution of problems more difficult. It "may do great harm to the vital interest of the entire people of Pakistan," while the advice tendered by him as a "true friend" would meet "the interest of the entire people of Pakistan and the interest of preserving peace in the area." The words "entire people of Pakistan" were meant to convince Yahya that Moscow was interested in preserving the territorial integrity and unity of Pakistan. Lest his message be misunderstood or deemed as uncalled-for interference, Podgorny stated that in appealing to him (Yahya), he was guided by the "generally recognised humanitarian principles recorded in the Universal Declaration of Human Rights and by concern for the welfare of the friendly people of Pakistan."[24]

Writing in *Komsomolskaya Pravda* under the heading "Events in Pakistan—Our Commentary," E Verin spoke of "the most serious political crisis in the history of Pakistan" as "undoubtedly strictly an internal affair of that State." He expressed "deep anxiety" as regards the actions of the Pakistani Army in the following words :

> These actions of the Army can be characterised as nothing else than crude arbitrariness and violence causing most serious anxiety to the Soviet people. The crisis which has arisen can and must be settled by political means. It should not be allowed to happen that the words "Civil War" appearing these days in the foreign press should become a reality....The Soviet people express a serious anxiety at the cruel steps taken against the population of East Pakistan. The Soviet people express their warm desire to their neighbour Pakistan that it resolve the difficult problems faced by the Republic by political means in the interests of the entire Pakistani people.[25]

In declaring that it was "imperative" that "immediate measures" be taken in East Pakistan for ensuring the stoppage of the further influx of refugees and for creating conditions of security for their safe return to their homes in a joint statement with India issued on 8 June 1971 or in Premier Kosygin's election speech two days later, the USSR was guided by the considerations mentioned in the preceding paragraphs. Kosygin asserted that a "peaceful solution" of the problems between India and Pakistan "would be in accord with the national interests of the peoples of India and Pakistan and the cause of preserving peace on the Hindustan peninsula." A different development of events, he warned, "would play into the hands of those internal and external forces which operate to the detriment of the interests of both India and Pakistan and pursue their own selfish aims."[26]

That Moscow had not given up hope of playing a pacifying role (similar to the one played after the 1965 Conflict) was evident from Kosygin's election speech on 9 June 1971. He observed : "As before we come out for the peaceful solution of all problems arising in relations between India and Pakistan and hold that the Tashkent Declaration continues to remain a good basis for this." Consequently, the Soviet Union seemed to assume a neutral posture. The Soviet press faithfully reproduced the accounts of border incidents and air space violations emanating from Karachi as well as New Delhi. Thus, *Pravda* of 24 June 1971 and 5 July 1971 carried side by side both the Indian and Pakistani versions about border incidents and as regards a Pakistani allegation about violation of their air space by Indian aircraft and the Indian Defence Ministry's denial thereof.

Writing in the *New Times* (No. 25, June 1971), A. Ulansky expressed his "deepest concern and anxiety" at the tension in the Indian sub-continent and the plight of the refugees. However, he did not go beyond demanding, in the name of peace and humanity, that "conditions be created in East Pakistan for the return of the refugees and that they be assured safety and the possibility to live and work in peace"—a phraseology sufficiently vague against which Pakistan could have no complaint. He expressed some doubts as regards Yahya's sincerity in transferring power to civilian hands. Bhutto had fully supported the military measures taken in East Pakistan in March 1971. However, Ulansky believed that he was insisting "now" on the transfer of power to the "elected representatives of the people." In the July issue of the *New Times* (No. 30), L. Kirichenko referred to the "chauvinist, great power policy" of China as fraught with dangers to the peoples of both India and Pakistan and to the cause of peace. He warned against Peking "exploiting the difficulties in Pakistan and the complications between that country and India" in an attempt "to catch the Pakistani leaders in its net."

Similarly, a commentary in *Izvestia* by V. Vasin in July 1971 avoided taking sides with India or Pakistan. It urged both countries, in identical terms, to make efforts to prevent a "further aggravation of the situation" in the sub-continent. Vasin stressed that the preservation of peace in the Indian sub-continent was "the only correct road meeting the national interests of the Indian and Pakistani peoples and the cause of universal peace." He warned against those forces that were "acting vigorously" and "using every possibility of intensifying tensions in that area in pursuance of their selfish interests." *Pravda* of 3 August 1971 showed a sympathetic appreciation of India's difficulties when it gave details of Pakistani war preparations and carried Yahya's statements to foreign televisions that his country was now on the verge of war with India. A few days later, it gave prominent display to the Indian Prime Minister's appeal to the Heads of 24 Govern-

ments and Moscow was reported to have conveyed its concern
to Islamabad over the trial of Sheikh Mujibur Rahman. Kosygin
was also reported to have written a letter to Yahya
expressing serious concern about his threats of a total war
against India.

Even after the conclusion of the Indo-Soviet Treaty in August
1971, Moscow continued to stick to a similar position. The
Joint Indo-Soviet Statement of 11 August 1971 reiterated the
"firm conviction" of both sides that there could be "no military
solution" and considered it necessary that "urgent steps" be
taken in "East Pakistan" for the achievement of a "political
solution." It did not specify that the solution had to be acceptable to the elected leaders of the people of Bangladesh. It called
for the creation of conditions ensuring the safe return of the
refugees to their homes because that alone would answer "the
interests of the entire people of Pakistan and the cause of the
preservation of peace in the area."[27] In the words of Rushbrook
Williams, this was read in Islamabad as a Soviet move *away*
from support from Bangladesh.[28] The use of the words "East
Pakistan" and "the entire people of Pakistan" undoubtedly
signified that Moscow was not in favour of either the
disintegration or the dismemberment of Pakistan. Vague
formulations, such as "no military solution" and "political
solution," at the same time, seemed to afford some satisfaction
to India as well. Moscow, thus, appeared to be pursuing a
skilful diplomacy—a veritable feat in tight-rope walking.

After the initialling of the Treaty, India could feel confident
as regards Soviet support but the language of the joint
communique seemed to convey a different meaning to Pakistan,
i.e. Moscow would probably not intervene in the crisis. On
19 August 1971, Victor Issraalyan, the Soviet Ambassador to
the UN, opposed the convening of a Security Council meeting
on the tense situation in the sub-continent on the ground that
the root of the tension was Pakistan's domestic problem.
It was for Pakistan, he said, to solve it by creating conditions
for the safe return of refugees to their homeland. This was,
indeed, a subtle way of doing things. The Soviet stand was
designed to meet Indian wishes about not holding meetings
of the Security Council, which would have been utilized by

the Western Powers in transforming the Bangladesh crisis into an Indo-Pakistan issue and for the stationing of UN observers on the border between India and Pakistan so as to freeze the situation. At the same time, such an eventuality, it seems, would have allowed Yahya to continue his repressive actions in East Bengal and permitted him to deal with own his domestic problem in his own way, and to take his own time as regards the creation of conditions for the safe return of refugees to their homeland.

On his return from Moscow on 9 September 1971, the Foreign Secretary of Pakistan stated that Soviet leaders fully agreed that the nature of Pakistan's political institutions and structure was an "internal affair" and that they had "reiterated their deep interest in the unity and integrity of Pakistan." A change in that regard was noticeable in Gromyko's speech before the General Assembly on 28 September 1971. He stated that the present situation in the region was tense and it was "not merely a domestic question." This change was partly designed to create a favourable climate for the Indian Prime Minister's visit to the Soviet Union. Gromyko, however, utilized the opportunity to express the hope that things would not go so far as military confrontation in the area and that restraint and reason would gain the upper hand.[29]

For obvious reasons, India was gravely concerned about the problem. The imposition of "an impossible burden," as a result of the influx of about 9 million refugees (the figure was 8.28 million on 31 August 1971) into India, endangered her "own progress and survival of her social and political institutions." Therefore, during her visit to the USSR, Mrs. Gandhi described it as "a threat to peace in the sub-continent."[30] She expressed her anguish that while "our restraint has been appreciated only in words" by the governments of the world, the basic issues involved and "the real threat to peace and stability in Asia are being largely ignored."[31] Premier Kosygin blamed the Pakistani authorities for creating "unbearable living conditions" by their "actions" which were responsible for the "mass flight of the population from East Pakistan" into neighbouring India. "Political settlement in

East Pakistan," he said, should "take into account the legitimate interests of its population," safeguard "its normal development and eliminate the threat of further aggravation of Pakistani-Indian relations." He appealed to Yahya Khan to take "the most effective steps for the liquidation of the hotbed of tension that has emerged."

Kosygin, however, desisted from making any specific reference to the fact that the tense situation created by the actions of the Pakistani authorities posed a direct or real threat to the peace and stability in Asia—as had been asserted by Mrs. Gandhi. The primary task in Kosygin's eyes was "to prevent the straining of relations between India and Pakistan." This was evident from his remark that the USSR was doing and would continue to do "its utmost for the maintenance of peace in that region and for the prevention of an armed conflict." The joint statement issued on 29 September 1971 reaffirmed :

> The preservation of peace demanded that urgent measures should be taken to reach a political solution of the problems which have arisen there, having regard to the wishes, the inalienable rights and lawful interests of the people of East Bengal as well as for the speediest return of the refugees to their homeland in conditions safeguarding their honour and dignity.

Speaking two days later, the Soviet President, N.V. Podgorny, referred to "the difficult and dangerous situation in the Hindustan sub-continent." The Soviet people, he said, were closely watching that situation. He believed that "the further sliding towards a military conflict must be prevented and that the tension there should be removed by means of an equitable political settlement with due account for the legitimate rights and interests of the peoples in that region."[32] The Soviet President, thus, counselled restraint on both India and Pakistan. He refrained from endorsing President Giri's interpretation of the political settlement—"a solution arrived at in accordance with the wishes of the chosen representatives of the people who were given a massive mandate in December 1970 elections."[33] The Kremlin, thus, seemed to adopt a cautious approach in the matter. It hesitated to identify itself with any particular type of political solution.

This indicated that Moscow was not willing to give up all its options *vis-a-vis* Islamabad.

A certain shift in the Soviet stand was, nevertheless, evident in the remarks of the Soviet leaders which held Pakistani authorities responsible for the influx of the refugees in India and for the creation of "the hotbed of tension" in the sub-continent. It was also clear in their references to the legitimate interests and rights of the people of East Pakistan, and the use of the words "East Bengal." All this might have been the result of Indian presuasion. After Mrs. Gandhi's visit to the USSR, there was a marked upswing in the criticism of Pakistan in the Soviet press. The Soviet Peace Committee urged the cessation of "reprisals" against Sheikh Mujib and other popular leaders of "East Pakistan." The USSR Association for the UN protested against "the crude violation" by the Pakistani authorities of the principles of the Universal Declaration on Human Rights. Protest meetings were held in Moscow, Leningrad, Minsk, Riga and other cities of the USSR against Pakistani repression in East Bengal. In the wake of Pakistan's criticism of the Kremlin's attitude, however, Moscow was also, at times, seen, reverting to seemingly neutral postures.

On 7 October 1971, the spokesman of the Pakistani Foreign Office objected to Kosygin's criticism of the Yahya regime's action. That action, he said, "was taken against anti-national elements in East Pakistan who had organised armed revolution against established authority and attempted to dismember the country." No country, including the USSR, he stated, would have tolerated such attempts. He also alleged that the recent Indo-Soviet Treaty had "encouraged India to step up provocative activities against Pakistan." He asked Moscow to take notice of "the aggressive disposition of the Indian armed forces against the Pakistan borders in both the wings." On 8 October 1971, a joint statement of the USSR and Algeria declared their "respect for the national unity and territorial integrity of Pakistan and India." The two states appealed to both New Delhi and Islamabad to find a peaceful solution to the problems confronting them "according with the principles of non-interference, mutual respect, good neighbour relations and the spirit of the Tashkent meeting."[34] Commenting on it, an Indian researcher has gone to the extent of describing it as "an example of Soviet diplomatic duplicity," an attempt, on the part of Moscow, to see a political solution of the problem which would not put a major strain on Soviet-Pakistan relations.[35]

Lest the above-mentioned pronouncement in the communique be misconstrued in India, Moscow immediately sought to allay New Delhi's apprehensions. A vigorous popular campaign advocating an end to reprisals against Sheikh Mujibur Rahman was mounted in the Soviet press. In a long commentary on the events in Pakistan, on 10 October 1971, *Pravda* accused the military *junta* of Pakistan of somehow trying to justify its action. Islamabad, it said, had adopted a "discriminatory policy" towards the eastern province ever since 1947. The commentator, I. Borisov, vigorously protested against the trial of Mujibur Rahman. He regarded it "an act of juridical reprisal." He not only demanded the release of the Awami League leader but also sought "a political settlement of the crisis in East Pakistan, a settlement which takes into account the will, inalienable rights and legitimate interests" of the people of that province. Such a settlement, he said, would facilitate the speedy and safe return of the refugees to their homes.[36]

Deputy Foreign Minister Firyubin expressed his full agreement with India's assessment of the tense situation in the sub-continent. That situation, the statement issued at the end of his talks in New Delhi said, "endangers the cause of peace in the area." This apparently signified that Moscow agreed with the Indian view that a military threat did exist which imperilled the security of India. Consultations that took place on his visit on 26 October 1971 were said to be not only in conformity with the existing procedure of annual bilateral consultations but also "under the provisions of Article IX of the Soviet-Indian Treaty of Peace, Friendship and Cooperation."[37] That Article provided that, in the event of either party being subjected to an atttack or threat thereof, the High Contracting Parties "shall immediately enter into mutual consultations in order to remove such threat and take appropriate effective measures to ensure peace and the security of their countries." To carry further conviction with India, a high-powered military delegation visited New Delhi with a view to assess India's defence requirements in the face of the threatened Pakistani aggression.

The chauvinistic hysteria and the "hysterical anti-Indian campaign in Pakistan," which enjoyed the "patronage of some in the Pakistani administration," was strongly criticized in an article in the *New Times* (No. 44) in October 1971. Commentator I. Borisov, at the same time, stated that the "bellicose statements" emanating from the leaders of reactionary religious and communal parties and organizations in India as well were seeking to use the tense situation on the Pakistani-Indian frontier to further their selfish political aims. With the two armies directly facing each other and with border incidents occurring intermittently, a single incautious move or a chance occurence, he said, might be enough for "the present tension" to flare up into an armed conflict with devastating, irreparable consequences. He dwelt on the harmful effects of the Indo-Pak Conflict of 1965 on the economic and political life of both countries. He recalled the *Tass* statement of 7 September 1965 and observed that words contained therein "are more timely than ever today" when the same external forces were adding to the tension on the Indian sub-continent. The pursuit of East Pakistani refugees and resistance groups by the Pakistani army, he said, had set off a chain-reaction of armed incidents on the border between East Pakistan and India, "and these have led to the present confrontation." I. Borisov then referred to the restraint shown by India and "sober appraisal of the consequences of a possible armed conflict" on which Yahya was harping "in his recent speeches." The preservation of peace on the Indian sub-continent, the Soviet writer asserted, required that urgent measures be taken to facilitate a political settlement of the existing problems with due consideration for the wishes, the inalienable rights and lawful interests of the population of East Pakistan—"measures that would ensure the quick return home of the refugees and guarantee their safety." He concluded by saying that the peoples of both India and

Pakistan needed peace, and that "their true friends" were doing all they could to prevent a military conflict between the two countries. In that connection, he recalled the words of Premier Kosygin.

In November 1971, the Soviet press found fault with the Yahya regime for displaying "Crush India" placards and provoking daily clashes on the border (*Pravda*, 19 November). It held Yahya's "violent measures" responsible for the creation of the critical situation in the sub-continent, thereby castigating those who equated India and Pakistan in the matter (*Pravda*, 21 November). It asserted that the situation arose due to the refugee influx caused by Pakistan's military administration (*Prvada*, 13 November). An article in the *Krasnaya Zvezda* stated that Pakistan had staked much "on a military solution of the problem of East Pakistan." It added : "This is precisely what creates a tense atmosphere and jeopardises peace in the sub-continent." However, Moscow still deemed it prudent not to completely identify itself publicly with India.

P. Mezentsev's commentary in *Pravda* (23 November 1971) admitted that the repressive action of the military authorities of Pakistan was the source of tension on the entire sub-continent. It acknowledged the fact that the influx of ten million refugees was entailing "a very heavy economic burden on India." It took note of the implications of staging demonstrations by chauvinistic elements, under official patronage, in West Pakistani cities, including Lahore, under the slogans of "waging a holy war against India" and "completely crushing" India, etc. Such actions, he said, were not at all conducive to normalizing relations between the two countries and could only further aggravate the situation. Despite all that, the Soviet commentator deemed it necessary to state that the refugee problem and "serious difficulties," it created in the relations between India and Pakistan should not become "the cause of military conflict between them." With the situation becoming more tense and frequent large-scale encounters occurring between Indian and Pakistani armed forces, concentrated along the border, the *Pravda* commentator counselled moderation on the two countries in the following words :

The refugee problem has created serious difficulties in the relations between India and Pakistan. However, it should not become the cause of a military conflict between them. The military administration should stop the reprisals against the East Pakistani population and take measures for millions of people to return home. Such a solution would, above all, be in accord with the interests of Pakistan itself and the cause of preserving peace on the sub-continent.[38]

In another *Pravda* commentary (26 November 1971) entitled "Indian Sub-continent Needs Peace," A. Moslennikov and V. Shurygin blamed the Pakistani military administration for the political crisis in East Pakistan which was said to have been the consequence of its refusal to hand over power to the duly elected representatives of the people. The East Pakistani refugee problem, both in scale and in nature, they stated, had become, an international problem, which inevitably created increasing tension in the relations between the two states and posed "a direct threat of a military conflict." Realizing the harmful consequences—economic, social and political—of an armed conflict, the Soviet commentators urgently called for a political solution of the crisis. They pinned their hopes on the sober voices "heard of late" not only from Mrs. Gandhi but also "on the part of individual politicians and statesmen in Pakistan."[39] Evidently, Moscow preferred to adopt a more or less neutral stance since it seemed anxious to preserve some influence in Pakistan. Even at that stage, it wished to prevent Islamabad from leaning too heavily on Peking. It was realized that a military showdown between India and Pakistan, would weaken both nations and create conditions of instability in the region, which were likely to be exploited by China.

India was, however, getting seriously perturbed by the intolerable situation. The massive exodus of refugees into India, the Indian delegate to the UN Third Committee stated on 18 November 1971, was a "threat to India's stability and security," and indeed, to her very existence. It was tantamount to "a civilian aggression," "an intolerable interference" in the internal affairs of India, "in fact, a new form of aggression."[40]

The Kremlin could neither ignore the insistent appeals of the leaders and people of Bangladesh, including the faithful East Pakistan Communist Party, nor completely write off "the

great country"—India—whose importance for Moscow increased considerably in view of the gathering clouds of Sino-
US rapprochement. Consequently, the Soviet Union often
showed a marked preference for India and an understanding of
the Indian stand in its criticism of Pakistani authorities. That
phenomenon was most clearly perceptible in Moscow's assurance to India that it had not supplied any military equipment to Pakistan in addition to what had already been supplied
in the past;[41] in its unabated arms assistance to India; in the
signing of the Indo-Soviet Treaty—a reinsurance for India
against Peking's involvement in any conflict between India and
Pakistan; and in its opposition to the convening of Security
Council meetings. The avowed purpose of such meetings was
to transform Pakistan's domestic problems into an Indo-Pakistan issue and utilize them for pressing the demand for stationing
observers on the borders of the two countries. Thus, the
intolerable situation with regard to refugees would have persisted
and, probably, it would have been frozen.

After 3 December 1971, when Islamabad launched large-
scale attacks on several Indian airfields, the Soviet Union gave
complete support to India. In such a situation, it was not
possible for the Kremlin to adopt an equivocal attitude. Apart
from military support and assistance, Moscow rendered valuable political support in the UN. The Soviet delegate to the
Security Council insisted on his proposal that the representative of Bangladesh should be invited to take part in the deliberations of the Council. Above all, he used his veto power,
which set at naught all attempts aimed at censuring India or
imposing a solution on her. It was realized that with the
emergence of an independent Bangladesh, friendly to both India
and the Soviet Union, Moscow would be in a better position to
meet the challenge posed by Sino-US *detente*. A more satisfactory balance of power in the Asian continent could thereby be
preserved. APN Commentator, Mikhal Krylov, in his commentary entitled "Stop Bloodshed and Ensure Non-Involvement of
Outside Forces," emphatically asserted that apart from "purely
humane motives," Soviet leaders had "other important
reasons" for preserving peace in the Indian sub-continent. He
noted with concern the support given by the USA and China's

"open encouragement" to the dangerous actions of Islamabad, which had disregarded the sober appeals of the USSR in the matter. He adjudged that the involvement of outside Powers in the conflict would bring about a further aggravation of the situation and declared that developments "in close proximity to its southern borders" could not but infringe upon the interests of the USSR's security.[42]

On the beginning of the 14-day War in December, Moscow realized the dangers inherent in the Chinese involvement in the Conflict. It came out strongly in support of India both in and out of the United Nations. The *Tass* statement of 5 December 1971 found fault with the Pakistani Government for trying to blame India for the "growing resistance by the East Pakistan population to the mass repressions and persecutions," and for aggravating relations with India by building up military preparations. It accused Islamabad of starting the war by bombing and strafing a number of towns in north-western India. The statement also warned the Governments of all countries of the world against "involvement in the conflict," which would lead to "a further aggravation of the situation in the Hindustan peninsula."[43]

The representative of Pakistan, Shahi, spoke in critical terms about the Indo-Soviet Treaty and of Soviet supplies of military hardware to India. He criticized Moscow for "making it possible" for India to launch "subversion and aggression" against Pakistan and yet seeking to invoke the Tashkent spirit. He took exception to the *Tass* statement of 5 December, which "in effect says that Pakistan was following a dangerous course in defending itself and resisting a military occupation and implied that Pakistan's action even posed a threat to the Soviet Union's security interests." Shahi also found fault with Moscow for referring to Pakistani attacks on 3 December and ignoring, as he said, "large scale attacks on East Pakistan from all sides, which commenced on 21 November."[44] The Soviet representative, Malik, refused to enter into an argument with Shahi but simply quoted the following innocuous excerpts from the *Tass* statement to refute Shahi's accusations :

Guided by concern for the maintenance of peace, the

Soviet Government repeatedly expressed to President Yahya Khan of Pakistan and to the Government of Pakistan its concern over the situation that had developed in the Hindustan Peninsula in connection with the events in East Pakistan....In approaching the Government of Pakistan with these considerations, the Soviet Government acted in accordance with the principles of humanitarianism, wishing the Pakistan people well in the solution, in a democratic way, of the complex problems facing the country......In the face of the military threat now hanging over Hindustan, to which not a single peace-loving country can remain indifferent, the Soviet Union calls for a speedy end to the bloodshed and for a political settlement in East Pakistan on the basis of respect for the lawful rights and interests of its people.[45]

In the United Nations, the USSR vetoed the Peking-backed US proposal calling for an immediate ceasefire and the withdrawal of troops in the sub-continent without any reference to the developments in Bangladesh which had been the root cause of the critical situation. At the same time, Moscow put forward its own draft resolution calling for a political settlement "in East Pakistan which would inevitably result in a cessation of hostilities." The resolution also called upon the Government of Pakistan to take measures to cease all acts of violence by Pakistani forces "in East Pakistan which have led to deterioration of the situation." The Soviet draft made no direct reference to a cease-fire or troop withdrawals.

In his statement, Malik defended India against the Chinese accusations that New Delhi had created the refugee situation. He denounced the attempt of both Pakistan and China—"its great protector"—and of "certain allies of Pakistan in their military blocs" for placing India and Pakistan on the same footing. He characterized the US draft resolution as one-sided, and, for that matter, unacceptable. He made a strong plea for inviting Bangladesh's representatives for participation in the discussion. Moscow also vetoed the draft resolution, submitted by Belgium, Italy and Japan, which called upon the Governments of India and Pakistan "as a first step for an immediate cease-fire and for a cessation of all military activities." That resolution vaguely referred to "efforts to bring about conditions necessary for the speedy and voluntary repatriation of the millions of the refugees to the homes." China was the only country that voted against the Soviet draft resolution.

Spartak Beglov's commentary in the Soviet press on 8 December 1971 described the influx of ten million East Pakistanis into India as "not a mere flow of refugees" but an event which drastically upset the balance of the Indian economy, "affecting its security in the widest sense of the word and the outcome of all its political campaigns at home." He then referred to "the evermore threatening statements from the Pakistani capital," and the warlike passions roused against India. "Mutual troop withdrawals" and "cease-fire" were not enough. The hotbed of war, he said, could not be extinguished without a simultaneous settlement in East Pakistan with account taken of the will expressed by the people.[46] APN Commentator, I. Plyshevsky, stated that the cessation of military actions between India and Pakistan did not mean the cessation of bloodshed in the Indian subcontinent. To limit oneself to the call for "early," "immediate" cessation of military operations, he said, was tantamount to condemning many more thousands of East Pakistanis to death and many more millions to become refugees. Consequently, what was important, he stated, was not only the cessation of military operations, but an immediate end to all bloodshed. Commenting on the US draft resolution which provided for the stationing of UN military observers on the Indo-Pakistani frontier, Plyshevsky observed that such a step would grant the Pakistani Military Administration an opportunity to continue with impunity its reign of terror against its political opponents—the overwhelming majority of the East Pakistani people. Their condition, he said, would worsen a hundred times as compared with what existed earlier. It would create an additional obstacle to "the saving of people by crossing the border." The UN Security Council would, thus, become "a shield for the terrorist actions of the Pakistani authorities."[47] The problem of the East Pakistani refugees, *Izvestia* Political Analyst, V. Kudryavtsev, stated, was not so much a matter of humanism as of politics, but "bourgeois pseudo-humanists shut their eyes to this."[48]

Victor Mayevsky's article in *Pravda* on 9 December 1971 accused Peking of playing "an instigator's role in the exacerbation of the situation on the Hindustan peninsula" and of pursuing "a policy of setting Asians against Asians, a policy openly resembling the USA's 'Guam Doctrine'." After denouncing China's "especially provocational role" in the Indo-Pakistan Conflict, he observed :

> On the one hand, the Maoists tried in every way to worm their way into East Pakistan and, with the help of their agents, preached a "people's war" there. On the other hand, they advertised their support for the military regime in Pakistan, striving to turn it into an instrument of their chauvinst, great power course in Asia. It is not difficult to see that the essence of Peking's position is to fan the Indian-Pakistani conflict, to pour oil on the flames. In so doing, the Maoists are pursuing their own selfish chauvinist aims. They are profoundly indifferent to the true national interests of the Pakistani people ; they regard Pakistan merely as a puppet in the unscrupulous game they are playing in the international arena.[49]

Commenting on "China's collusion" with the United States in denying Bangladesh's representatives an opportunity to participate in the debate and in trying to push through a US-sponsored pro-Pakistan resolution, *Pravda* of 6 December 1971 remarked :

> A group of countries, headed by USA, which were joined by the representatives of the People's Republic of China, managed to turn down the proposal about inviting to the Council's meeting representatives of the Bangladesh national liberation movement and thus created from the very start of the meeting an atmosphere which is not conducive to an objective discussion of the causes which created the dangerous situation in the Hindustan peninsula.[50]

Analyzing the basis and significance of the identical stand taken by both Washington and Peking in the UN on the Indo-Pakistan War, a commentary in the *Sovietskaya Rossia*—an organ of the CPSU—accused both China and the USA of giving the West Pakistan military *junta* promises of arms aid before it embarked on war with India. It added :

A weakening of India and Pakistan as a result of the

present war would play into the hands of Peking great-power chauvinists who have been dreaming of establishing their supremacy in Asia. It would also play into the hands of the American imperialists since this war exhausts and divides forces capable of opposing jointly the neocolonialist designs of the USA.[51]

The *Izvestia* Political Observer, V. Kudryavtsev, on 12 December 1971, stated that by giving military assistance to the Pakistani Government both Peking and Washington not only provoked Pakistan to attack India but also helped it in the cruel suppression of the Bengali people. In so doing, he added, Peking had proceeded solely from selfish motives of establishing its domination in Asia. Kudryavtsev accused the ruling Maoist group in China of "fishing in troubled waters" and of taking advantage of the artificially magnified contradictions between individual Asian countries. Writing again in *Izvestia* on 18 December 1971, V. Kudryavtsev exposed the hypocrisy of the "peace-makers"—the USA and China—by stating that they had adopted a one-sided approach to the question of putting an end to the conflict on the Hindustan peninsula.[52]

In a despatch from New York on 17 December 1971, *Pravda* accused Peking of ignoring "the liberation character of the East Pakistan population's struggle and the role of India, which became a victim of aggression by Pakistani forces on its western border." China was criticized for its profound indifference to the East Bengalis' liberation struggle. The Maoists, it said, simply regarded Pakistan as a trampline for the realization of their own chauvinistic aims. The Chinese delegation at the UN, it added, had defended "injustice and violence." In another attack on the identical roles of China and the USA in the Indo-Pakistan Conflict, *Pravda* observed :

The events in the Hindustan peninsula have torn down the mask from Peking leaders to show to the whole world that they are marching hand in hand with the stranglers of the freedom of the peoples and that they are driven by selfish chauvinist motives. If not formally, then actually Peking has converged with the inspirers and organisers of the anti-Communist blocs—SEATO and CENTO.[53]

After the Indian Government ordered a cease-fire and Pakistani troops surrendered in Bangladesh, the Soviet representative desired that the Security Council take a decision welcoming "the cessation of hostilities in East Pakistan." It should also express hope that the cease-fire would be observed by both sides, which would guarantee, without delay, the "unimpeded transfer of power to the lawful representatives of the people elected in December 1970." The Soviet draft resolution in the matter called for an immediate cease-fire and the cessation of all other military actions "along the entire border between India and West Pakistan and along the cease-fire line of 1965 in Jammu and Kashmir." While welcoming the Indian decision of an unilateral cease-fire, Moscow asked Pakistan to take an identical decision without delay. The resolution also called upon all Member States of the UN to render comprehensive assistance for the speediest cessation of military actions and to refrain from any steps which could impede the normalization of the situation on the Indo-Pakistan sub-continent.[54]

After much deliberations, the Security Council, on 21 December 1971, adopted resolution 307, which demanded a durable cease-fire and the cessation of all hostilities until withdrawals take place, as soon as practicable, of all armed forces. It called upon all concerned to take all necessary measures to preserve human life and for the observance of the Geneva Convention of 1949. It also enjoined upon them to apply, in full, its provisions concerning protection of wounded and sick POWs and the civilian population. Explaining Moscow's abstention on that resolution, the Soviet representative noted the positive factors contained in the resolution as regards a cease-fire, withdrawal of troops, and the attention given to the humanitarian aspects of the problem. At the same time, he pointed out that the resolution also contained certain provisions, e.g. the reference in the second preambular paragraph to the General Assembly resolution of 7 December 1971, to which the USSR could not agree. He observed that the Soviet Union had voted against the Assembly resolution because it was "one-sided in nature" and did not take account of the specific features, the unprecedented nature and the complexity of those events which took place in "East Pakistan as a result of repressions against the East Pakistani population." He stated that it was precisely those occurences which constituted the main cause of the serious friction that arose in that region "leading to the unleashing of the military conflict as a result of the attack on India by Pakistan armed forces."[55]

Writing in *Izvestia* on 23 December 1971, V. Kudryavtsev observed that though the Security Council resolution included important points which promoted the normalization of the situation in the Indian sub-continent, it, nevertheless, failed to stipulate that "only the elected representatives of East Pakistan can decide on its destinies."[56]

An important aspect of Soviet policy was condemnation of Peking's role in the Indo-Pakistan War, the refutation of Chinese allegations and charges levelled against Moscow, and the exposition of Peking's true designs. Thus, on 4 December 1971, the Soviet representative, Malik, stated that Peking's "chatter, prattle and demagogy about social imperialism" was playing into the hands of only the imperialists, drawing numerous countries, including Pakistan, into "military aggressive blocs." China was criticized for defending "military dictatorship, terror and oppression."[57] After describing social imperialism to be "as great an absurdity as fried ice," Malik refuted the base slander, particularly slander against the friendship between India and the Soviet Union, by the "Chinese traitors to socialism." Peking's accusation that the Soviet intention was to conquer the Indian sub-continent and launch further aggression against China was considered by Malik as a "fairy story" meant for "little children or great fools." He apprised the non-aligned countries, the small and medium-sized countries, of the true Chinese intentions of subjecting them to its influence and control.[58] In his statement before the Security Council on 13 December 1971, Malik accused the Maoist clique of "setting Asians against Asians" and pursuing "the hypocritical two-faced policy" of promoting, inciting and exacerbating the political crisis in East Pakistan by its concept of the so-called "people's war" and, at the same time, broadcasting its support for Pakistan in an

attempt to turn it into an instrument of its chauvinistic
course of aggrandizement in Asia for the purposes of strengthening its influence and control over the Indian peninsula,
as well as over the whole of Southeast Asia. By provoking
an aggravation of the crisis in East Pakistan and inflaming the
Indo-Pak Conflict, Malik said, the Maoists were trying to
attain their "expansionist, selfish, great-power chauvinist
purposes" with total indifference to "the national interests
both of East Pakistanis as well as the Pakistani people as a
whole."[59]   In his subsequent statement of 15 December 1971,
Malik referred to "a United States-Chinese duet." He
observed : "Peking is interested only in one thing : to exploit
the situation and to strengthen its position in East Asia and
in the Indian sub-continent."[60]

Pravda's Political Commentator, V. Mayevsky, accused
Peking of playing "a doubly treacherous game." On the one
hand, it incited the East Pakistani populace to "struggle
against the Punjabi, *i.e.* West Pakistani landowners,"
thereby interfering in the affairs of East Pakistan. In this
connection, reference was made to the booklet, *To Bengali
Revolutionaries*, which contained excerpts from the works of
Mao and Lin Piao and was circulated in East Pakistan
by Chinese agents and pro-Chinese elements with Peking's
financial assistance. On the other hand, China sought to
strengthen its ties with the ruling circles of West Pakistan
and rendered them military, economic and political support for attacking India. Mayevsky thereby concluded that
Peking was not in the least concerned with the interests of the
Pakistani people. It was only interested in "turning Pakistan
into an instrument of Peking's great-power chauvinistic policy
in Asia and pushing Pakistan into an armed conflict with
India." Peking's hypocrisy in posing as champions of "state
sovereignty and territorial integrity," of the idea of self-determination, and as fighters against "splitting and subversive
actions" was laid bare by referring to Chinese moral and material
support to the Nigerian secessionist, Ojukmu, who tried to set
up the separate state of "Biafra." By showing solidarity with
the USA, the Soviet commentator observed, Peking actually
encouraged the US imperialists to militarily intervene in the

Indian subcontinent under the pretext of discharging their "commitments" under the CENTO and the SEATO. He added : "China's stand certainly was one of the factors which encouraged the US to send the ships of the Seventh Fleet to the Indian Ocean." Immediate ceasefire, as demanded by the Chinese representative, he pointed out, could only mean "a continuation and aggravation of the conflict" in the Indian sub-continent.[61]

Another commentary in *Izvestia* by V. Kudryavtsev on 29 December 1971 exposed the Maoist leaders' contention as regards the events in East Pakistan being the "domestic affair" of Pakistan by referring to "domestic affair" claims of Vorster's racist government in South Africa and the Portuguese colonialists in Mozambique, Angola and Guinea (Bissau). By aligning itself with the military regime of Pakistan and "the US imperialists" in the national liberation struggle of the people of East Pakistan, Peking proved that it was "more concerned with its maneouvres for realising its hegemonistic aspirations than with the destinies of nations." Since the Peking leadership had always displayed a derisive attitude to its own national minorities and since the foreign policy of a state was a continuation of its domestic policy, the Soviet commentator remarked, Peking's stand as regards the events in the Indian sub-continent was a logical outcome.[62]

Writing in the *New Times* under the caption "Now That The Guns Are Silent," Dimitry Volsky observed that the two-week war "provoked by the Pakistani authorities' policy of ruthlessly suppressing the people's movement in East Bengal brought defeat to those who were to blame for it." From the very beginning, he said, the question of a ceasefire was inseparable from that of eliminating the root causes of the crisis. India, he remarked, had fought for a just cause and the sympathies of all progressive people were on her side. In politically aligning themselves with Washington in helping the Pakistani generals, the Soviet commentator added, the Chinese rulers had "virtually become co-partners" in Western military blocs. By showing themselves as "totally unscrupulous," they had broken "all class principles and betrayed the cause of national liberation and social progress."[63]

The statement of the Soviet Foreign Ministry on 18 December 1971 expressed satisfaction at the cessation of hostilities and considered it conducive to the achievement of "an effective political settlement of problems associated with the conflict." The statement urged all countries "to assist in every possible way in quickly restoring peace on the Indian sub-continent and to refrain from any steps which might complicate the normalization of the situation."[64]

G. Yakubov's long article in *Pravda* reproached Peking for consistently trying to weaken, isolate and discredit India with a view to furthering its own hegemonistic designs in Asia. Pakistan, he said, would not have launched military operations against India on 3 December 1971 "if it had not been aware of instigating support from outside." An enormous share of the responsibility for the conflict, he stated, rested with the Chinese leaders "who sow animosity between peoples and act as instigators of wars." According to the *Pakistan Times*, he added, Peking began supplying 400 fighters and bombers, tanks and anti-aircraft installations to Pakistan. Instead of giving any help in overcoming Indo-Pak differences, Yakubov observed, the Chinese leaders hindered "in every way" the settlement of disputes between the two countries. They provoked Pakistan to anti-Indian actions "in the hope of drawing Pakistan into the net of their geo-political strategy." In this regard, the Soviet writer cited Peking's role in the UN in frustrating Moscow's attempts towards the cessation of hostilities between India and Pakistan and measures taken to guarantee a political settlement. He then remarked :

> The Indo-Pakistan conflict made clear the provocative nature of the foreign policy course of the Peking leadership, a course aimed at creating and fanning up hotbeds of tension. When guns were roaring Peking added fuel to the fire, fomenting hostility between India and Pakistan. At the same time, while warming their hands by the fire so kindled, the Peking leaders and their American imperialist partners posed as "peace-makers," demanding hypocritically a cease-fire. Now that the fire had ceased, instigating calls are coming daily from Peking urging Pakistan leaders to 'carry forward the war to a victorious end.'[65]

The Kremlin's role during the Indo-Pak War of 1971 had been in marked contrast to the attitude it had adopted during the 1965 Conflict. In 1965, Moscow had adopted a fundamentally neutral stance. It concentrated upon "the immediate cessation of military operations, the halting of the tanks and the silencing of the guns" without bothering as to "the causes of the origin of the conflict"—without seeking to determine "who is right and who is to blame," as Kosygin's messages to Ayub and Shastri dated 4 September 1965 put it. In 1971, however, Moscow laid considerable stress on the "source of tension." The Security Council, Malik stated on 4 December 1971, "has not the right to close its eyes to the cause of the emergence and the deterioration of the situation." The questions of a cease-fire and of a political settlement, he added, were closely and inseparably bound together. They had to be tackled simultaneously. Moreover, unlike 1965 (when Moscow had joined hands with Washington in exerting pressure on both India and Pakistan in effecting the cessation of hostilities and calling upon third parties to desist from interference), the Soviet Union, in 1971, publicly and unequivocally supported India. The Indo-Soviet Treaty, Maslennikov observed, acted as "the shield which protected South Asia from the interference of outside forces during the Indo-Pakistan conflict."[66] The change in Soviet policy during the Bangladesh crisis was primarily due to the fact that the circumstances in 1971 were quite different from those existing in 1965. In the 60s, Moscow and Washington shared similar views about Peking exploiting the situation in the subcontinent. But with Sino-US rapprochement looming large on the horizon in 1971 and Washington's attempts to intimidate India, the Kremlin could not have obviously remained indifferent to the promotion of its interests in South Asia.

7

USSR-Pak Relations After 1971

USSR-Pak relations were put to severe strain during the Bangladesh Crisis. In that context, a Pakistani writer has observed as follows :

> Relations between the USSR and Pakistan, which had considerably cooled since April 1971, thenceforth deteriorated rapidly. The Russian Government suspended its economic aid to Pakistan and the Russian experts working on various projects left the country. The Soviet import organization advised the Afghan Bank-i-Milli not to permit any movement of Pakistani goods into Afghanistan which serves as the overland transit route for Pakistan-USSR trade. Sea trade was also suspended and after November 1971 no Soviet ship came to pick up cargo from Karachi.[1]

After Islamabad disregarded Podgorny's friendly advice, started war against India, and began to look towards Peking and Washington for sustenance and support, the Kremlin was left with no choice but to come out in open support of India. After China vetoed the Soviet draft resolution, which would have otherwise been adopted, Moscow effectively blocked the adoption of all those resolutions which would have been tantamount to exerting of international diplomatic pressure on India. The USSR also rendered necessary military assistance for ensuring a successful outcome of the freedom struggle in Bangladesh.

Z.A. Bhutto found fault with the Soviet President for addressing a letter to Yahya Khan. In "dictating a political solution for the crisis in East Pakistan," he observed, the Soviet Union chose to forget its own history, "her own military interventions for self-preservation even beyond her borders in Hungary and Czechoslovakia," and called upon the Government of Pakistan to find a particular kind of solution to a problem that exclusively concerned the people of Pakistan. Bhutto was, thus, quite critical of the Soviet role during the Bangladesh Crisis and the Indo-Pakistan War of 1971.

However, after Bhutto became President of Pakistan, he seemed anxious to repair the damage done to USSR-Pak relations by not forgetting to see the Soviet ambassador in Islamabad, when he called on the Chinese and American envoys. It is, indeed, noteworthy that while Bhutto in retaliation to announcements of recognition to Bangladesh, went to the extent of severing diplomatic relations with a large number of countries (he even left the Commonwealth after UK recognized Dacca) he desisted from snapping ties with Moscow when the latter recognized Bangladesh. The maintenance of good relations with Moscow helped Islamabad in a number of ways. It prevented the USSR from aligning itself too closely with India and against Pakistan. It enabled Bhutto to reiterate his desire of having bilateral relations with all the three Great Powers, though this did not mean that Islamabad could not be closer to some than to others. Bhutto could also thereby assume a posture of pursuing an independent foreign policy and claim affinity with the Third World. Moreover, by renewing its contacts with Moscow, Islamabad could hope that economic and technical assistance for the completion of projects in hand with Soviet collaboration would, at least, be continued and that it would have no difficulty in obtaining spare parts for equipment already supplied.

During Bhutto's visit to Kabul in January 1972, it was reported in the press that Pakistan was no longer averse to the idea that "she should cooperate in the possible arrangement for allowing easy flow of traffic on the Asian Highway and open her borders with Afghanistan and India for the purpose."[2] Even if it had nothing to do with the Soviet pro-

posal of Collective Security in Asia or the idea of regional economic cooperation, steps in that direction were very likely
to be appreciated by the Kremlin. It signified an improvement over Pakistan's earlier opposition in the matter. It was,
therefore, not without significance that the resumption of
Soviet supplies of machinery to Pakistan was announced soon
after Bhutto's Kabul visit. In this connection, it is also important to recall that it was in Moscow's interests not to
push Pakistan into too much dependence on China. Here,
it is significant to note that the Soviet Union had not completely stopped its economic and technical assistance to Islamabad
even during the Bangladesh Crisis.

At one time, the USSR seemed to have entertained some
doubts about India's non-capitalist growth and her status of a
"National Democratic State." Nevertheless, it entered
into a Treaty of Friendship with India in 1971, and looked
forward to the latter playing a significant role in the region.
That, however, did not mean that Moscow had concentrated all
its efforts on India and neglected Pakistan. With the defeat
of Pakistan and the emergence of Bangladesh, Peking's capacity to maintain an artificial balance or parity between India
and Pakistan had no doubt suffered a setback. However, China
is unlikely to abandon its policy of playing up one sub-continental Power against the other in order to regain its influence in the region, and in particular to counter Soviet moves
in the area. Though China had sought to use Pakistan as
its major "strong point" in the Middle East and the Indian
Ocean area and exploit the contradictions between India
and Pakistan, a Soviet commentator remarked, Peking had
nevertheless made "some peaceable gestures to India in 1971,"
i.e. before the Bangladesh crisis erupted into an Indo-Pak conflict. In the opinion of a Soviet analyst, the true aims of Peking
were "in no way concerned with the interests of the two countries."[3]

With Mao's changed posture towards non-alignment (this
was discernible from Peking's message to the Lusaka Conference of Non-aligned Nations : previously, the Chinese attitude had been quite negative), Moscow did not rule out
the possibility of Peking utilizing the non-aligned countries

against the USSR, as one of the "super powers," in what the Soviet commentator, D. Vostokov, termed, its "great power designs."[4] The prospect of a strong regional Power, *viz.* India, remaining closely aligned with its main adversary—the USSR—was not quite appealing from Peking's point of view. However, before Peking could make any move in the direction of weakening Indo-Soviet friendship or think of making some friendly gestures towards India, it had to watch the situation and see that some settlement was first reached between the countries of the sub-continent.

The Soviet Union, on its part, did not wish to completely write off Pakistan, particularly after having spent so much money and effort in the past. It was hardly in Moscow's interest to leave Islamabad at the mercy of Peking or tie it down to the bandwagon of Sino-US collusion. With Sino-American *detente* coming on the surface, India's importance is bound to loom large in Moscow's calculations. With her victory in Bangladesh and her peaceful nuclear explosion, India has become a leading Power in the region and will be playing a significant role in South and Southeast Asia. However, Soviet concern for safeguarding its borders and securing its southern flank from hostile influences, as also the necessity of preserving conditions of peace and stability near its frontiers, induced Moscow to persistently cultivate Islamabad. Considerations of mutually beneficial trade, the importance of an overland route to strengthen Moscow's trade ties with Pakistan, Afghanistan and India, and the scheme of Collective Security in Asia are likely to weigh heavily with the Kremlin. Moreover, the need to contain and guard against Peking's nefarious influence, competition with the USA and China on a world scale, and its desire to play a global role also accounted for Moscow's sustained interest in Pakistan.

Accordingly, when President Bhutto arrived in Moscow at the head of a 58-member delegation on 16 March 1972, he was received at the airport by Premier Kosygin. Speaking at a luncheon in honour of the visiting Afghan Premier, two days earlier, Kosygin offered to help find a political settlement between India and Pakistan. He, however, coupled that offer with a revival of the Soviet proposal for a Collective Security System in Asia. The Soviet Union, he added, would "continue to contribute to the political settlement of disputed issues between the states of the Indian sub-continent in the interest of peace and mutual understanding."[5] Speaking at a luncheon meeting during Bhutto's visit to Moscow, Kosygin commended the willingness of both India and Bangladesh to hold talks with Pakistan. He advised Bhutto to adopt a realistic approach in the matter by discarding his policy of confrontation and replacing it by "a policy of peace and cooperation between the states of Hindustan and achieve agreement on the establishment of peace and tranquility on the India-Pakistan frontier."[6]

The joint communique, issued at the end of Bhutto's visit, stated that the Pakistani President was prepared to take steps towards establishing peaceful conditions in the sub-continent. In that connection, Bhutto attached great importance to the cessation of hostile propaganda by the countries of the sub-continent against each other. Moscow, however, refrained from expressing any opinion in the matter. It seemed that although "great attention in the talks" was given to the exchange of views on the situation in the Indian sub-continent, nothing tangible seemed to have come out of the talks. In the Indo-Soviet joint statement of 5 April 1972, for instance, Moscow favoured "direct negotiations between the governments of India, Bangladesh and Pakistan" for arriving at a peaceful political settlement of the problems obtaining in the area. Thus, Bhutto's bid to seek Soviet support for securing the release of the Pakistani POWs and the vacation of territory occupied by India in West Pakistan did not seem to have borne fruit. A similarity of views of the governments of the USSR and Pakistan was reflected in their demand as regards the implementation of the 22 November 1967 resolution of the Security Council on West Asia in their desire "to establish a fair and lasting peace" in that region. The two sides also demanded the withdrawal of all foreign troops from Indo-China in order to ensure peace and security in the area, and the implementation of the inalienable rights of the peoples of Indo-China so that they could independently decide their destiny in accordance with their national interests and without any outside interference. Both sides agreed that the United Nations was "an important instrument of peace and security."

The main achievement of Bhutto's visit was in the field of bilateral relations. It was agreed that USSR-Pak trade and economic, scientific, technical and other relations, which had been disrupted as a result of the events in the area in 1971, should be restored. The term of the USSR-Pak agreement on economic and technical co-operation was extended and the two sides agreed to hold talks to introduce appropriate changes therein. This signified that the USSR would resume its assistance to Pakistan in geological prospecting, in power engineering and in building a metallurgical works in Karachi. The two sides also agreed to explore avenues of expanding economic and technical cooperation in other fields as well. As regards trade, the two sides agreed to immediately resume trade transactions and conclude, as soon as possible, a new trade agreement till 1974 which envisaged a further expansion of trade between the two countries. In order to further strengthen relations, it was agreed to hold a regular exchange of opinions between the two governments on questions of mutual interest.[7] Thus, Bhutto's visit to Moscow, as Radio Pakistan put it, resulted in "breaking the ice" and injecting "some warmth in the frozen relationship."

While attaching "especially great importance" to what Brezhnev called "the progressive strengthening of our friendship with India and with the great Indian people," the Soviet Communist Party chief, at the same time, emphasized : "We are also for good relations with Pakistan; no conflicts and no contradictions in interests divide us from that country." The recent visit of President Bhutto to the USSR, he added, "showed that the necessary prerequisites for the development of good relations between our two countries exist." Brezhnev stated that the Soviet people were "consistent advocates" of the establishment of relations of lasting peace and good neighbourship among India, Pakistan and Bangladesh. They regarded it as "a substantial contribution to the normalization of the political climate throughout Asia."[8]

Accordingly, when Mrs. Indira Gandhi and Z.A. Bhutto reached an agreement at the Simla Summit meeting on 2 July 1972 with regard to the non-use of force, the withdrawal of armed forces from the areas under each other's occupation and the delineation of the line of control in Jammu and Kashmir, which was not to be altered by either side, it was promptly welcomed by the Kremlin. Even before the Summit, Commentator Arkad Moslennikov, writing in *Pravda* on 2 June 1972, observed that all sincere friends of India, Pakistan and Bangladesh hoped that statesmanlike wisdom would prevail at the talks. He expressed the hope that ways would be found for a peaceful settlement of the problems of the Hindustan peninsula, which would benefit not only the peoples of that region but all peace-loving mankind.

Writing in *Izvestia* on 5 July 1972, V. Nakaryakov characterized the Simla Agreement as "a major step towards peaceful cooperation" and "a real step forward on the way of ensuring peace and friendship between India and Pakistan." That important document of peace, he said, signified the beginning of an entirely new approach to relations between the two neighbouring countries. He expressed "great satisfaction" at the successful outcome of the Summit and described the Agreement as "a victory for the forces of peace and progress, a triumph of the policy of peaceful coexistence of states." The Soviet commentator then went on to quote Brezhnev's remarks at the 15th Congress of the Soviet Trade Unions. The Soviet Party Chief had stated that Moscow's relations with India had continued to improve throughout the years. At the same time, Brezhnev stressed : "We stand also for good relations with Pakistan, with which we have no conflicts and no controversies to strain our relations." After thus quoting Brezhnev, the Soviet writer observed : "Everyone who can evaluate things realistically cannot but welcome the outcome of the Simla negotiations." He concluded by saying : "The agreement signed may, nay it must, become the cornerstone of the foundation on which an edifice of peace and cooperation will be erected by the joint efforts of the peoples of the sub-continent."[9]

In the beginning of 1973, the Pakistani press carried

editorials and reports relating to large-size trawlers of the Soviet Navy, equipped with highly sophisticated electronic equipment used for coastal spying, as having been frequently spotted in the Arabian Sea, particularly near the coast of Pakistan. Thus, an editorial in the *Tameer* on 18 January 1973 stated that these huge fishing trawlers were not only "stealing fish from Pakistani waters" but were also being used to keep *liaison* with "some political fish as well." The paper referred to the notorious Soviet conspiratorial temperament and their intricate espionage system. It demanded that the Soviet trawlers be forbidden from interfering in Pakistani territorial waters in order to "safeguard national security and protect national fish resources." The *Peking Review* reproduced with satisfaction all such Pakistani reports, which exposed the "spying activities" of the Kremlin. The Chinese weekly also gave publicity to another Pakistani paper, the *Nawai Waqt*'s denunciation of Moscow's designs to the effect that the USSR extended "help to India in bisecting Pakistan" and attempted "to bring Pakistan under her influence."[10]

A month later, the Chinese news media carried further Pakistani press reports of the merciless plundering and draining of Pakistan's fish resources by Soviet trawlers. As a consequence of Soviet activities, the *Peking Review* observed, some 400 trawlers in the 1200-trawlers strong Pakistani fishing fleet were lying idle and between 6,000 and 6,500 fishermen were rendered jobless. About 50,000 family members and dependents of the unemployed fishermen were said to be facing starvation. Due to reduced fish hauls, a loss of about Rs. 150 million in foreign exchange in a year had also been incurred. Furthermore, the Chinese weekly quoted from the *Pakistan Times*' report of 23 February 1973 to the effect that Soviet intrusions had caused a sharp rise in fish prices in local markets.[11] All this signified that China did not wish good relations between the USSR and Pakistan to develop and strengthen. Peking also sought to exploit the situation when opportunities presented themselves for creating misgivings and difficulties in the relations of the two countries.

USSR-Pak relations received a temporary setback when

a large *catche* of Soviet-designed machine guns, suitable for
guerilla warfare, was unearthed in the Iraqi Embassy in
Pakistan on 10 February 1973. These arms were obviously
meant for Baluchi separatists who were active in Iran.
They might have been meant for use by the disaffected
elements on the Pakistani side of Baluchistan as well. The
Soviet Union's proposal about an Asian Collective Security
System also came to be criticized by Bhutto. The Pakistani
President raised the question : Asian security "against
whom ?"[12] Evidently, Bhutto—the champion of a "special
relationship" with Peking—did not wish to displease China.

Partly to assure Moscow as regards Islamabad's desire to
maintain good relations with all the great Powers but mainly
to secure Soviet help as regards the release of over 90,000
Pakistani POWs in India, Bhutto dispatched, in the beginning of February 1973, A.H. Pirzada as his Special Emissary
to the USSR. While in the Soviet Union, Pirzada spoke
highly of the USSR as "a great country...an Asian country
too and a neighbour of Pakistan." He referred with appreciation to Brezhnev's remark, on 21 December 1972, in his
report devoted to the 50th Anniversary of the Formation
of the USSR. In that report, the Soviet leader had stated :
"There are good prospects for the promotion of good relations
with Bangladesh, and Pakistan." Conveniently ignoring any
reference to Bangladesh, Pirzada emphasized the fact that
there existed the most extensive opportunities for developing
friendly relations between Pakistan and the Soviet Union.
He expressed gratitude for the latter's economic assistance,
particularly in prospecting mineral resources and for developing the national economy. He then emphasized "the
important role of the Soviet Union in normalizing the situation on the Hindustan sub-continent."[13]

It is significant to recall here that, before Pirzada was
sent to Mosow, a senior Soviet diplomat had reportedly
suggested that India should take the initiative in the further-
ance of the Simla Agreement. Pirzada signed a cultural
agreement with the Soviet Government, which provided for
the exchange of scientists, teachers, students, films, books
as well as radio and television programmes. He also held

talks on improving economic and trade ties, especially for securing the reactivation of earlier aid commitments with regard to geological prospecting and the construction of a power generation and a metallurgical plant in Karachi. However, he did not seem to have cut much ice with Soviet leaders with regard to the issue of Pakistani POWs. On the contrary, the Kremlin was said to have impressed upon him the need to take speedy cognizance of the realities, the necessity of strengthening peace and friendly relations in the sub-continent and of preventing regional differences from being exploited by outside forces.[14]

Even after extending diplomatic and other support to India in the 1971 Conflict, which had resulted in the break-up of Pakistan, Moscow sought to cultivate friendly relations with Islamabad. The Kremlin played host to President Bhutto and agreed to extend the economic and technical agreement with Pakistan. It ensured that unutilized credits (out of $464 million worth of credits, given by the USSR to Pakistan since 1961, only $168 million were said to have been utilized by Pakistan) would be disbursed to Islamabad. Here, it is pertinent to recall that, in December 1972, a Soviet delegation had arrived in Pakistan to discuss proposals for the re-scheduling of the repayment of Soviet credits totalling $80 million by Pakistan. The talks covered Soviet aid already in the pipeline and commitments of future assistance.[15]

In March 1973, it was reported that the Soviet Union and Czechoslovakia had signed agreements with Pakistan releasing Islamabad from the obligation to repay credits utilized in Bangladesh when it was East Pakistan. An official statement, issued from Rawalpindi on 10 March 1973, stated that the accord with Moscow would pave the way for progress on a number of Pakistani projects, including a steel mill in Karachi, a power station at Guddu and high-frequency transmission lines and the supply of radio transmitters. The statement further added that Czechoslovakia had agreed to postpone repayments due between May and June 1973 connected with projects in Pakistan.[16] On 27 April 1973, a three-year trade agreement was signed between Pakistan and the Soviet Union.

Pakistan, thus, seemed to be reactivating its so-called policy of "equi-distance" with all the three great Powers—the USA, the USSR and China. Soon after the separation of Bangladesh, Islamabad enthusiastically renewed its friendly relations with Washington, obviously for reasons of obtaining economic aid, which was required for the restoration of the economy, as also for its continued growth, and for reasons of obtaining "military assistance if only in the form of spare parts for the large proportion of American equipment in the Pakistani military."[17] Washington, on its part, promptly resumed its economic assistance to Pakistan. From July 1972 to April 1973, the United States and the Aid-Pakistan Consortium delivered more than $340 million to Islamabad in commodity-aid for the on-going Indus River projects and programme loans. Although Pakistan formally withdrew from the SEATO, it resumed its full participation, at Ministerial level, in the CENTO—an alliance system specifically directed against the USSR. In doing so, Islamabad took into account "the Indo-Soviet defence treaty," as an official of the Pakistan Foreign Office stated. Pakistan's sliding back into the embrace of either Washington or Peking or both was not in Soviet interests. Moscow, therefore, appeared keen to re-establish its presence in Islamabad. It could thereby hope to neutralize the harmful influence of and compete successfully with rival Powers.

Rapprochement between India and Pakistan and the establishment of stable conditions in the sub-continent were most desirable from the Soviet point of view. Accordingly Moscow tried to impress upon Pakistan that its future lay in cultivating normal relations with India and Bangladesh and not on the road that China and the United States preferred it to traverse. Commenting on the Chinese vote on the admission of Bangladesh, *Pravda* observed that it was also realized by realistic circles in Pakistan that Peking's attitude neither served the long-term interests of Pakistan nor facilitated normalization of the situation in the sub-continent. Moscow stressed the futility of Yahya's adventurist policy that pushed him into a military conflict with India, and which, ultimately, had ended in Pakistan's defeat.

A special commentary published by *Tass*, on the eve of

Pakistan's National Day in March 1973, stated that the
former Pakistani military rulers sought "to distract the
people's attention from domestic problems by inciting anti-
Indian psychosis and anti-Sovietism by militarisation and cooperation in anti-Soviet military blocs." It described Bhutto's
policy as "sober-minded" and spoke of the "fruitful results"
of the Simla Agreement. The Soviet commentary quoted
Bhutto as saying : "The sooner Bangladesh is recognised,
the better it will be for both countries." *Tass* then warned
against "the reactionary forces in the country, the right
wing parties and religious fanatics," who were doing all they
could to impede the recognition of Bangladesh. Discussing
President Bhutto's efforts to develop the national economy
and improve relations with the Soviet Union, the *Tass*
commentary observed :

> The people of Pakistan are faced with difficult prob-
> lems—economic development, democratic social reforms and
> solution of complicated nationalities problem. All these
> can be solved, provided the old and harmful course of
> enmity and militarisation is given up and a policy of friend-
> ship and cooperation with all countries, most of all with
> neighbouring countries—India and Bangladesh—is pursu-
> ed.[18]

Undoubtedly, there are certain elements within Pakistan
who speak of China and the USA as dependable friends
and seem to find fault with Moscow for consistently backing
India over the years. Some even go to the extent of blaming
the Kremlin for the break-up of Pakistan. However, there
are also other forces, which positively assessed the Soviet role
in the Indian sub-continent. Thus, the National Awami
Party leader, Khan Abdul Wali Khan, asserted that the Soviet
Union was not responsible for the separation of East Bengal.
He went on to remark :

> Till the last moment, Russia tried to save the integrity of
> Pakistan by insisting on a political solution [to the East
> Bengal problem]. President Podgorny wrote to Yahya Khan
> to seek a political solution. But this advice was not accept-
> ed. Before the fall of Dacca, Russia moved a resolution
> in the Security Council, appealing for an immediate end
> to the war and a political solution. Had this appeal been
> accepted, Pakistan would have stayed united today.[19]

The emergence of Bangladesh as a secular, democratic People's Republic, and its separation from the Islamic theocratic state of Pakistan, signified a severe blow to the "two-nation" theory on which Pakistan was said to have been founded. However, as a strong defender of the faith and a champion of the ideology on which Pakistan was said to be based, Bhutto did not think that the "two-nation" theory was rendered inapplicable in the wake of Pakistan's dismemberment. The independence of Bangladesh, so vociferously proclaimed by the authorities in Dacca, he said, could only be predicated upon "her distinctive Muslim character and separateness." Bangladesh, Bhutto observed, was "in fact the former Muslim Bengal." Dacca's claim of being a secular state, he said, in no way, altered that fact. He even went to the extent of asserting that "secularism, in the sense of tolerance and rejection of theocracy" was "inherent in Islamic political culture." He, thereby, endeavoured to salvage the ideology of Pakistan from the outmoded concept of theocracy.

Bhutto disagreed with the assertion that Pakistan "has lost her *raison d'etre* owing to the emergence of Bangladesh" on the ground of what he called "the verifiable historical fact" that Pakistan was originally intended to comprise only the northwest zone of the South Asian sub-continent. The word "Pakistan," he said, was coined with reference to areas which the state would include—"P" stood for Punjab, "A" for the Afghan frontier, "K" for Kashmir, "S" for Sind and "Tan" for Baluchistan. He remarked that, at that stage, Bengal was not included within Pakistan. Bhutto further stated that the "famous Lahore Resolution," adopted by the Muslim League on 23 March 1940, demanded the establishment of two independent states in the Muslim majority areas in the northwest and the north-east zones. Whether "the two Muslim communities decide to combine under a single sovereignty," as they did in 1946-47 and for a quarter century thereafter, or whether "they continue to live apart, as they do now," Bhutto observed, "the bases of their statehood" remained as it was established in 1947. He added : "Bangladesh owes her existence to Pakistan, if there had been no Pakistan, there would have been no Bangladesh."

Despite the death and destruction mercilessly unleashed on unarmed civilians in East Bengal by Pakistani military personnel in 1971, Bhutto appeared quite hopeful about the future course of relations between Pakistan and Bangladesh. He did not seem to give much credence to the hostile posture his country had adopted towards the sovereign People's Republic of Bangladesh, *e.g.* non-recognition, refusal to repatriate stranded Bangladesh nationals in Pakistan and the inclusion in the constitution of Pakistan of a provision providing for re-absorption of the former East Pakistan into Pakistani territory. Evidently, Bhutto believed that estrangement between Pakistan and Bangladesh would not last long and that, in course of time, it would even be possible for them to take a joint or similar stand against India. He did not seem to have abandoned his policy of confrontation with India and the concept of maintaining a "just balance" in the sub-continent for all time to come. His remarks about "factors that unite us in mutual sympathy" with "our brethren in Bangladesh," the sharing of "a common historical aspiration and culture," the struggle waged "together to achieve independence from both Western imperialism and Hindu domination," are highly significant in that regard.

The maintenance of a "just balance" in the Indian sub-continent was stated to be in the interests of the global Powers as also those of the neighbouring countries. It was asserted that Pakistan would "never accept the concept of Indian hegemony in the sub-continent." The attempt of any state of the sub-continent to dominate the area, Bhutto observed, would only result in instability. He was obviously trying to impress upon Dacca as well as the global Powers—the USA, China and even the USSR—the necessity of following "a balanced policy in relation to the states in the sub-continent." Bhutto assured that his country would try to preserve "friendly and balanced relations with all world Powers" in so far as it was "compatible with our self-respect and dignity." In this connection, Bhutto did not forget to mention the military assistance Moscow had rendered to India since 1965, which was said to have been "dramatically augmented" in 1971. That had resulted in an "unprecedented disparity between India's and Pakistan's military strength." Bhutto then referred to the Kremlin's role during the Bangladesh Crisis and the Indo-Pakistan War of 1971. Whatever might have been the Soviet motives in entering into the Treaty of Friendship with India, that "pact," Bhutto stated, "certainly gave India the backing, both military and psychological, to embark upon her armed aggression." He also pointed to the strong diplomatic support Moscow had rendered to India in the Security Council, thereby holding Moscow responsible for the dismemberment of Pakistan. Bhutto, however, soon realized the futility of indulging in mud-slinging with regard to past events. He did not wish to completely write off Moscow from his scheme of furthering Pakistani interests. He, therefore, hastened to dwell on the "marked improvement, evidenced recently," in his country's relations with the Soviet Union, especially after his visit to Moscow in March 1972. Bhutto also expressed his earnest hope that "the estrangement" between the USSR and China would not impede the development of that process.[20]

The term "Muslim nationalism," as applied to Pakistan, was, indeed, quite misleading in view of the religious universalism and the existence of a large number of Muslim States in various parts of the world. Pakistan's "unidimensional nationalism based on religion alone", with its disregard of the "factors of geography and local tradition,"[21] was, perhaps, the only thing of its kind. It might have been considered useful in extending Pakistani influence over the adjoining areas inhabited by Muslims. The bond of religion alone, however, was found wanting in preserving the unity of the two wings of Pakistan. The emergence of Bangladesh amply proved that a sense of free and equal participation in the political and economic life of the country is an important factor in keeping two peoples of a nation united. According to Saleem M.M. Qureshi, a Pakistani writer, the separation of erstwhile East Pakistan *"appeared"* to have dealt "a mortal blow to the very concept of Muslim nationalism." "East Bengal," he adds, *"seems* to have rejected the idea of religion as the basis of nationality by adopting secularism as its official creed." The use of the words "appeared" and "seems" indicates that, in the opinion of Qureshi, the "Islamic basis" of truncated Pakistan had not been undermined and that Islamabad's capacity to join hands with West Asian Muslim States remained.

In so far as the "new Pakistan is more homogeneous—geographically, economically, linguistically and culturally...," it appears to have emerged as a stronger rather than a weaker state. Saleem Qureshi is not quite sure of the rejection of "Muslim nationalism" in Bangladesh either. He observes :

> Inspite of the apparent rejection of Muslim nationalism by East Pakistan, today's Bangladesh is in reality one of its two successors. The war against West Pakistan perforce made the East Bengali nationalism local as well as antipodal to the ideological Pakistani nationalism and it compelled Bengali Muslims to repudiate Muslim nationalism. The Indian support for their cause further made them play up their cultural rather than their religious identity. However, it remains to be seen whether this alienation from Muslim nationalism is permanent.... It may well be possible that once again Bengali Muslims will decide to claim their Muslim legacy. Bangladesh nationalism may eventually lay as good a claim to be the successor to Muslim nationalism as the nationalism of truncated Pakistan. After all, Bangladesh now is the next largest Muslim nation to Indonesia and the very fact that it exists as a political entity separate from the culturally similar West Bengal is evidence enough of the survival of one form of Muslim nationalism.[22]

The leader of the National Awamy Party NAP(M), Professor Muzaffar Ahmed, in an interview with an Indian journalist in May 1973, stated that the notion of a "Muslim nation" or Islamic nationalism was absurd, "false and hypothetical," and even contradictory to the concept of Bangladesh nationalism. Nevertheless, it was still regarded "a living and active force continuing to have its impact on the minds of many of our people."[23] Maulana Bhashani, the leader of the NAP(B), does not seem to like the phrase "Muslim Bengal," yet he considers himself to be a religious person, does not exclude his religion from his socialism and takes pride in his concept of Islamic socialism.[24] The Dictionary of National Biography, published by the Indian Institute of Historical Studies in May 1974, states that after his victory, *viz.* the creation of Pakistan, Jinnah had virtually disowned the "two-nation" theory by declaring that Pakistan would be a secular and not a Muslim State. It is further stated that he never genuinely believed in that theory. He adopted it only as a fighting technique to achieve his political objective.[25] Likewise, it can be said that it is not without some purpose that Bhutto is seen laying considerable emphasis on his "Muslim Bangla" theme. Addressing the UN General Assembly on 20 September 1973, he observed :

> The separation of two parts of Pakistan has by no means weakened, far less invalidated, the basic premises of Pakistan's ideology....Whether the two Muslim communities decide to combine under a single sovereignty, as they did in 1946-1947 and for 25 years thereafter, or whether they constitute two separate sovereignties as they do now, the basis of their statehood remains as it was established in 1947. Although this separation is a reality, it does not undermine our sense of identity nor does it so alter the situation in South Asia as to justify a lack of equilibrium or the establishment of a dominance in state relationships within the sub-continent.[26]

From the above remarks, it appears quite obvious that Islamabad would seek to enlist Dacca's support for reactivating its policy of acting as a counterpoise to India and endeavour to neutralize India's power and influence in the sub-continent. Pakistan seems quite hopeful of playing the game of power politics in the 1970s and 1980s, similar to the one it had played in the 1950s and the 1960s, in conjunction with Dacca and/or with the help of such friendly Powers as may lend a helping hand to it. The circumstances in which the diplomatic recognition of Bangladesh by Pakistan had taken place had given some credence to Bhutto's protestations of fraternal feelings for "Muslim Bengal." The mediation of Arab emissaries on the eve of the Islamic Summit in Pakistan made Bhutto's task with regard to the recognition of breakaway Bangladesh easy (blunting the Rightist opposition to that action) and enabled Mujibur Rahman to make a concession about the release of the 195 POWs, indicted for war crimes. It also brought Bangladesh within the fold of Islamic summitry. As Bangladesh and Pakistan have begun to deal directly with each other, it should not be difficult to settle the outstanding political problems left over by the 1971 War. It is expected that the financial issues relating to the sharing of the assets and liabilities of the united Pakistan will also be sorted out in due course of time and diplomatic relations established.

Whether Pakistan would seek to exploit the Muslim sentiment in Bangladesh to create trouble for India or endeavour to normalize its relations with New Delhi in the interests of peace remains to be seen. Admittedly, the leaders of India, Pakistan and Bangladesh are and must be regarded as primarily responsible for the maintenance of conditions of peace and stability in the sub-continent. A great deal would, however, also depend on outside Powers. For instance, the policy of military pacts with and arms assistance to Pakistan, pursued by Washington in the 1950s had three significant effects within Pakistan, viz. to strengthen the armed services within its political system; to strengthen the central government against other centres of authority in the society; and to strengthen Pakistan against India.[27] The direct results of each one of these were in that order : the military coup of 1958 which brought Ayub at the helm of affairs; the feeling of discontent and exploitation in other provinces, leading to the separation of East Bengal; and the desire of the military rulers of Pakistan to settle problems with India by resorting to force, as was the case in 1965 and again in 1971.

Thus, the induction of a foreign powerful nation, viz., the USA, in the affairs of the Indian sub-continent was not only responsible for cataclysmic changes in the area but also compelled other major Powers, especially the USSR and China, to refashion and readjust their policies towards the countries of the region.

Similarly, Chinese hostility towards India produced significant changes in the attitudes of the nations of the sub-continent. It also compelled other great Powers to reorder their priorities and modify their policies. Pakistan's special relationship with China is directly related to that phenomenon as also the parallelism in the policies of the two super Powers towards the problems of the Indian sub-continent in the 1960s. Ayub's venture in taking up arms against India in 1965 was as much the result of the confidence generated by Washington's arms assistance as the product of Peking's

encouragement and incitement. If Yahya felt disinclined to
seek a political solution of the East Bengal problem in 1971
and pursued the reckless policy of bloody repression in the
eastern wing, it was again due to the mistaken belief that
his allies, the USA and China, would come to his rescue, when
the need arose, and that he would thereby be able to keep East
Bengal under subjugation.

Moscow is well aware of the anti-Soviet nature of Chinese
activities throughout the world, particularly on its periphery.
The Kremlin would, therefore, continue to cultivate relations
with Pakistan. Writing on the occasion of the 25 years of
USSR-Pak diplomatic relations, Professor Yuri Gankovsky,
Vice-President of the Soviet-Pakistani Cultural Relations
Society, traced the beginnings of the all-round, mutually beneficial and fruitful cultural, economic and political relations
between the two countries as far as 2,000 years back. He described Bhutto's visit to the USSR in March 1972 as "an
important and fruitful event in the history of Soviet-Pakistani
relations." He welcomed the positive changes that were
noticeable in Pakistan's foreign policy. Among these, he
cited : the signs of *detente* in relations with India ; the withdrawal from the SEATO ; the recognition of North Vietnam
and the establishment of diplomatic relations with East
Germany and North Korea. Professor Gankovsky then
went on to remark that the record of friendly relations
between the Soviet Union and Pakistan, in the last 25 years,
"provides convincing proof that they are not based on the
transient needs of the moment, but stem naturally from the
long-term, vitally important interests of the peoples of the
USSR and Pakistan."[28]

The Kremlin's attitude towards India and Pakistan had,
in the past, been based and would, in the future, continue
to be based on its evaluation of the objective conditions
existing, at a given time, in the countries of the Indian sub-
continent, and the requirements of its national interests and
regional and global needs. In the changing international
enviornment, Moscow's postures towards both India and
Pakistan had also undergone changes with the changing needs
and circumstances of the times. In the 1950s, Soviet policy

towards Pakistan was, to a great extent, in the nature of a reaction to American strategy in Asia. In the 1960s, it was primarily conditioned by its competition with China. With Sino-US rapprochement coming into existence, Soviet policy towards the Indian sub-continent is likely to be primarily influenced by considerations of neutralizing the joint thrust of China and the USA in South Asia.

In order to counter the unfavourable effects of Sino-US rapprochement and to meet the Chinese challenge in Asia, Moscow is likely to assign a higher priority to India. Because of her size, population and superior military strength, including nuclear capacity as demonstrated by her recent peaceful nuclear explosion, India could prove very useful to the Kremlin. The USSR might even consider India "as the first line of defence of the Russian Central Asian frontiers in a future military confrontation with China."[29] But, Moscow cannot possibly afford to ignore the existence of Pakistan in close proximity to its borders. Moreover, reasons of countering Chinese influence and considerations of keeping India within a system of checks and balances (with a view to keep New Delhi amenable to Soviet influence) compel the USSR to maintain a foothold and a political presence in Islamabad.

The Soviet Union could effectively tarnish China's image as a champion of national liberation wars in the wake of the Bangladesh Crisis. Moscow's stock also rose higher in the sub-continent, particularly in India and Bangladesh. Its relations with Pakistan, however, suffered a temporary set-back. In order to repair the damage caused by the 1971 War, Moscow has endeavoured to renew its economic and political contacts with Islamabad and to resume its assistance for various projects in Pakistan. Although USSR-Pak relations in the immediate post-1971 period had not reached the level of cordiality, which they had attained in the aftermath of the Tashkent Declaration, there can hardly be any doubt that the USSR would endeavour to exert itself in order to further improve its relations with Islamabad. Pakistan continues to be important, very important, for obvious geo-strategic and political reasons. Pakistan's strategic location in close proximity to Soviet borders makes it incumbent upon Moscow to keep it immune from hostile influence, that of China in particular. A friendly Pakistan can serve many a useful purpose for the USSR. Hostile Chinese and American influences can thereby be kept in check. It can also enable Moscow to keep India on her toes—constantly looking to the Kremlin and not take the USSR or its support for granted. Thus, Moscow can have a better bargaining position vis-a-vis both India and Pakistan provided it plays its cards well. Besides, the USSR can thereby hope to realize its schemes of an overland route through Afghanistan to the Indian Ocean, regional economic cooperation and Asian Collective Security, if it cultivates friendly relations with Pakistan. Cordial relations with Islamabad could also help the Kremlin in extending its connections with West Asian Muslim States, with which Pakistan has quite close relations.

The preservation of the status quo in the Indian sub-continent would enable Moscow to maintain its dominating position of influence—a position which it has labouriously built over the years. Therefore, the Soviet Union is very likely to be interested in the establishment of a stable regime in Pakistan —a regime which would be inclined to normalize its relations with the other States of the sub-continent and thereby help in creating stable and peaceful conditions in the region. The pursuit of an adventurist policy on the part of Islamabad in Kashmir or any attempt by Indian leaders to recover the Pakistani-occupied Kashmir is bound to disturb the status quo, create tension and instability and inevitably involve outside Powers. The USSR is expected to view with disfavour all such destabilizing situations or tendencies. Any upheaval in the sub-continent is also likely to adversely affect and put strains in the growing US-USSR detente. Moreover, conflict or the heightening of tension in the Indian sub-continent is likely to afford Peking an opportunity to fish in troubled waters. China's interference cannot but be detrimental to the Soviet Union's interests. In the years ahead, China and the Soviet Union are expected to be the main competitors for influence in South Asia. For the USA, sub-continental affairs may be of peripheral interest and the sub-continent an area of low priority. For the two Communist Powers, on the contrary, the region is of vital concern to their national interests.

How exactly the USSR's relations with Pakistan will develop in the future is, indeed, quite difficult to forecast, for other Powers are not likely to remain idle. Much would depend on the emerging power pattern in a changing world—the state of relations among the great Powers (Sino-Soviet relations, US-USSR and Sino-US relations), the internal conditions within Pakistan and its relationship with India, as also India's posture in the world, especially New Delhi's relations with the USA, the USSR and China.

8

USSR and Bangladesh

THE sympathetic attitude adopted by Moscow towards Bangladesh during and after its freedom struggle created favourable conditions for the development of friendly relations between the two countries. The support rendered by the Soviet Union proved very helpful for the cause of the liberation of the people of Bangladesh. The vetoing of all undesirable resolutions in the Security Council ensured the successful conclusion of the freedom struggle, thereby ushering in the sovereign People's Republic of Bangladesh. Moscow followed this up by diplomatic recognition, in the face of Pakistani threats of snapping USSR-Pak relations, and extended much-needed economic assistance for the reconstruction of the war-ravaged economy of the newly-born Republic.

Unlike Washington and Peking, Moscow had expressed, as early as 2 April 1971, its concern about the "repression" and "persecution" of the people of East Bengal. It had taken serious note of the tragedy of 10 million refugees and demanded a political solution of outstanding problems on the basis of "the wishes, the inalienable rights and lawful interests of the people of East Bengal."[1] It did not hesitate to condemn "the sanguinary suppression by the Pakistani authorities of the basic rights and the clearly expressed will of the population of East Pakistan, ruthless terror against millions of people of that part of the country" and the overt violation of the Universal Declaration of Human Rights.

In his statements in the Security Council in December 1971, the representative of the Soviet Union asserted that the military conflict in the Hindustan Peninsula was "the direct-consequence of a series of acts of oppression, mass repression and violence" committed for months with a view to suppress "the clearly expressed will of 75 million East Pakistanis." "The people of East Pakistan," he said, were obliged "to respond to this and rebuff it by means of armed resistance." The question of a cease-fire and that of recognition by Pakistan of the expressed will of the East Pakistan population, he observed, were organically and inseparably bound together—the political settlement being indissolubly linked with a cease-fire.[2]

A little later, the Soviet delegate did not hesitate to declare that "only the people of East Pakistan in the persons of their elected representatives can decide their future fate with regard to whether they will remain part of Pakistan or form a separate independent State" as well as "the question of resumption of talks or contacts of any kind on relations with the Pakistan Government."[3] On 15 December 1971, the Soviet representative stated that India could agree to a cease-fire and withdraw her troops only if an assurance was given that the Pakistan Government would also withdraw its troops from East Pakistan and that "a political settlement is achieved there by peaceful means by the lawful representatives of the East Pakistan population." For that purpose, he added, it was essential to transfer power to those elected by the people, "the representatives of the party that won a majority at the December 1970 elections." The Pakistan military authorities, he further stated, were incapable of ensuring normal conditions for the safe return of "all East Pakistan refugees from India" and that such conditions could be brought about "only by new authorities consisting of and appointed by the legitimate representatives of the East Pakistan people and elected by that people."

A cease-fire, the Soviet representative observed, must be accompanied by the transfer of power to the representatives of the majority Party in East Pakistan, who were elected in December 1970.[4] He submitted a resolution on 16 December 1971, which welcomed the cessation of hostilities in East

Pakistan and expressed hope that the state of cease-fire would be observed by both sides, which would guarantee, without delay, unimpeded transfer of power to the lawful representatives of the people elected in December 1970.[5] The strong support extended by the USSR both in and outside the UN for the cause of Bangladesh's liberation naturally evoked feelings of admiration among the people of Bangladesh for the Soviet Union.

A Pakistani writer has alleged that, with a view to establish its foothold in Dacca, Moscow not only extended full diplomatic support to the Bangladesh liberation movement but also exerted its influence for inducting the pro-Soviet East Bengal communists in the broad-based Consultative Committee. (That Committee had been formed to direct the Liberation Front.) Moscow, he says, also pleaded for the inclusion, in the delegation of Bangladesh to the UN, of the Communist leader, Professor Muzaffar Ahmed, and for the exclusion of the pro-West Khondkar Mushtaque Ahmed, who was later removed from the post of Foreign Minister of Bangladesh, presumably at the behest of the Kremlin.[6] How far these allegations are true, is, indeed, difficult to say. It is no doubt true that on 3 June 1971, the pro-Moscow Indian newspaper, the *Patriot*, had claimed that the Awami League could not provide "seasoned leaders" capable of organizing a guerilla war. The Awami League, it added, could only succeed if it cooperated with the left-wing parties. While the Bangladesh freedom struggle was on, the Indian Communist Party (CPI) paper, the *New Age*, in its issue of 10 October 1971, carried the 18-point programme issued by the Communist Party of Bangladesh for a National Liberation Front.

After Bangladesh emerged as an independent and sovereign nation, the Communist Party (which was founded in 1948 but had been banned in Pakistan since 1954) came to be revived on 31 December 1971 wlth the reopening of its headquarters in Dacca. During the freedom struggle, the East Pakistan wing of the Party was renamed as the Communist Party of East Bengal. It later became the Communist Party of Bangladesh (CPBD). That the CPBD enjoyed the blessings of the USSR and was aligned with Moscow was beyond doubt. The pro-

Soviet CPI weekly organ, the *New Age*, in an article on 2 January 1972, proposed a national government for Bangladesh. It conceded that such a proposition would be unacceptable to the ruling Awami League. Nevertheless, it urged unity amongst "patriotic forces" at all levels and desired that the Consultative Committee be made more effective. On 20 January 1972, a Moscow Radio commentary stated that although the CPBD was "not large," its contribution to the liberation struggle had been "not at all insignificant." Its active co-operation with the Awami League Government was said to be essential for the reconstruction of the country. The Soviet commentary recalled that it was at the behest of the Communists that the Awami League government-in-exile had set up an All-Party Cabinet Consultative Committee. The commentary then emphasized the importance of united action by "various parties and partriotic forces."

A delegation of the CPBD, led by Abdus Salam, visited Moscow in July-August 1972. The CPBD participated in the Bangladesh elections held on 7 March 1973. However, failure to obtain any seats in the elections by pro-Soviet groups and the landslide victory of the Awami League signified that Moscow could not hope to exercise any leverage in the local politics of Bangladesh. The Soviet Union could not have been happy with the formation of the CPBD (Leninist). The leaders of that Party had criticized China's role in the liberation struggle of Bangladesh. But they had, at the same time, expressed their oneness with the anti-revisionist policy of Peking in the international Communist movement. The emergence of the CPBD (L) led to a further split among the Communists in the new State. Already there was the CPBD (Marxist) and the pro-Soviet CPBD.

The first relief supplies from the USSR to Bangladesh were flown to Dacca on 20 January 1972. On 25 January 1972, the Soviet Union recognized Bangladesh and, soon after, diplomatic relations came to be established. The letter of recognition was sent as a message from Nikolai Podgorny, President of the Presidium of the Supreme Soviet of the USSR and Alexei Kosygin, Chairman of the Council of Ministers, to President Abu Sayeed Choudhury and Prime Minister Mujibur Rahman of Bangladesh. It conveyed "friendly wishes of peace, well-being and successes in consolidating the state sovereignty" of Bangladesh and "in building a peaceful democratic republic." The message also expressed the hope that the two countries would "successfully develop fruitful friendly relations" which, it was confidently stated, met "the vital interests of the peoples of our two countries, the cause of strengthening universal peace."[7]

On 7 February 1972, a barter trade agreement providing for an exchange of goods—Russian materials and equipment against traditional exports from Bangladesh—worth Rs. 20 crores both ways was signed. On the same day, the Soviet airline, Aeroflot, inaugurated a weekly Moscow-Dacca service—the first scheduled international route through Bangladesh. Two days later, *Pravda* announced that Sheikh Mujib had been invited to visit the USSR at the beginning of March. On 25 February 1972, a four-member Russian economic delegation assured the Foreign Minister of Bangladesh as regards the resumption and speedy completion of the Russian projects located in the territory of Bangladesh. Among these projects were the Ghorasal power project and the installation of two powerful radio transmission lines. On 2 March 1972, Moscow agreed to unlock the flow of aid amounting to 38 million roubles (Rs. 3.80 crores) previously negotiated with Pakistan for those projects.[8] A sum of 5 million roubles was also earmarked as commodity assistance.

The Prime Minister of Bangladesh, Sheikh Mujibur Rahman, paid an official visit to the Soviet Union from 1 to 5 March 1972. In the joint declaration issued at the end of the visit, Sheikh Mujib expressed his gratitude for the "active and consistent support" given during the freedom struggle and "for the assistance rendered by the Soviet Union." He also apprised Soviet leaders of his Government's programmes for economic recovery, the consolidation of public order and improvement of the living standards of the people. The two sides noted with satisfaction that the first steps in the development of cooperation between the two countries—the signing of the trade agreement, the establishment of sea and air communications between them and the initiation of contacts between trade unions, youth and other social organizations—testified to the existence of vast opportunities for all-round cooperation and the consolidation of friendship between the peoples of the two countries. Further development of "friendly relations and fruitful cooperation" in the political, economic, scientific, technical and other fields was deemed to be in the interests of the peoples of the two countries and in "the interests of the common struggle against imperialism and neo-colonialism."

It was reiterated that the two countries should strive to expand trade and develop ties and contacts in the fields of science, art, literature, education, public health, press, radio, sports and in other fields. In order to gain "a deeper mutual acquaintance with the life, culture and achievements" of the peoples of the two states, it was stated, in the joint declaration, that the USSR and Bangladesh would promote cooperation and direct links between governmental bodies and social organizations, including trade unions, youth and women's organizations, as well as enterprises and cultural and scientific institutions. It was further agreed that the experts of the two countries would meet in the near future to work out specific proposals for further development of cooperation in the economic, cultural and other fields.

The two sides also signed an agreement with regard to Soviet assistance in the construction of a thermal power station, a radio broadcasting station, an electrical equipment plant, as well as in geological prospecting for oil and gas. Moscow further agreed to assist Dacca in the reconstruction of the latter's merchant marine and of railway transport and in the development of marine fisheries. It was also stated in the joint declaration that the USSR would help in the training of national cadres for various branches of the industry and agriculture of Bangladesh. Moscow also agreed to provide consultative services for the rehabilitation of industry and helicopters for improvement of air communications within the interior areas of the country. The two sides agreed to expand trade and to hold "regular political consultations" between the two governments "at various levels on all important matters involving the interests of both the states."

The emergence of the new independent state of Bangladesh

was considered "an outcome of the triumphant national liberation struggle of the people of Bangladesh." That struggle, the
joint declaration stated, had clearly revealed the attitude of
different states to the just cause of the people of Bangladesh.
It had also shown who were the foes of the People's Republic
of Bangladesh.

As for the situation in the sub-continent, it was stated in
the Kosygin-Mujib joint declaration that the governments of
all countries of the region should direct their efforts towards an
early normalization of relations. The two sides observed that
a genuine political settlement in the subcontinent could only
be achieved through negotiations between the states directly
concerned, "without outside interference and having regard to
the actual situation, on the basis of the legitimate rights and
interests of its peoples."

On other international issues, the two sides declared that the
seven-point proposal of the Provisional Revolutionary Government of South Vietnam constituted "a realistic and constructive basis for a peaceful political settlement of the Vietnam
problem." The full implementation of the resolution of 22
November 1967 was likewise considered the basis for achieving
"a stable and just peace" in West Asia. The Bangladesh
Government highly appreciated the efforts of the Soviet Union
and other socialist countries aimed at convening an All-Euro-
pean Conference on Security and Cooperation in Europe. It
also extended its support to the decision to convene a world
disarmament conference. (A resolution in that regard had been
adopted by the UN Assembly on the initiative of the USSR.)
Finally, the leaders of the two countries extended their full
support to the activities of various friendship societies established in their countries. It was further stated that they attached
great importance to the development of personal contacts at all
levels between the Soviet Union and Bangladesh. The two
sides declared their mutual intention to increase exchanges of
visits by statesmen and representatives of social, scientific, cultural and other organizations of the two countries.[9]

Addressing a news conference on his return to Dacca on 7
March 1972, the Foreign Minister of Bangladesh, Abdus
Samad Azad, observed : "We are not aligned to any super

Power, but we have only accepted the hand of friendship and help offered by the USSR for rebuilding our economy from the ashes of war." He added that Moscow had committed large-scale assistance to Dacca which would go a long way in facilitating a speady recovery of his country's economy. He discounted reports about Soviet military assistance to Bangladesh.

Economic cooperation between the Soviet Union and Bangladesh developed rapidly after Mujib's visit. On 21 March 1972, a Soviet salvage delegation arrived in Dacca, and on the next day, it signed an agreement providing for free Soviet assistance in restoring normal conditions for navigation in the seaports of Bangladesh. On 2 April, *i.e.* within a few days of the signing of the salvage operation agreement, the first two of a flotilla of 20 Soviet ships arrived in Chittagong to clear the approaches and ports of Chalna and Chittagong of mines and sunken ships which impeded shipping traffic.[10] Within a short period "as a result of their ceaseless and skilled work," the Bangladesh Ambassador to the Soviet Union observed later on, blocked jetties were not only made safe for navigation, but were also made wider and deeper. The rehabilitation of the Chittagong port, he stated, was "of crucial importance" because it was making a significant contribution to the rehabilitation of the entire economy of Bangladesh.[11]

On 9 May 1972, a four-member Russian oil expert team arrived in Dacca. Its leader observed that drillings in Jaldi and Simutang in the Chittagong Hill tracts had been completed. He was hopeful that large deposits of natural gas would be discovered in the Simutang region.[12] According to a report in June 1972, Moscow had bought 50,000 tons of rice from Thailand through Singapore merchants for shipments to Bangladesh.[13] Exchange of visits between the two countries became a recurring phenomenon. A cultural agreement was concluded between the two countries in Dacca in December 1972. It laid the foundation for close cooperation between the two countries in the field of culture and education.

When the question of the admission of Bangladesh into the United Nations came to be discussed in the UN forums,

Moscow rendered strong support in the matter and even co-sponsored draft resolution S/10771 in the Security Council. That resolution had proposed that the Council should recommend to the General Assembly the admission of the People's Republic of Bangladesh as a member of the United Nations. In his statement on 24 August 1972, the representative of the USSR stated that Bangladesh "without any doubt entirely meets all the requirements, without exception, which the United Nations Charter in Article 4 lays down for membership of the United Nations." The Government of Bangladesh, he added, had solemnly proclaimed that it accepted the obligations contained in the Charter and undertook to fulfil them. Bangladesh, he emphasized, had been officially recognized by 86 members of the world community; it had already been accepted as a member of the world community and had become a member of a number of specialized agencies and was moreover a peace-loving State. Commenting on the Chinese draft resolution in the matter, he observed that it was in direct contradiction to Article 4 of the UN Charter—it arbitrarily expanded the Charter requirements and hence was anti-constitutional. It was an attempt to foster discriminatory practices in the matter. The Chinese draft, the Soviet delegate pointed out, undermined the fundamental provisions of the Charter and cast doubts on the principle of the universality of the Organization.[14]

After Bangladesh's application for membership of the UN came to be vetoed by the Chinese delegation, the Soviet representative, Malik, replied to the Chinese charges levelled against Moscow. He stressed that Peking's veto on the admission of Bangladesh was an act against the interests of the national liberation movements of the oppressed peoples in general and the national liberation movement of the people of East Bengal in particular. The Chinese veto, Malik stated, was contrary to the interests of the developing countries as a whole, and against the interests of the developing State of Bangladesh in particular. It deprived the people of Bangladesh of UN support and aimed at Dacca's isolation. It was an act contrary to the development of healthy tendencies and to the improvement of the atmosphere in the Indian sub-continent and in the continent of Asia as a whole. Malik accused Peking of "inciting distrust, enmity and hatred among the countries of that area" by pursuing a policy of favouritism in the Indo-Pakistan sub-continent. Moreover, the Chinese stand was characterized by the Soviet delegate as an act contrary to the principle of universality and detrimental to the interests of the UN itself. He considered it contrary to the UN Charter, as Peking was trying to impose anti-Charter provisions and conditions in respect of the admission of new members to the world organization. Malik stated that while the Chinese propagated the theory of struggle against the super Powers "for their political demagogic purposes" they were actually behaving as a super-super-Power in the UN by using the veto against Dacca's entry. These "clumsy manoeuvres and crude anti-Soviet tactics," he added, could not mislead people as regards Peking's real designs and motives.[15]

The Security Council was unable to take any decision because of the Chinese veto. The question of the admission of Bangladesh, therefore, came to be considered in the General Assembly. Two resolutions were submitted. The one sponsored by Yugoslavia and 22 others expressed the desire that Bangladesh be admitted to the UN at an early date. The other 16-Power draft expressed the desire that the parties concerned should make all possible efforts to reach a fair settlement of pending issues. It called for the repatriation of POWs in accordance with the Geneva Conventions of 1949 and the relevant provisions of Security Council resolution 307 (1971). After consultations, both resolutions were simultaneously adopted without debate and without a vote. Summing up the consensus, the President of the General Assembly stated that the admission of Bangladesh to the UN should be viewed along with the over-all solution of the existing political, legal and humanitarian problems. It was essential, he said, to view the "simultaneous adoption of two resolutions as constituting an inter-dependence between these two viewpoints." He also welcomed the Simla Agreement. The second resolution, mooted by Pakistan's supporters, was meant to create the impression that the question of Dacca's admission could not be resolved until other problems, particularly that of the POWs, were settled.

In his statement, the Soviet representative laid much emphasis on the 23-Power resolution, the adoption of which, he said, would definitely expedite the admission of Bangladesh to the UN. The early and unconditional admission of Bangladesh, he stated, would correspond with the interests and the task of the further normalization of the situation on the Indian sub-continent. It would, he said, contribute to the subsequent successful solution of all pending problems, thereby meaning that Dacca's entry in the UN was a condition precedent for progress on other issues. The Soviet representative demanded the cessation of confrontation and considered the Simla Agreement between India and Pakistan "a positive and significant step in the normalization of the situation." Commenting on the second draft resolution, he observed that he interpreted it as an expression of the wish that in the South Asian sub-continent *all the parties* concerned would make efforts, in a spirit of collaboration and respect for each other's sovereignty, to settle *all* the problems pending between them. However, that was an issue other than "the immediate one of the admission" of Bangladesh—the item on the agenda. By that he clearly meant that while Dacca's entry in the UN could brook no delay, the settlement of the other issue could wait. He firmly objected to the imposition of any further requirements or conditions in the further consideration of Dacca's admission to the UN. Such an approach, he remarked, would be discriminatory. It would place Bangladesh on an unequal footing with other States and would be a violation of the UN Charter, Article 4 in particular. He decried any attempt that would create a harmful precedent for the UN and its prestige. By obstructing Dacca's admission in the UN, the Soviet representative added, the Chinese were hampering the establishment of stability in the sub-continent, perpetuating tension and conflict and serving "the interests of the imperialists."[16]

The strong support rendered by the Soviet Union for the admission of Bangladesh in the UN further strengthened the strong bonds of friendship already existing between the two countries. An agreement on the exchange of radio and television programmes was signed in Dacca on 22 November 1972. The agreement, which was to remain in force for two years and could be automatically extended by another two years, provided for the exchange of news materials, music recordings and television films, and other material of interest to radio and television on the political, economic and cultural life of the two countries. In December 1972, a cultural pact providing for the mutual exchange of personnel and knowhow was signed in Dacca. Syed Nazrul Islam, Minister for Industries, went to Moscow to participate in the 50th anniversary of the founding of the USSR on an invitation from the Soviet Government.

In assessing the situation in Bangladesh before its first elections in March 1973, the Soviet Commentator, Yuri Logovskoy, made a positive evaluation of the Awami League Government's work. He particularly appreciated the nationalization of the jute and other leading industries, banks, insurance companies and export trade; the adoption of an agrarian reform law; adherence to a non-aligned foreign policy; and the establishment of diplomatic relations with North Vietnam. He emphasized the role of democratic and progressive forces, especially that of the National Awami Party led by Muzaffar Ahmed (NAP-M) and the pro-Soviet Communist Party (CPBD). At the same time, he did not forget to mention the harm that was being done to the country by rightist forces, supported by the American intelligence agency, and the "ultra-left, Maoist-type opportunist elements objectively in league with the Right." During the armed struggle for independence, he said, these ultra-left Maoist-type elements either preferred to sit out the storm in safety or went to the extent of approving the supply of Chinese weapons to Islamabad, which were being used against patriots. He observed : "Now they have launched a noisy campaign to draw attention to themselves. How irresponsible this campaign is may be judged by the fact that its organizers claim that independence has given nothing to the people." He then asked : "Could this be qualified as anything but mockery of the memory of those who gave their lives for freedom ?"

The ultra-left, the Soviet writer observed, "is speculating on shortages of food, the high cost of living and other objective difficulties encountered by the young republic, and conducting a vicious smear campaign against the countries that supported the Bangladesh people in their just struggle." As regards foreign policy, most of the ultra-left groups, he stated, "steer a pro-

Maoist course." Their home policy platform was nebulous and they had "no realistic positive proposals to offer which might win popular support." On the contrary, the Soviet author pointed out, many leaders and rank-and-file members of the NAP(M) took an active part in the fight for an independent Bangladesh. That Party, he said, endorsed the nationalization programme of the government, gave "a high appraisal" of the support given by the Soviet Union to the Bangladesh liberation struggle and underscored the importance of Soviet-Bangladesh cooperation in the restoration of the latter's economy.

As for the pro-Soviet Communist Party (CPBD), the Soviet commentator stated that, from the outset, it had waged a consistent struggle "in defence of the national and class interests of the working people." The demands it advanced for an end to large-scale land tenure, nationalization of foreign capital, guarantees of the right to work, and an independent foreign policy, he said, won it prestige among the working people. In 1971, he stated, the Communists took part in organizing armed resistance and fought in the ranks of guerilla detachments. During that period, its membership "grew notably, and so did its influence." It had also entered the Consultative Committee of the Political Parties. Canvassing for the support of the Communist Party in the coming elections in Bangladesh, the Soviet author observed :

> It [Communist Party] supports the democratic measures taken by the Government to strengthen the country's economic independence and improve the people's living conditions and also its peaceable foreign policy. The Communists are contesting the elections under the watchword of unity of all national patriotic forces in support of broad socio-economic reforms in the interests of the masses.[17]

It was, thus, quite evident that in the Bangladesh elections, Soviet sympathies were all along with the NAP(M) and with the Moni Singh-led CPBD in particular. Muzaffar Ahmed's NAP could very well have secured a good number of seats, had it not been for its ill-advised pronouncements and agitation against Sheikh Mujibur Rahman—the most popular leader and Father of the Nation—all of which cost it dearly. The Communist Party had a very limited following in the country, and therefore, it put up only four candidates for the elections. They failed to obtain any seat. However, the Soviet Union sought comfort in the fact that the rightist parties and the ultra-left Maoist-type elements had also fared miserably in the elections. The ruling Awami League swept the polls and won a landslide victory.

When Sheikh Mujib reassumed the Prime Ministership of Bangladesh after the elections, he was warmly congratulated by Premier Kosygin. In a message, he described Mujib as "the real patriot of Bangladesh standing for strengthening national independence," for democracy, for peace and friendship among nations. Kosygin then expressed his confidence that relations of "lasting friendship and fruitful cooperation" between the Soviet Union and Bangladesh would be "further developed to the benefit of the peoples of our two countries in the interest of strengthening peace."[18] *Pravda* also hailed the landslide victory of the Awami League as a convincing mandate for the Government's progressive course for independence, non-alignment and neutrality, "for further advance of democratic and radical socio-economic reforms in the country, for normalization of the situation in South Asia, for durable peace in the area and throughout the world." It expressed satisfaction over the defeat of the so-called Inter-Party Action Committee, which had been formed during the elections and had raised anti-India and anti-Soviet slogans.[19]

Inaugurating the Asian Peace Conference in Dacca in May 1973, at which the Sheikh was presented the World Peace Council's highest award—the Juliot Curie Medal—the Bangladesh Prime Minister criticized the augmentation of Pakistan's armed strength by the big Powers. He blamed Islamabad for not recognizing the reality of Bangladesh and for not favourably responding to the Indo-Bangladesh Joint Declaration of 17 April 1973. That Declaration had offered a package deal providing for the repatriation of Pakistani POWs and civilian internees, with the exception of those required for trial in Dacca, the repatriation of the Bengalees detained in Pakistan and the return of those persons in Bangladesh who had declared their allegiance to Pakistan. It, thus, separated the humanitarian problems from the political issues. Although Mujib referred to his earlier suggestion that South and Southeast Asia be declared a zone of peace, he, as also the Bangladesh Foreign Minister, Kamal Hossain, avoided making any direct reference to the system of collective security in Asia. The question of an Asian Security System, it might be recalled, was broached at the Peace Conference in Dacca by Kamalov, the leader of the Soviet delegation, as well as by Romesh Chandra, Secretary-General of the World Peace Council. However, this lacunae was partly made up when Bangladesh's delegate to the Peace Conference, Sheikh Fazlul Huq Moni, an important member of the Awami League Organizing Committee, moved a declaration on Asian security which urged Asian countries to work together to evolve a policy of mutual cooperation and security and laid down certain guidelines for such a policy.[20]

Though relations between the Soviet Union and Bangladesh are expected to remain friendly, how long the present cordiality—born of the strong bonds forged during the liberation struggle and the critical period of the emergence of Bangladesh and the subsequent material and moral support rendered by the Kremlin—will last, is, indeed, difficult to say. Much would depend on the developments within Bangladesh and the changing international situation. Dacca, devoted as it is to a policy of secularism, socialism, democracy and non-alignment (like New Delhi) would very much like to continue its fruitful contacts and friendly intercourse with Moscow. At the same time, Bangladesh would like to diversify its political and economic relations so as to maintain rapport with other important centres of power in the world. That would enable Dacca to avoid excessive dependence on both the USSR and India. Bangladesh would thereby gain greater manoeuvrability in the world and would be able to obtain much-needed economic and technical assistance from all possible sources in order to build its economy.

It is not surprising that soon after the establishment of diplomatic relations between Washington and Dacca, the USA became the largest single aid-giver to Bangladesh, with a total aid of the order of $451.94 million between 16 December 1971 to 31 March 1974. According to a study of the US Agency for International Development, India with $339.9

million was the second and the USSR the fifth largest aid-giver with $134.83 million.[21]

As already noted in the previous Chapter, Pakistan has recognized Bangladesh and the problem of the POWs, including the 195 indicted for war crimes, as also that of the exchange of Pakistani and Bangladesh nationals, has been satisfactorily resolved. Direct contacts between the two countries have commenced and the establishment of diplomatic relations is not far off. With the normalization of Pakistan-Bangladesh relations, there seems no reason for China to remain indifferent or hostile to Dacca. As early as March 1972, Peking had offered a trade deal, which Dacca had spurned because of the absence of diplomatic recognition. After Pakistan and China are able to establish their diplomatic presence in Bangladesh, Bhutto is likely to exploit the Muslim sentiments of the people of Bangladesh, and Peking, on its part, would endeavour to use the leftist-Maoist extremist groups to subserve its own ends. Both Pakistan and China are likely to make individual as well as combined efforts to loosen the strong bonds of friendship existing between Bangladesh and India on the one hand, and the USSR, on the other. Moscow and New Delhi have, therefore, to remain vigilant in the matter.

As early as 10 January 1972, the *Novosti* Press Agency (APN) commentator, D. Volsky, in a commentary entitled "Instigators From Peking," interpreted Chou En-lai's remark that "the fall of Dacca...will lead to endless strife on the South Asian continent"—on the day military operations ceased, as instructions given to the relevant Chinese services about fanning the cinders of the dying-out conflict and stubbornly pouring oil on its smouldering coals. He accused Chinese leaders of not giving up their policy of sowing the seeds of distrust and kindling enmity. In that connection, he referred to the *Hsinhua* Agency's attempt to accuse India of "plundering East Bengal economically"—a wilful distortion of India's decision to purchase East Bengal's main export article, jute, which had for months been lying without use in warehouses. He added that the Chinese politicians, "who dream of foiling the normalisation of the situation in East Bengal and embroiling Bangladesh with India," had not given up their nefarious schemes.[22]

During the March 1973 elections in Bangladesh, the NAP (B) (the National Awami Party led by Maulana Bhashani) ceaselessly carried on an anti-India campaign through election leaflets and posters. It relentlessly criticized Sheikh Mujib's Government for its alleged subservience to New Delhi. India was vigorously blamed for the economic ills of Bangladesh. New Delhi was accused of reducing Bangladesh to a mere captive market and of promoting smuggling of essential goods and commodities. The party circulated a handbill listing ten charges against the Bangladesh Government. Of these, as many as nine, were, in fact, charges levelled against India. Allegations about Dacca entering into "secret pacts" with India, which were said to be detrimental to the sovereignty of Bangladesh, were also made. Other Parties in the forefront attacking India were the CPB(L), the pro-Chinese Communist Party (Leninist), BCP (Banglar Communist Party) and the affiliated Bangla Chattra Union. There seems little doubt that after the establishment of diplomatic relations between China and Bangladesh, Peking would seek to utilize these parties not only for fomenting trouble and discontent within the country, thereby making things difficult for Mujib, but also for undermining the friendly relations existing between India and Bangladesh and between the USSR and Bangladesh.

In the beginning of June 1973, Maulana Bhashani carried his anti-India tirades still further by launching a campaign for the boycott of Indian goods, with a bonfire of Indian goods and the picketing of shops selling them. He even threatened *jehad* (holy war) against India. He stated that Pakistan had looted crores of rupees from Bangladesh, but, after the latter had attained independence, it was India which had looted wealth from the country. He advocated "gherao" of Government offices and called upon the members of the armed forces and the police force to join the people's movement. He also called for friendship with Pakistan and China. Although Bhashani failed to arouse a spontaneous anti-Mujib movement, his anti-India and communal propaganda appeared to be providing fuel to "Muslim Bangla" activists. These activists were said to be operating in a fairly organized manner, particularly in the Chittagong Hill tracts, which provided a good sanctuary near the border with Burma, whose tribal population was said to be loyal to Pakistan's Minister, Raja Tridib Roy. It was known that ever since independence, Maoist extremist groups had been making common cause with the rightist communal parties, which had gone underground. Both considered India a common enemy and both had found a common spokesman in Maulana Bhashani. Thus, "communalism had been buttressed by the cult of violence of Maoists."[23]

After the Indian and Bangladesh Prime Ministers reached agreement on boundary demarcation (16 May 1974), Maulana Bhashani, the leader of the pro-Peking National Awami Party (B), gave no credit to them for resolving issues that had eluded solution for a whole generation. On the contrary, the Chief of the six-Party Opposition United Front (Maulana Bhashani) not only protested against the retention of some portion of Berubari by India but also demanded that New Delhi should "return" Muslim majority areas including Karimganj of Assam and Murshidabad of West Bengal to Bangladesh.[24]

Addressing a function organized by the *Bharat-Bangladesh Maitry Samiti* (Indo-Bangladesh Friendship Association) in Dacca to celebrate Bangladesh's Independence Day towards the end of March 1973, the Indian High Commissioner, S. Dutt, warned against the harmful effects of the propaganda being made by certain elements in the country. He described the friendship between Bangladesh and India as quite natural. It was determined by geographical and historical ties and had deeper roots. It did not depend on any one person. Dutt went on to assert that the false propaganda aimed at creating misunderstandings between the two peoples had even surpassed the technique of Goebells. In this connection, he referred, in particular, to the propaganda that about Rs. 2,000 crores had been transferred to India through smuggling—a piece of falsehood that defied rational comprehension. Dutt did not deny that there was smuggling across the border. He castigated those who indugled in such activities as anti-social elements on both sides of the border. He added that since the borders were guarded, people could not have crossed over without the knowledge of anyone. Referring to propaganda against the fish and jute trade, the Indian High Commissioner observed that Bangladesh needed coal, cement and many other things from India and if it did not supply goods in exchange, it would have to pay in hard currency.[25]

An independent member, Kamrul Islam Mohammed Salauddin, speaking in the Bangladesh Parliament on 13 April 1973, criticized the Indo-Bangladesh Friendship Treaty and demanded good relations with China, as also with the Islamic States. His remarks showed that there were certain forces and persons in Bangladesh who shared their thoughts with the leaders of Peking and Islamabad. Salauddin described the Indo-Bangladesh Friendship Treaty as "unequal," which was said to stand in the way of "making friendship with China." It was due to that Treaty, he said, that Peking was not favourably responding to Dacca's offers of friendship. He did not rule out the possibility of India, at some future date, endeavouring to establish her hegemony over Bangladesh. He referred, in particular, to clauses 9 and 10 of the Treaty, according to which, he stated, if India was involved in any war, Dacca would be forced to follow suit.[26] Obviously this misplaced criticism was intended to malign India.

Under the Treaty of Friendship, Cooperation and Peace Between India and Bangladesh, initialled on 19 March 1972, the two nations are committed not to enter into or participate in any military alliance directed against the other party, to refrain from any aggression against the other and not to allow the use of their territory for committing any act that might cause military damage or constitute a threat to the security of the other High Contracting Party (Article 8). The two parties are also bound to refrain from giving any assistance to any third party taking part in an armed conflict against the other party and in case either party was attacked or threatened with attack the two sides would immediately "enter into mutual consultations" in order to take appropriate effective measures to eliminate the threat and thus ensure the peace and security of their countries (Article 9). Furthermore, the two parties are obliged not to undertake any commitment, secret or open, toward one or more States which might be incompatible "with the present Treaty" (Article 10). Nowhere is it mentioned in the Treaty that the parties would be compelled to take action against their will. The commitments and obligations undertaken by the two countries are meant to safeguard their mutual interests and they are not designed to benefit only one side to the disadvantage of the other.

There is every likelihood that friendly relations between the USSR, India and Bangladesh would continue to develop. But, as the well-known saying goes : there are no permanent friends and no permanent enemies—only interests are permanent. Changes in the internal situations of countries and in international environment cannot be ruled out and circumstances often make strange persons bedfellows. For instance, even in the case of Bangladesh, misgivings, suspicions and unfriendly acts during the Crisis on the part of Washington were soon forgotten and fruitful relations came to be established with the USA. Likewise, Pakistani crimes and atrocities were not allowed to stand in the way of promoting Dacca's national interests. Thus, it was decided to concede the Pakistani demand with regard to the 195 POWs who had earlier been indicted for war crimes. Peking's denunciation of Mujibur Rahman and its opposition to Dacca's entry in the UN is also bound to disappear from the peoples' memories after the establishment of diplomatic relations between the two countries.

Like the USA and the USSR, Islamabad and Peking would soon be establishing their diplomatic presence in Dacca. In view of the growing Sino-Soviet rift, the main challenge to the Soviet position would emanate from China—its arch rival. The main thrust of this challenge might not be in the economic field, because even when Peking begins to extend economic aid to Dacca, its capacity to provide aid would most likely remain limited as compared to that of the USSR. China's challenge to the Soviet Union is most likely to take the form of an attempt to exert its influence over the Maoist extremist elements within Bangladesh with a view to create problems for Mujib, as also for others. One might recall that the Maoist extremists, such as Mohammed Toha's EPCP-ML (East Pakistan Communist Party-Marxist-Leninist) at first kept aloof from the Bangladesh liberation struggle, presumably on Chinese advice. Subsequently, however, it exerted itself to wrest the leadership of the liberation movement in Bangladesh from the hands of Mujib's Awami League-oriented *Mukti-Bahini* in an attempt to transform Bangladesh into a Communist State. That such a communist state would have been dominated by China was evident from the fact that, after his visit to Peking in 1970, Toha began to insist that the immediate launching of armed insurgency and the formation of Naxalite-style terrorist squads in East Pakistan were indispensable.[27]

The West Bengal CPM (Communist Party-Marxist) sought to establish an identity of interests between West Bengal and East Bengal on the grounds that the former was a kind of "colony" of India, just as the latter had been a "colony" of West Pakistan. Its assertion of West Bengal's right to secede from India on the basis of the demand for the "right of self-determination for the nationalities in India" cuts no ice. It might, however, be recalled that the CPM, though regarded revisionist by Peking, has marked Maoist characteristics in its ideological preferences. According to Van der Kroef, what was particularly noteworthy was that the CPM was moving "significantly closer toward the Chinese Communist position of support for ethnic secessionists in South and Southeast Asia (e.g., in Nagaland and Upper Burma)." Moreover, it had been sympathetic to the idea of a united (and preferably a "red") Bengal State comprising West Bengal and Bangladesh. Van der Kroef adds: "There are those in Bangladesh who would look upon such a consummation with sympathy."

The whole struggle for Bengali freedom against Islamabad "has had a widespread, politically radicalizing effect." Even within the Awami League, slogans like "Land to the Tillers" and demands that workers be "the owners of the means of production" (as Sheikh Mujibur Rahman himself put it in his

May Day message in 1970) have not been uncommon. The official commitment of the "People's Republic of Bangladesh" to socialism, Van der Kroef adds, "provides a further framework for West Bengal CPM and Naxalite interaction with the Maoists and other political currents in the new state." That China's sympathies had all along been with the Maoist elements in Bangladesh was quite discernible from Peking's disapproval of Mujib's denunciation of "extremists" (*i.e.* Maoist guerillas), who refused to surrender their arms, and his "persecution" of EPCP-ML armed partisans.[28]

Although leftist pro-Chinese groups might have suffered a great deal during and after the emergence of Bangladesh, they have not completely disappeared from the scene and are far from being a spent force. After China establishes its diplomatic presence in Dacca, it will no doubt seek to renew contacts with them and resurrect their influence by providing them both sustenance and support. These Maoist elements share with others the dream of a united Bengal or a "Greater Bengal" as Maulana Bhashani calls it. In an interview with an Indian journalist, the National Awami Party leader emphatically stated :

> Bengal is an entity by itself, with an ideology of its own, a soul of its own...it is a nation by itself...I believe that your Bengal too in the near future will liberate itself from the clutches of India in the same way as our Bengal has already done so from those of Pakistan. And the two will unite and form Greater Bengal.[29]

Professor Muzaffar Ahmed, the leader of the NAP (M), has adopted a somewhat ambivalent attitude in the matter. He acknowledges the scientific fact of a Bengali nation, based on language and culture. He speaks of an independent Bangladesh and an "autonomous state of Bengal within India" as coming within the framework of that Bengali nationalism. For instance, he observed : "We do not make any distinction between the Bengalis on either side of the border." Moreover, he considers all talk on Bangladeshis being "a nation by themselves" as merely motivated by a desire to assuage Indian "misgivings about Greater Bengal, that is, to prevent the slogan of United Bengal from being raised on both sides of the border."[30]

Thus, there seems a great possibility of China exploiting the discontent and frustration of the people in Bangladesh and the popular resentment in West Bengal for the purpose of launching and encouraging the united "Red Bengal" movement. "Neither India nor the USSR," Van der Kroef observes, "can permit Bengali nationalism to develop—but Peking can." The spectre of a united "Red Bengal," he adds, might well be the indicated Chinese counter-move to Soviet-Indian rapprochement in the South Asian international political arena. He, therefore, considers a united Bengali state ideal as "the difficult but likely tactic for the CPM, the Naxalities and the EPCP-ML." Mutual rivalries between these groups and their more ephemeral fronts, he states, "may well make such an objective as unlikely of implementation as the certainty that New Delhi, backed by its Soviet friends," would never permit (1) a peaceful West Bengal secession and (2) its merger in a Peking-influenced, united Bengal state. For the CPBD, therefore, as much as for its Moscow-oriented CPI counterpart, "Bengali radical nationalism is likely to become an important—perhaps the principal—tactical 'enemy' in the near future." But this enemy, Van der Kroef reiterates, "is but an element in the Sino-Soviet power struggle now likely to intensify in the years ahead in the South and Southeast Asian area."[31]

The popularity of the CPM and the CPML—strong advocates of such unification—is, at present, at a low ebb. Moreover, there is no distinctive organizational matrix for the attainment of that objective. Therefore, the chances of a unified Bengali State emerging in the near future seem quite remote. However, the ideal of one Bengali nation and feelings of Bengali nationalism are not completely absent from the minds of intellectuals, the Maoist underground and the CPM ancillaries. It is a question of the "extremists"—the CPM and the Naxalities in West Bengal and the EPCP-ML and Maoist groups in Bangladesh joining hands and making common cause against the "bourgeois" governments of Indira Gandhi's Congress in India and Mujib's Awami League in Bangladesh. Much would depend on the extent to which Muslim nationalism in Bangladesh can make common cause with non-communist Bengali nationalism in West Bengal and the degree to which both will be prepared to support a possible CPM-Naxalitie-EPCP informal alliance towards an independent United Bengal State. In this syndrome, the *People's Daily* warning to India, about not rejoicing too soon over her victory in the 1971 War and Bhutto's strategy of activating cooperation with "Muslim Bengal," seem quite ominous. It is not unlikely that, if circumstances appear favourable, Pakistan would not hesitate to lend a helping hand to China in the possible break-up of a part of India. By severing West Bengal's links with India, Islamabad would be avenging its humiliating defeat in the 1971 War, which had resulted in the separation of East Bengal from Pakistan.

For the moment, developments such as the movement for an independent, united Bengali State, as a writer put it, "seem highly speculative—as speculative as was the movement towards an independent Bangladesh fifteen or even ten years ago." At the same time, that writer asserts that Bengali nationalism and the issue of a separate Bengali state "are and remain the hidden factor" in the continuing confrontation between the Naxalites and their overt enemies—the CPM—on the one hand, and the Gandhi Government and its CPI allies, on the other, just as it is a principal background dynamic within Bangladesh as the Mujib Government seeks to checkmate its Maoist elements. Quoting West Bengal's top police officials to the effect that "the Naxalite has not been destroyed" and that the social and economic conditions that promoted the development of the insurgency persisted, that writer observes : "The radical fusion of the two parts of the Bengal nation...is not an improbable prospect."[32] Maulana Bhashani had prophesied that, within five years, West Bengal would embark on a mass struggle "to free itself from the domination of India, and within twenty years my dream of a Greater Bengal will come true."[33]

There can hardly be any doubt that such an eventuality (a united "Red" Bengal State) would, indeed, have dangerous implications for the peace and stability of the sub-continent. It would be very harmful to the interests of the Soviet Union as also those of India. China, on the other hand, could feel very happy about it. For obvious reasons, Moscow would endeavour to defeat the attainment of the objective of a United Bengal

State and render all possible assistance to strengthen the hands of the Indira Gandhi and Mujib Governments. To that end, it would not hesitate to extend economic assistance, diplomatic support, arms supplies, and even political support. The CPI could be seen cooperating with Mrs. Gandhi's Congress Party as the pro-Soviet CPBD (Communist Party of Bangladesh) and NAP(M) being advised to cooperate with the Awami League. Indeed, a three-party alliance of the Awami League, CPBD and NAP(M) has already been formed to face the challenge of Maoist and other extremist parties. Professor Muzaffar Ahmed, leader of the NAP(M), has vouchsafed full support to all progressive steps of the Awami League Government. He has also expressed the view that his Party was most concerned and most determined to maintain and continually strengthen friendship with India.[34]

Whether Sheikh Mujibur Rahman will be able to solve his internal problems and overcome his internal difficulties and stand on his own or be compelled to "alter his sub-continent perspective to placate the rightists as well as the pro-Chinese left,"[35] would depend on his ability to face the situation and the cooperation and assistance he manages to secure within the country and from friendly countries. In so far as the USSR is concerned, it will, no doubt, render all possible help, in its own interests, to ensure conditions of peace and stability within Bangladesh and, indeed, within the whole of the Indian sub-continent.

9

Conclusion

PAKISTAN'S close proximity to Soviet borders has been an important factor in the Kremlin's attitude towards Islamabad. Accordingly, Moscow naturally felt concerned about the presence of US bases in Pakistan. It had all along endeavoured to keep Pakistan away from hostile groupings or influences, be that of either the USA or China or both. The Kremlin could never think of writing off Pakistan altogether, though it often deemed it necessary to take countervailing measures to safeguard its vital national interests. Despite the slogans that were raised about "*Hindi-Rusi-Bhai-Bhai*," Indo-Soviet relations had all along been based on considerations of India's utility in Soviet calculations as regards its regional and global requirements. For similar reasons, Moscow had never missed any opportunity to cultivate relations with Pakistan. That has always been the case—throughout the Stalin period, the Khrushchov Era and the contemporary Brezhnev-Kosygin phase.

That Stalin was not averse to cultivate normal relations with Pakistan was evident from the neutral posture he adopted on the Kashmir issue, the establishment of diplomatic relations, and from his desire to have fruitful contacts and mutually beneficial trade relations. Moreover, it was also evident from the invitation extended to Prime Minister Liaquat Ali Khan to visit the Soviet Union. If much headway could not be made in USSR-Pak relations during the Stalin period, it was not so much due to apathy or indifference on the part of the Kremlin as to the Pakistani ruling elite's reservations and lack of response.

The rulers of Pakistan aspired to reap greater benefits by aligning themselves with the Western Powers. The USA, with its superior military and economic resources and tremendous political influence in the world, held greater attraction for Karachi. Washington was considered more suitable by Pakistan in helping it overcome its economic difficulties and in facilitating the realization of Pakistani objectives in the international field, particularly the settlement of the Kashmir problem to its satisfaction. The United States, on its part, felt attracted towards Pakistan because of the latter's strategic location and close proximity to the Soviet Union. The construction of US bases in Pakistan was considered very useful, in the event of a possible conflict, in mounting crippling attacks on the military installations in the Ural region and the industrial complexes of Soviet Central Asia. The Kremlin even suspected that Karachi's willingness to cooperate with Washington might enable the latter to lure "the Arab countries to enter the military bloc and putting pressure on India."[1]

After Stalin's demise, Malenkov stated that the "Soviet Union attaches great importance to the successful development of relations with Pakistan and to strengthening of every kind of relations between the two States."[2] No favourable response was, however, forthcoming from Pakistan, which persisted in its attempt to consolidate its links with the United States. In the circumstances, Moscow could not have remained indifferent to the steadily growing rapport between Pakistan and the USA, especially in the direction of forging a military alliance which was directed against the USSR. The Kremlin endeavoured to dissuade Karachi from following such a "dangerous course." After Pakistan joined the Western alliance systems and cast its lot with the enemies of the USSR, Moscow reacted by extending full support to India on Kashmir and to Afghanistan on the Pakhtoonistan issue—the two most vital questions concerning Pakistan. In the face of keen competition with Washington, the Kremlin felt that it had no alternative but to forge closer and friendlier relations with India, which, like the Soviet Union, was vehemently opposed to the Western alliances.

If, during the Khrushchov Era, USSR-Pak relations were marked by tension and much bitterness and Indo-Soviet relations by growing friendship, it was not the result of any sentiments on the part of the Soviet leader. Pakistan's firm alignment with the West and the establishment of hostile bases on its territory prevented Moscow from developing cordial relations with Karachi. India's policy of non-alignment, on the other hand, seemed to serve the Kremlin's regional and global needs perfectly well. Not only was India free from any hostile bases or influences, but her opposition to Western alliances and their policies of economic and political domination as also her campaign against racial discrimination and coloni- alism, suited Soviet foreign policy requirements of under- mining the Western Powers' image, prestige and power.

India's geo-political position, her size and population, policy of non-alignment, and the existence of a widespread pro-Soviet leftist movement—all these were, indeed, important factors that weighed heavily in the Kremlin's calculations. Nonetheless, Moscow's preference for India was largely determined by the utility that the latter had in serving its regional and global needs.

The rising influence of the Anglo-American bloc in India in the wake of the Sino-Indian Conflict and the existence of dismal economic conditions (Washington had made special food shipments to India to enable her to tide over the bad crop years of 1964-66) and political instability in the second half of the 1960s were viewed with concern in Moscow. The USSR had made intermittent efforts to develop friendly relations with Pakistan. When the first opportunity presented itself, as was the case in the early 60s and more particularly in the post-Tashkent period, the Kremlin proceeded to cultivate relations with Islamabad in a big way. Thus, Moscow adopted a non-partisan approach in Indo-Pak disputes and began to extend large-scale economic and technical assistance to

Pakistan. It even started supplying military hardware to Islamabad, to which India had objected. All this was done to subserve Soviet national interests. The USSR thereby hoped to secure the termination of US bases in Pakistan, prevent Islamabad from closely aligning itself again with Washington and wean Pakistan away from China—which was seen emerging as a rival and hostile Power. Friendly relations with Pakistan were also considered necessary for establishing an effective Soviet presence in Islamabad which could enable Moscow to exert a wholesome influence over both India and Pakistan. The Kremlin could thereby also hope to ensure the establishment of stable and peaceful conditions in the Indian sub-continent. The creation of such conditions was most desirable from the viewpoint of Soviet national interests because of the region's close proximity to Soviet borders. It also deprived rival Powers of any pretext or opportunity for intervening in South Asian affairs. It could, thus, keep the sub-continent free from any hostile presence or influence.

Unstable conditions within Pakistan and Yahya's unsympthetic attitude towards Soviet proposals regarding regional economic cooperation and Asian Collective Security led Moscow to suspend its arms deliveries to Islamabad in 1970. Soviet concern about the East Bengal tragedy was reflected in Podgorny's letter of 2 April 1971. Yahya might have listened to his advice as regards a political settlement in the matter, had there been no extremist forces' pressure within Pakistan and had Yahya not received any sustenance and support which he managed to secure from other Powers, China in particular. Washington seemed inclined to favour a political solution of the Crisis. However, the USA found it more convenient and safer to hold its hand partly because of China and partly for fear of spoiling its relations with Pakistan.

Sino-US rapprochement and Bhutto's visit to China in November 1971 affected Soviet perception of its regional and global interests. In the circumstances, Moscow deemed it prudent to render strong political support to India by concluding a Treaty of Friendship and Cooperation with New Delhi.

With the outbreak of war between India and Pakistan and with both Peking and Washington closely aligning themselves with Islamabad and rendering all possible support thereto, the Kremlin had no other alternative except that of rendering unequivocal and all-out support to New Delhi. At such a critical juncture, the adoption of any other course of action would have caused resentment in New Delhi, resulted in irreparable damage to Indo-Soviet relations, and would have led to the undoing of all the gains secured, over the years, through massive doses of economic and military aid. In the initial stage of the Bangladesh Crisis, the USSR adopted a cautious attitude. It appeared quite anxious to lessen the tension between India and Pakistan. However, circumstances compelled Moscow to assign a higher priority to India and to show a marked preference for New Delhi. The prospect of India agreeing to some settlement of the problem, under the auspices of the Western Powers, during Mrs. Gandhi's visit to the US and Europe, could hardly have appealed to the USSR. However, before events could take such a turn, Moscow deemed it necessary to support India more openly, as was done during N. Firyubin's visit io New Delhi towards the end of October 1971. A report in the *Daily Telegraph* even went to the extent of asserting that the Soviet Deputy Foreign Minister had tried to dissuade Mrs. Gandhi to postpone her visit to the Western capitals.[3]

Changes in the international environment in the wake of President Nixon's visit to China compelled Moscow to take counter-viling measures or reinsurance actions to safeguard its national interests. It should, however, be remembered that despite their sympathy for Bangladesh's freedom struggle Soviet leaders had adopted a cautious approach in the matter. Evidently, the Kremlin was keen to retain a working relationship with the military rulers of Pakistan. Moscow's pleas with regard to a "political solution" and its insistence on sparing Sheikh Mujibur Rahman's life were guided by considerations of arriving at a political settlement of the pro- blem — a settlement which could have preserved the unity of Pakistan and avoided a military confrontation between India and Pakistan. Moscow, it seemed, did not openly wish to

take the side of any one country for fear of damaging its
relations with the other.

In the fast-changing international environment, due to Sino-
US rapprochement in particular, the conclusion of the Indo-
Soviet Treaty was of great significance to India. The influx
of ten million refugees had created a very critical situation
for India. She did not merely face a serious financial crisis
but grave political problems as well. According to the *Economist*, the immediate problem was two-fold : "how to pay for
them and how to send them back whence they came."[4]
International aid was necessary in the short term. However,
even when the refugees came to be regarded as an "international responsibility," no new major commitments were being
made. Of the total amount donated by the largest aid giver
(USA) for relief and rehabilitation, about 70% went to
Pakistan and only 30% to India.[5] Thus, neither any massive
economic assistance for the relief and rehabilitation of the
refugees was forthcoming nor any political solution in East
Bengal (which would have ensured the safe return of refugees
to their homes) seemed in sight. In the circumstances, there
was a danger that "the Awami League leadership would
disintegrate and that the League would be transformed into
either an all-Bengal regional nationalist movement, or a guerilla
Communist movement increasingly dependent upon Chinese
support, or both."[6] "As the resistance movement grows and
its base widens," Sisir Gupta observed, "it will inevitably
acquire far more radical qualities than it now possesses."
The radicalization of the resistance movement was, indeed, a
pre-condition of its success. Sisir Gupta added : "If the
struggle in Bangladesh has to be waged on many fronts, it
cannot be conducted by moderates alone."[7]

Border incidents with Pakistan were constantly on the
increase. There was every likelihood of the crisis escalating into
an Indo-Pak conflict. In these circumstances, India could
not afford to ignore possibilities of Great Powers' intervention
in sub-continental affairs. Moreover, 1971 was neither 1965
nor 1962. The international environment was altogether different
in 1971. Commenting on Henry Kissinger's summer consultations

in New Delhi, an Indian observer remarked : "In case of war
with Pakistan, Kissinger is supposed to have said, China would
come in and India would not get any American help as she
had in the Sino-Indian War of 1962."[8] Obviously, Washington
could not be counted upon to support India against Pakistan.
At a time when President Nixon was anxiously seeking to
normalize his country's relations with Peking, as part of his
global diplomacy, "he would not as a matter of course
follow policies irritating to China." The global priorities of
US policy, at that time, were "in maximum contradiction
with regard to India and in maximum harmony with regard
to Pakistan."[9] In these circumstances, a non-partisan attitude
on the part of Washington or parallelism in the policies of
the two super Powers *vis-a-vis* China seemed out of the question.
Therefore, India deemed it necessary to take some precaution-
ary reinsurance measures.

The most significant measure Mrs. Gandhi took was to
enlist firm Soviet support by concluding a 20-year Treaty of
Peace, Friendship and Cooperation with the USSR. India thereby offset both the Chinese and the American roles—"the
Chinese by presenting them with a Soviet military 'guarantee' in
support of India, and the Americans by cancelling out such UN
activity as Washington might attempt, "[10] in the world organization. Soviet support also offset any adventurist American
action in the Indian Ocean. Not only had the USSR supplied
India with $730 million worth of arms since 1965 (as compared
to $70 million worth of US arms sales to both India and Pakis-
tan since 1965), but it even agreed to sign a treaty, which,
"together with new arms deliveries and military consultations,
gave India additional assurance of Soviet political support as
the crisis mounted."[11]

After thus analyzing the situation, a US scholar (Wayne
Wilcox) makes some observations which are quite understand-
able if viewed from the standpoint of Pakistan and Sino-US
rapprochement. He speaks of Soviet support being "decisive in
giving India the military confidence to move" and of "a
Russian guaranteed invasion to occur with only the US protest-
ing." He used a phraseology almost similar to what Peking had

used when he stated : "The Soviet 'crime' was apparently 'aid-ing and abetting'—not directly committing the offense, but using it to enhance its position in South Asia and the Indian Ocean." The Soviets, he added, had followed, not led, the Indians, and whatever status the Russians had attained in the sub-continent was a consequence of Indian policy.[12]   The Chinese went even further. They spoke of the "Indian aggression against Pakistan" as being the direct result of Soviet incitement, encouragement and support.

The conclusion of the Indo-Soviet Treaty in August 1971 signified that Moscow had a great stake in India and her secu-rity for obvious strategic reasons—the necessity of countering a Sino-US thrust in the sub-continent on Pakistan's behalf. How-ever, the Kremlin deemed it prudent not to give up its earlier policy of caution. This was partly because Moscow feared that a military conflict between India and Pakistan would "play into the hands of those internal and external forces which operate to the detriment of both India and Pakistan."[13]   The continu-ance of a tense situation and the prolongation of a protracted guerilla struggle was, in the long-run, fraught with serious dangers. It would have resulted in the weakening of both India and Pakistan and even created conditions for the take-over of the resistance movement by Maoist elements. However, in view of Sino-US backing for the Pakistani ruling *junta*, Moscow's capacity to influence the opinions and decisions of Yahya Khan towards sanity and reason was bound to be very limited.

The signing of the Indo-Soviet Treaty did not imply that Islamabad had ceased to be factor in Soviet policy. In the USSR-India joint communique, issued after the conclusion of the Indo-Soviet Treaty, mention was made, presumably at Soviet insistence, of "the interests of the entire people of Pakistan." Subsequently, in the Soviet-Algerian joint communique as well, the Kremlin did not forget to lay emphasis on "respect for the national unity and territorial integrity of Pakistan."

Islamabad, naturally enough, felt very much concerned about the Indo-Soviet Treaty.[14] Nevertheless, Pakistan deemed it neces-sary to make "all-out efforts to maintain bilateral relations with the Soviet Union."[15] Obviously, Islamabad could not hope to gain anything by the deterioration of relations with Moscow. At unofficial levels, there was much open criticism of the Indo-Soviet Treaty. Bhutto described it is "a pact of aggression" which was bound to embolden New Delhi to embark on an adventurist policy *vis-a-vis* Pakistan and China. Qayyum Khan and Maududi also criticized the Treaty as posing a serious threat to Pakistan. *Dawn,* however, took a different view. It suggested that the Treaty did not give India more elbow room. In fact, it reduced it because Moscow did not want a war in the sub-continent and, therefore, would certainly want India to tread very carefully.[16]

Even when Bhutto and Agha Shahi made frontal attacks against Moscow in the UN, the Kremlin desisted from replying in kind to their severe criticism and denunciation of Soviet policy. It is also significant to note that when the situation created by the Indo-Pak War of 1971 was over and the separation of Bangladesh had become a reality, the Kremlin reverted to its policy of wooing Pakistan by resuming its economic aid and renewing its political contacts. Moscow sought to reactivate its policy of neutralizing Pakistan and preventing it from moving too close to China or the United States or both. The events of 1971, thus, seemed an aberration in USSR-Pak relations. The Bangladesh Crisis and the Conflict of 1971 did not create any lasting or irreparable breach in their relations. Bhutto's visit to Moscow and the resumption of Soviet aid amply proved that.

With the official recognition of the People's Republic of Bangladesh by Pakistan and the settlement of the problem of Pak POWs and civilian internees, including that of the 195 POWs indicted for war crimes, the chapter of the 1971 War has come to an end. These problems were gradually sorted out by a series of bilateral and trilateral meetings, held among the leaders of the three states (India, Pakistan and Bangladesh) at Simla (July 1972), New Delhi (August 1973), Lahore (March 1974) and New Delhi (April 1974). These contacts have ushered in the process of normalization of relations in the sub-continent. Whether this trend will ultimately lead to the creation of durable conditions of peace and stability would depend on the leadership of the three countries, their domestic compulsions, as also on the attitude of outside Powers, especially China, the USSR and the USA.

In so far as Pakistan was cut to size, shorn of its inflated notions of seeking parity with India, on the basis of borrowed strength, and made to accept the altered power relationship in the sub-continent, the 1971 War may be said to have created more favourable conditions for peace and stability in the region, on a more realistic basis, in the future. The commitment of both India and Pakistan to a peaceful solution of mutual differences under the Simla Agreement implied "a Pakistani abandonment of the military option in Kashmir."[17] Furthermore, the commitment with regard to a bilateral solution of problems could well be interpreted to mean that Pakistan had forsaken its reliance on outside intervention, including UN mediation, observation or involvement, in Kashmir. Likewise, the firm agreement of December 1972 on the line of actual control in the State of Jammu and Kashmir augurs well for stabilizing Indo-Pak relations on a sound footing and reducing the necessity for either side's dependence on outside Powers for security or other reasons.

However, as soon as India withdrew her forces from Pakistani territory, Z.A. Bhutto (both as President of Pakistan and subsequently as its Prime Minister) began to harp on the well-known Pakistani theme of self-determination for the people of Jammu and Kashmir. The line of actual control in Kashmir, he stated, could not be construed as an international boundary. In these circumstances, it might seem doubtful if Pakistan would accept "India's explication for the Simla Agreement, rendering the old 1949 UN-supervised ceasefire line irrelevant and making the new bilateral arrangement exclusively 'a bilateral responsibility',"[18] and altogether stop seeking UN involvement in the Kashmir issue. Pakistan has also made up its losses (in tank, aircraft, etc.) of the 1971 War and considerably augmented its armed might. Pakistan's defence budget for 1974-75 reached an all-time high with a total allocation of Rs. 560 crores, as compared with Rs. 340 crores for 1972-73 and Rs. 423 crores for 1973-74. This higher allocation was announced soon after Bhutto's statement that Pakistan must defend itself against what he called "India's nuclear blackmail."[19] Despite augmentation of its military strength, Pakistan can hardly feel confident about having an edge over India. With the emergence of Bangladesh and the explosion of a peaceful nuclear device by India, the balance of forces in the sub-continent has obviously tilted in favour of New Delhi. In the altered power relationship, it would, indeed, be quite risky for Islamabad to seriously think of military confrontation with India for the solution of the Kashmir problem. However, one cannot rule out, for all time to come, the possibility of Pakistan re-energizing and internationalizing the Kashmir problem on the political plane when conditions within the State of Jammu and Kashmir permit the same or when Islamabad is able to count on the Great Powers' support in the UN.

In this context, it is worth recalling that Bhutto had all along been a strong advocate of the so-called "liberation" of Kashmir. He had believed : "If a Muslim majority area can remain a part of India, then the *raison d'etre* of Pakistan collapses....Pakistan is incomplete without Jammu and Kashmir, both territorially and ideologically."[20] In private conversations, however, Bhutto seemed to have adopted a softer line in the matter. He confided to an Indian journalist that the struggle for self-determination of the people of Jammu and Kashmir was not inspired from outside and, therefore, the problem could not be solved by "outside support."[21] He had also committed Pakistan, under the Simla Agreement, not to use force to alter the *status quo* in Kashmir and to seek a bilateral solution of the issue. However, as recently as 19 May 1974, while commenting on India's peaceful nuclear explosion, he stated : "Pakistan will neither give up the right of self-determination for Kashmiris, nor will it accept India's hegemony in the sub-continent."[22]

Subsequently, in his reply (dated 6 June 1974) to Prime Minister Indira Gandhi's letter, Premier Bhutto imputed military motives to India's scientific and space research, and considered it a matter of grave concern not only to Pakistan but "to all countries which border on the Indian Ocean." While stating that he did not wish to be deflected from the policy of establishing Indo-Pak relations on "a rational neighbourly basis," he, at the same time, considered India's peaceful nuclear explosion as introducing "an unbalancing factor" in the process of "step by step" normalization and prejudicing what he called the "equilibrium and tranquility in the subcontinent." Thus, he blamed India for undermining the process of reconciliation between the two countries. He made no mention whatsoever of the Simla Agreement. On the contrary, he raked up the Kashmir plebiscite issue, accused India of dismembering Pakistan and alleged that India was planning a nuclear navy.[23]

In the wake of India's peaceful nuclear explosion, Pakistan unilaterally put off indefinitely the Indo-Pak talks, on restoring postal, telecommunication and travel facilities between the two countries that were scheduled to be held in Islamabad on 10 June 1974, thereby impeding or delaying the process of normalization in the sub-continent. Mrs. Gandhi's assurances to Bhutto, soon after the nuclear explosion, about India's peaceful intentions and her commitment to settle all her differences with Pakistan peacefully through bilateral negotiations in accordance with the Simla Agreement did not seem to carry conviction with Islamabad. Whether Pakistani moves at hampering the process of reconciliation are a temporary phase to suit the exigencies of the domestic situation, a deliberate attempt at the behest of China, or a measure to probe the possibilities of alienating Bangladesh from India remains to be seen. However,o ne thing seems certain that the desire on the part of Pakistan to reactivate the Kashmir issue within or outside UN forums, and to create tension in the subcontinent still exists. The vigorous pursuit of such a course of action would largely depend on domestic compulsions and the encouragement and support it receives from outside Powers, particularly China.

The China factor is bound to remain an important consideration in Soviet calculations, particularly in determining policy towards the Indian sub-continent. For that matter, Moscow would continue to assign a higher priority to India than to Pakistan and view with concern the emergence of any tense situation in the sub-continent. This was reflected in V. Shurigin's article (13 June 1974) in which he sympathetically viewed "a considerable increase in the international prestige of India"

in recent years and positively assessed her "big contribution to
the cause of normalising the situation in the Asian continent."
The Soviet commentator then referred to the forces inside the
countries of the sub-continent and outside them, that were
opposed to normalization of relations between the three States—
India, Pakistan and Bangladesh. These forces, he stated, were
pursuing their own interests and were seeking to impede the
positive process of the establishment of an atmosphere of peace
and good-neighbourliness in South Asia. V. Shurigin added :
"They use artificial pretexts to aggravate the situation, to sow
the seeds of distrust and animosity between India and Pakistan
in the first place."[24] These remarks were clearly directed against
the Chinese, who were also accused of distorting the essence
and character of Indo-Soviet friendship and cooperation. But,
at the same time, the Soviet commentary was a subtle way of
telling the Pakistani Premier that he should not take an alarm-
ist view of India's peaceful nuclear explosion; that he should
try to adjust himself to the changed power relationship in the
region; and that he should not do anything which would go
against or reverse the process of normalization in the Indian
sub-continent. Even after disbursing $8,228 millions in econo-
mic grants and credits to India and $3,438 millions to Pakistan
during 1947-70, Washington was unable to induce New Delhi
and Rawalpindi towards an enduring sub-continental peace
which would have served its global as well as regional interests
vis-a-vis its adversaries—the USSR and China. Whether Moscow
would be able to bring about a lasting reconciliation between
India and Pakistan, thereby ensuring durable conditions of
peace and stability in the region, and prevent its rivals from exploiting the situation to their own advantage and for subserving
their own interests remains to be seen.

Gone now is the West Pakistani hold over East Bengal
and with it the problems it gave rise to, leading to insecurity
and tension in that region. Gone is the fomentation of
communal trouble by repression of the Hindu minority in the
erstwhile East Pakistan ; gone the assistance rendered to
Naxalites, Naga and Mizo rebels by providing training
facilities, supplies or a secure base for operations and retreat,
often in collaboration with Chinese attempts at infiltration

and subversion. Gone also is the threat of waging a two-front war against India. The 1971 war seems to have paved the way for stabilization of the situation in the north-eastern part of India. With the emergence of a friendly Bangladesh, the threat of extremist leftist groups, based on Peking's capacity for infiltration and subversion, has also, to a great extent, receded in the background. Thus, propitious conditions seem to have been created for ensuring a peaceful and stable atmosphere in the region. But how long this situation will last is, indeed, difficult to say.

With the growing *detente* in the United States' relations with both the Communist Powers—the USSR and China—it might be becoming more apparent, as Wayne Wilcox believes, that South Asia "was peripheral to American vital interests, economic and strategic."[25] To Moscow and Peking, however, the Indian sub-continent has been and continues to be an area of direct political and strategic interest affecting their vital national interests. With the constantly developing strains in Sino-Soviet relations, the main challenge or competition which the Kremlin now faces emanates from Peking. In a booklet entitled "What is Peking After?" a Soviet specialist on China (Ernst Henry) asserted that South Asia is the kingpin of a multi-pronged strategy formulated by China to emerge as a super Power. China is the "only 'unsatisfied' external Power active in southern Asia." This is conceded even by the American scholar (Wayne Wilcox.) The two super Powers, he says, are more interested in defusing "third area" conflicts as indeed they have done in respect of the explosive "Two Germanies—Berlin" problem.[26]

One may argue that Moscow would prefer to strengthen India's position, both regionally and internationally, believing that to be to its advantage for maintaining a proper balance in Asia and also in the world *vis-a-vis* its main rivals—the USA and China. At the same time, it seems, that Moscow would like to preserve its influence in Pakistan, partly for reasons of minimizing the interventionist and destablizing role of other interested Powers, particularly China—its arch rival. The establishment of Indian primacy in the sub-continent, to a certain extent, makes for constraint on the part of Islamabad. The events of 1965 and 1971 should have convinced Islamabad that "strategic accomodation is a more rational and desirable policy than an unstable, unreliable, and illusory balance of power based on fickle and distant external 'balancers'."[27] Likewise, Mrs. Indira Gandhi also realizes that a stable, democratic, and united West Pakistan is very much in India's interests, for it is only then that outside Powers' intervention in sub-continental affairs can be prevened. All this augurs well for peace and stability in the region.

The role of the great Powers in the maintenance of stable conditions in the sub-continent, as stated earlier, is equally, if not more, important. Despite *detente* between the super Powers, rivalry and competition between the USA and the USSR continues. Washington, on its own, and probably in conjunction with Peking, is bound to exert itself to preserve a modicum of influence in the Indian sub-continent. Peking will undoubtedly endeavour to create a sphere of influence for itself. Thus, the two, individually or jointly, may seek to strengthen their ties with Islamabad, establish and further develop their relations with Dacca, try to loosen Indo-Soviet ties, and, for that matter, even think of effecting a rapprochement with New Delhi. The renewed interest of the USA and China in the Indian sub-continent, however, may not all be in the interests of peace and stability in the area. Peking, on its own or in concert with Washington, may attempt to reactivate its diplomacy of playing one Power against the other in the sub-continent, sow seeds of discord, and encourage Maoist and extremist elements to establish their stronghold in the countries of the region.

Pakistan, as already noted, has emerged, after the separation of East Bengal, a viable and coherent unit, with its economy stronger and its military strength further reinforced. Arms assistance from external Powers is very likely to fortify the officer corps in the Pakistani armed forces against other competing groups interested in the democratization and development of the country. It is also likely to enhance Islamabad's military capabilities and, along with it, Pakistan's expectations as well. It is significant to recall that the strength of the military establishment in Pakistan, "in part produced by American assistance in the 1950's and 1960's, was one of the factors crippling democratic development and political stability in the country," and the problem still remains.[28]   It is also worth noting that Islamabad has never hesitated to think in term of settling the Kashmir dispute by resort to force whenever it felt confident of its armed might.   Even after Pakistan's defeat in the 1971 War, Bhutto has not given up his advocacy of self-determination for the Kashmiri people.

Will the external Powers, China in particular, realize that the Military Establishment no longer constitutes a stabilizing force within Pakistan? Will they recognize that "Pakistan's best interests lie with a strategic accomodation with India and an end to the Kashmir dispute" and discourage false dependence on themselves?   Will they allow India and Pakistan to abide by their commitments under the Simla Agreement of July 1972, by which Kashmir, which had poisoned relations between India and Pakistan for so long, is considered a bilateral matter? All these are important, moot and sixty-four dollar questions.   The responsibility for maintaining peace and stability in the Indian subcontinent lies as much on the shoulders of the leaders of the countries in the region as on the attitude of the outside Powers.

Bangladesh does not pose a security problem to any country.   It also does not represent a major prize between the great Powers. Nevertheless, its importance in regard to creating conditions of stability and durable peace in the region cannot be under-estimated.   While law and order has come to be established, the economic condition of the country is far from satisfactory. These afford ample opportunity to extremist (leftist, Maoist) forces for fomenting trouble for Dacca as well as New Delhi.   Moscow, it seems, is expected to have little interest in influencing the pro-Soviet Communist Party and the NAP (Muzaffar Group) "to lay siege to a friendly govern-ment" in Bangladesh.   But from Peking it may be futile to have similar expectations.   It is no doubt true that China's involvement in local politics has been greatly undercut by the suppression of leftist pro-Chinese groups during and after the emergence of Bangladesh. The pro-Chinese forces, an American scholar has observed, "were never large, and if any still exist, have no access to Peking since there are no relations between the two sides."[29] However, this is only a transient phase for Peking is bound to establish diplomatic relations with Dacca in the near future.

It is pertinent to recall here that China, which had earlier vetoed Bangladesh's application for admission in the UN, allowed a unanimous resolution to be adopted, without vote, by the Security Council on Dacca's entry into the World Organization on 10 June 1974. Speaking in the debate, the Chinese representative expressed his Government's readiness to develop neighbourly relations with the countries of the sub-continent. He, however, added : "The Chinese Government would always firmly support the peoples of South Asia in their struggle against hegemonism and expansionism."[30]

The two super Powers, it seems, favour the resolution of the problems of the sub-continent through negotiations among the countries directly concerned. By rendering support to the Simla and New Delhi agreements, Moscow has, indeed, given ample indication of its preference for a bilateral solution of the problems. The US representative, speaking at the time of the Security Council approval of Bangladesh's UN membership, also appreciated the efforts of the leaders of India, Pakistan and Bangladesh "to initiate a process of regional reconciliation." He fully endorsed "the concept that regional problems should be solved by negotiation among the nations most immediately involved in the region itself."[31] These remarks appear quite encouraging for promoting stability in the region. Whether the two super Powers would exert themselves, stand together and coordinate their moves towards ensuring conditions of peace and stability in the sub-continent or fall apart, practise power politics and, in doing so, extend their support, one way or the other, to China would depend on the prevailing circumstances and the international situation at the time. It cannot be predicted. One can only say that the attitude of the two super Powers will have an important bearing on sub-continental affairs.

Since Bangladesh has common affinities in history, language and culture with West Bengal, there is every likelihood of the leftist groups in the two places making common cause in establishing a "United Bengal." For the moment, the advocates of this cause seem to be lying low, and for that matter, China, for the time being, is also maintaining studied silence. The question is : Will Peking try to exploit the situation ? Will it, thereby, seek to reap benefits when a movement to that effect is activated or gains momentum ? When that happens, it would, indeed, create a very destabilizing situation in the north-eastern region of the Indian sub-continent, the repercussions of which are not likely to remain confined to that part alone. Thus, a good deal would depend on how the leaders of India, Pakistan and Bangladesh manage their affairs—domestic and foreign—and the attitude the great Powers (China, the USSR and the USA) adopt towards sub-continental problems.

Notes

CHAPTER 1

1. Samin Khan, *Pakistan : Ideology-Constitution-Laws-Foreign Policy* (Karachi, 1961) 114-5 and 127.

2. UN Document S/PV. 1114 (11 May 1964) 4-5.

3. Government of Pakistan, Department of Advertising, Films & Publications, *Foreign Relations* (Karachi, 1956) 58.

4. Quoted in *Dawn*, 23 Mar 1965. Emphasis added.

5. *Ibid.*, 14 Aug 1964.

6. *Ibid.*, 23 March 1965.

7. Article by Hameedudin Qureshi. *Ibid.*

8. UN Document S/PV. 1247.

9. "Pakistan—Ideological Basis and Historical Role" by A.T.M. Mustafa, *Dawn*, 14 Aug 1964. Emphasis added.

10. Samin Khan, n. 1, 96.

11. Maulana Maudoodi observed : "If a secular and Godless, instead of Islamic constitution, was to be introduced...what was the sense in all this struggle for a separate Muslim homeland ? We could have had it all without that." Quoted in Hugh Tinker, *India and Pakistan* (London, 1962) 207.

12. UN Document S/PV. 1115 (12 May 1964) 12.

13. Nafis Ahmad, *The Basis of Pakistan* (Calcutta, 1947) 188.

14. When Syed Abu-l-Ala Maududi replied in the negative to the question whether the fighting in Kashmir was a *jehad* or not in May 1948 and was quoted by Kabul and Srinagar radio stations to that effect, Pakistan information services answered by denouncing him and recalling that he opposed partition. Leonard Binder, *Religion and Politics in Pakistan* (California, 1961) 136-7.

15. Government of Pakistan, Department of Publications, *Prime Minister's Statement on Foreign Policy* (9 Dec 1956) (Karachi, undated).

16. *Morning News*, 24 Mar 1965.

17. Choudhuri Rahmat Ali, *Pakistan : The Fatherland of the Pak Nation* (Cambridge, England, 1947) 331, 277 and 374. Emphasis added.

18. *Foreign Relations*, n. 3, 46.

19. Nafis Ahmad, n. 13, 185-6.

20. *New York Times*, 20 Dec 1951.

21. W. Norman Brown, *The United States and India and Pakistan*, 2nd edn. (Cambridge, Mass, 1963) 342.

22. Geoffrey Wheeler, *Racial Problems in Soviet Muslim Asia* (London, 1962) 61.

23. Sir Olaf Caroe, "Soviet Imperialism in Central Asia," *Foreign Affairs* (Oct 1953) 141.

24. K. Sarwar Hasan, *Pakistan and the United Nations* (New York, 1960) 54-5.

25. Geoffrey Wheeler, n. 22, 16.

26. Stalin, *Marxism and the National Colonial Question* (London, 1942) 53 and 163. Cited in Sir Olaf Caroe, n. 23, 140.

27. G. W. Choudhury and Parvez Hasan, *Pakistan's External Relations* (Karachi, 1958) 9.

28. Samin Khan, n. 1, 129.

29. *Dawn*, 12 Jul 1957.

30. See J.P. Jain, *China Pakistan and Bangladesh* (New Delhi, 1974) 1-18.

31. Samin Khan, n. 1, 5

32. Nafis Ahmad, n. 13, 160-1 and Foreword.

33. Quoted by B. Shiva Rao in a letter to the editor, *Hindu*, 15 Dec 1961.

34. Nafis Ahmad, n. 13, 44-5.

35. *Ibid.*, 165-6, 181 and 170-1.

36. *New York Times*, 15 Apr 1950.

37. *Times*, 10 Jan 1949.

38. *Ibid.*, 11 Jan 1951.

39. *New York Times*, 15 Sep 1951.

40. Major General Fazal Muqueem Khan, *The Story of the Pakistan Army* (Karachi, 1963) 154.

41. *Al-Ahram*, 4 Mar 1966. "Some circles in Washington and London may even have toyed with the idea of affecting the Moslems in Central Asian Republics of the Soviet Union and those in the Sinkiang Province of Mainland China by making Pakistan an economically viable and militarily strong ally of the Western democracies." George J. Lerski, "The Pakistan-American Alliance : A Revaluation of the Past Decade," *Asian Survey* (May 1968) 406. British experts, Sir William Barton and Sir Olaf Caroe, argued that Pakistan and not India was the key to West Asian defence. *Ibid.*, 402.

42. Aslam Siddiqi, *Pakistan Seeks Security* (London, 1960) 130-1 and 159-60.

43. Keith Callard, *Pakistan : A Political Study* (London, 1957) 314 and 321.

44. *New York Times*, 22 Mar 1952.

45. *Ibid.*, 19 Apr 1953.

46. *Pakistan News Digest* (Karachi) (15 Nov 1954) 7.

47. *Pakistan Horizon* (1961) 87.

48. *New York Times*, 2 May 1963. Since 1960, US aid has been primarily channeled through the World Bank's Aid-to-Pakistan Consortium, which consists of the USA, West Germany, the UK, Canada, France, Japan, Belgium, the Netherlands and Italy. According to Qutbuddin Aziz, the Consortium's aid pledge to Pakistan between 1960 and 1965 totalled $2.103 billion, nearly half of which was from the United States. *Christian Science Monitor*, 4 Apr 1966.

49. Callard, n. 43, 321.

50. *Dawn*, 10 Mar 1958.

51. J.P. Jain, n. 30, 25 and 76-7.

52. Choudhury and Hasan, n. 27, 13.

53. "To me neutralism seems suspiciously like 'fencemanship' " which could not withstand when put to the test. Cited in Callard, n. 43, 321.

54. Siddiqi, n. 42, 34-5 and 132-3.

CHAPTER 2

1. B. Ashe, "Political Parties in India," *World News and Views* (30 Dec 1939) 1173.

2. V. Balabushevich and A. Dyakov. "Indiia i Vtoraia Imperialisticheskaia Voina," *Mirovoe Khoziaistvo* (Dec 1940) 53-68. Cited in Raghunath Ram, *Soviet Attitude and Policy Towards Pakistan 1947-68*, Ph.D. Thesis of Jawaharlal Nehru University, New Delhi, 1973, 3.

3. *Ibid.*, 3-4. See also David N. Druhe, *Soviet Russia and Indian Communism* (New York, 1959) 237.

4. Raghunath Ram, n. 2, 5.

5. P.C. Joshi, *The Indian Communist Party* (London, 1942) 33 and 27.

6. Quoted in Gene D. Overstreet and Marshal Windmiller, *Communism in India* (Berkeley, 1959) 213-6.

7. See S. Melman, "Polozhenie v Indii" in *Mirovoe Khoziaistvo i Mirovaia Politika* (Nov-Dec 1942) 46-7. Cited in Bhabani Sen Gupta, *The Fulcrum of Asia* (New York, 1970) 43.

8. A. Dyakov, "Sovremennaia India" ("Contemporary India") *Bolshevik* (Feb 1946) 44-51. Cited in Raghunath Ram, n. 2, 7-8.

9. See "August Resolution," *For the Final Assault : Tasks of the Indian People in the Present Phase of Indian Revolution* (Bombay, 1946).

10. See E. Zhukov's article "Velikaia Oktiabrskaia Sotsialisticheskaia Revoliutsiia i Kolonialnyi Vostok" ("The Great October Socialist Revolution and the Colonial East") *Bolshevik* (Oct 1946) 43. Cited in Overstreet and Windmiller, n. 6, 249.

11. A. Dyakov, "The Situation in India," *Pravda*, 21 Oct 1946 as translated in *Soviet Press Translations* (28 Feb 1947) 6.

12. *New Times* (18 Apr 1947) 31.

13. *Pravda*, 12 and 16 May 1947. See Gene D. Overstreet, *The Soviet View of India : 1945-1948*, M.A. Thesis of Columbia University, New York, Feb 1953. Cited in Bhabani Sen Gupta, n. 7, 49-50.

14. E. Zhukov, "Ko Polozhenie v Indii," *Mirovoe Khoziaistvo i Mirovaia Politika*, No. 23 (1947) 3-14. Cited in Nirmala Joshi, *India and the Soviet Union : A Study of Non-Official Attitudes and Contacts 1917-1947*, Ph.D. Thesis of Jawaharlal Nehru University, New Delhi, 1973, 218.

15. A. Dyakov, "The New British Plan for India," *New Times* (13 Jun 1947) 12-5.

16. See John H. Kautsky, *Moscow, and the Communist Party of India* (New York, 1956) 24. See also Dyakov, n. 15 and Zhukov in *New Times* (Jul 1947).

17. *Bol'shaia Sovetskaia Entsiklopediia* (Moscow) Vol. 18 (8 Jan 1953) 73. Cited in Raghunath Ram, n.2, 15-6.

18. *Bol'shaia Sovetskaia Entsiklopediia*, Vol. 15 (12 Sep 1952) 79. Cited in Raghunath Ram, n. 2, 16.

19. K.P.S. Menon, *The Lamp and the Lampstand* (London, 1967) 28.

20. A. Dyakov, *India vo Vremia i Posle Vtoroi Mirovoi Voiny 1939-1949* (Moscow, 1952). Cited in Devendra Kaushik, *Soviet Relations with India and Pakistan* (Delhi, 1971) 31.

21. A.M. Dyakov, "Partitioned India," *New Times* (14 Jan 1948).

22. Y.V. Gankovsky and Gordon-Polonskaya, *A History of Pakistan* (Moscow, 1965) 100.

23. Dyakov, n. 21.

24. *Dawn*, 3 Apr 1949.

25. F. H. Soward and R.M. Fowler, *The Changing Commonwealth*, Proceedings of the Fourth Unofficial Commonwealth Relations Conference, 1949 (Toronto, 1950) 40.

26. N. Gladkov, "In Pakistan—Travel Impressions," *New Times*, No. 21 (24 May 1950) 22.

27. *Dawn*, 10 Jun 1949.

28. *Ibid.*, 11 Jun 1949.

29. K. Sarwar Hasan, *Pakistan and the Commonwealth* (Karachi, 1950) 29.

30. See Liaquat Ali Khan, *Pakistan* : *Heart of Asia* (Cambridge, 1951).

31. M.S. Venkataramani and H.C. Arya, "America's Military Alliance with Pakistan : The Evolution and Course of an Uneasy Partnership," *International Studies* (Jul-Oct 1966) 79.

32. *Pakistan Horizon* (Mar 1956) 46.

33. K. Sarwar Hasan, *The Strategic Interests of Pakistan* (Karachi, 1954) 2-3.

34. *New Times*, (22 Dec 1955) Documents, 26.

35. Sir William Barton, "Pakistan's Claim to Kashmir," *Foreign Affairs* (Jan 1950) 307.

36. Mustaq Ahmad, *The United Nations and Pakistan* (Karachi, 1955) 140.

37. See J.P. Jain, *China Pakistan and Bangladesh* (New Delhi, 1974).

38. *New Times* (12 Jul 1950) 19-20.

39. *Literaturnaia Gazeta*, 25 Jul 1950.

40. *New Times*, No. 28 (1950).

41. *Ibid.*, No. 4 (1951).

42. *Ibid.*, No. 8 (1951).

43. See Raghunath Ram, n. 2, 27-8.

44. *Pravda*, 27 Oct 1950.

45. *Christian Science Monitor*, 27 Jun 1950.

46. *Dawn*, 10 and 22 Mar 1951.

47. *New Times*, No. 13, 33 and 37 (1951).

48. *Pravda*, 3 Aug 1952.

49. *Literaturnaia Gazeta*, 25 Jun 1952.

50. See Raghunath Ram, n. 2, 41-4.

51. UN Document S/PV. 570 (17 Jan 1952) 13-8.

52. *Ibid.*, S/PV. 610.

53. *Pravda*, 1 Aug 1953.

54. See Raghunath Ram, n. 2.

55. *Pravda*, 29 Mar 1952. Cited in J.A. Naik, *Soviet Policy Towards India* (Delhi, 1970) 39.

56. *Pravda*, 27 Feb 1949.

57. *New Times*, No. 32 (1948).

58. *Pravda*, 26 Jul 1948.
59. *Ibid.*, 28 May 1949.
60. *Ibid.*, 9 Sep 1949.
61. *New Times*, No. 11 (1950).
62. *Pravda*, 2 Dec 1948.
63. *Ibid.*, 21 Nov 1949.

CHAPTER 3

1. *New York Times*, 9 and 13 Oct 1947.
2. M.A.H. Ispahani, "Pacts and Aid," *Pakistan Horizon* (1966) 188.
3. G.M. Kahin, *The Asian-African Conference*, (Ithaca, 1956) 20.
4. *Washington Post*, 10 Mar 1963. Cited in Khalid B. Sayeed, "Pakistan and China," in A.M. Halpern, *Policies Towards China : Views from Six Continents* (New York, 1965) 257.
5. *New Times*, No. 52. (22 Dec 1955) Documents, 26-7.
6. N. A. Bulganin, N.S. Khrushchov, *Visit of Friendship to India, Burma Afghanistan : Speeches and Official Documents* (Moscow, 1956) 202-3.
7. A. Pronin, "Pakistan Affairs," *New Times*, No. 42 (1954) 13-5.
8. See E. Zhukov, "The Bandung Conference of Asian and African Countries and its Historic Significance," *International Affairs* (Moscow) (May 1955) 18-32.
9. *New York Times*, 15 Sep 1954.
10. *Pakistan Times*, 24 Apr 1955.
11. Government of Pakistan, *Foreign Relations* (Karachi, Mar 1956) 40.
12. *Times* (London) 26 Mar 1956.
13. Government of Pakistan, Department of Publications, *Prime Minister's Statement on Foreign Policy* (9 Dec 1956) (Karachi, undated).
14. *New Times*, No. 30 (1957) 19-20.
15. Cited in Bhabani Sen Gupta, *The Fulcrum of Asia* (New York. 1970) 71.
16. *New Times*, No. 51 (1958) 15-16.
17. *Pravda*, 28 Mar 1959. Cited in Raghunath Ram, *Soviet Attitude and Policy Towards Pakistan 1947-1968*, Ph.D. Thesis of Jawaharlal Nehru University, New Delhi, 1973, 129.
18. *Pravda*, 17 Mar 1959.
19. *Izvestia*, 2 Dec 1953. Cited in Raghunath Ram, n. 17, 63-4.
20. *Dawn*, 4 Dec 1953.
21. *Ibid.*, 19 Dec 1953.
22. *New Times*, No. 15 (1954) 22.
23. *Pravda*, 28 Mar 1954.
24. *Dawn*, 31 Mar 1954.
25. *Ibid.*, 5 May 1954.
26. *Dawn*, 25 May 1958.
27. *Ibid.*
28. *Ibid.*, 13 Jan 1959.
29. *Pakistan News Digest*, 15 Mar 1959.

30. *News and Views from the Soviet Union* (Soviet Embassy, New Delhi) (21 Mar 1959) 5.

31. *Soviet News*, 26 Mar 1959.

32. *News and Views from the Soviet Union* (17 May 1960) 3-4.

33. *Dawn*, 15 May 1960.

34. *Pakistan News Digest*, 1 Nov 1959.

35. *Dawn*, 27 Oct 1959.

36. *Ibid.*, 19 Nov 1959.

37. *Pakistan Affairs* (Pakistan Embassy, Washington) 1 Dec 1959.

38. *Christian Science Monitor*, 17 Dec 1959.

39. Mohammad Ayub Khan, "Pakistan's Perspective," *Foreign Affairs* (July 1960). In a speech on 30 April 1959, Pakistan's Ambassador to the United States, Aziz Ahmed, spoke of a "common danger" facing the sub-continent and offered "a scheme of joint defence" to India, thereby making Pakistan "its defence shield lying as it does across the historic invasion routes to India in the north-west and approaches to that country from south-east." But this offer was likewise conditional on "the impediments," such as Kashmir and the dispute over the Indus waters being eliminated "first." *Hindu*, 3 May 1959.

40. *Hindustan Times*, 15 May 1974.

41. *Morning News* (Karachi) 24 Mar 1960.

42. *Pakistan Horizon* (1960) 12.

43. Text released by the Embassy of Pakistan, Washington.

44. *Pakistan Times*, 25 Mar 1956. K. Petrov, writing in *Izvestia* on 23 March 1956, dwelt on Pakistan developing mutually beneficial trade relations with the USSR and obtaining modern equipment that was essential for its industrial development from Socialist countries "without having to undertake any political or military obligations in payment." *Current Digest of the Soviet Press* (2 May 1956) 41.

45. *Dawn*, 12 Jul 1959.

46. *Pakistan Times*, 12 Jul 1959.

47. Interview with *Le Monde*. See *Dawn*, 1 Aug 1959.

48. *Pakistan Times*, 2 Aug 1959.

49. *Dawn*, 22 Apr 1960.

50. *Pakistan Horizon* (1961) 90.

51. *Dawn*, 5 Mar 1961.

52. *Pakistan Horizon* (1961) 250.

53. *Dawn*, 15 and 12 Jun 1961.

54. See S. M. Burke, *Pakistan's Foreign Policy : An Historical Analysis* (London, 1973) 300.

55. See Raghunath Ram, n. 17, 176.

56. *Pravda*, 30 Dec 1955. Cited in Devendra Kaushik, *Soviet Relations with India and Pakistan* (Delhi, 1971) 75.

57. *Current Digest of the Soviet Press* (28 Sep 1955) 17-8. Cited in Werner Levi, "Pakistan, the Soviet Union and China," *Pacific Affairs* (Fall 1962) 216.

58. *Pravda*, 29 Apr 1954.

59. *New Times*, No. 8 (16 Feb 1956) Documents, 19.

60. *Pakistan Times*, 13 Jun 1959.

61. Raghunath Ram, n. 17, 136.

62. *Pakistan Horizon* (1961) 345.

63. *Pravda*, 3 Apr 1961.
64. Foreign Broadcast nformation Service, *Daily Report*, 2 Feb 1962.
65. UN Document S/PV. 1016, 18.
66. Zulfikar Ali Bhutto, *The Myth of Independence* (London, 1969) 158.
67. Bulganin and Khrushchov, n. 6, 114.
68. *Dawn*, 30 Mar 1956.
69. S.M. Burke, n. 54, 297-8.
70. *New Times*, No. 50 (1962).
71. *Pravda*, 19 Sep 1963 and Burke, n. 54, 299.
72. See Wayne Wilcox, *The Emergence of Bangladesh* (Washington, 1973) 8.
73. *Dawn*, 26 Jun 1963.
74. See S.M. Burke, n. 54, 300.
75. UN Document S/PV. 1091.
76. Raghunath Ram, n. 17, 178.

CHAPTER 4

1. *Pakistan Times*, 30 Sep 1967.
2. Mohmmad Ayub Khan, *Friends Not Masters* (London, 1967).
3. Zubeida Hasan, "Pakistan's Relations with the USSR in the 1960's," *World Today* (Jan 1969) 34.
4. *Dawn*, 8 Apr 1965.
5. *Ibid.*, 10 Feb 1971.
6. *Pakistan Horizon* (1965) 187.
7. Mohammad Ayub Khan, *Speeches and Statements* Vol. VII, Jul 1964-Jun 1965 (Karachi, undated) 182.
8. *New Times*, No. 20 (1965) 15.
9. *Pravda* Statement, 9 May 1965 as translated in *Current Digest of the Soviet Press* (2 Jun 1965) 25.
10. *Dawn*, 14 Jul and 11 Aug 1965.
11. *Morning News*, 21 Aug 1965.
12. *Link*, 21 Aug 1965, 9.
13. *Pravda*, 4 Sep 1965.
14. UN Document S/PV. 1237. Emphasis added.
15. *Ibid.*, S/6671.
16. *Pakistan Horizon* (1965) 428-30.
17. *Ibid*, 430-1.
18. UN Document S/PV. 1247.
19. *Ibid.*
20. *Ibid.*, S/6685.
21. *Current Digest of the Soviet Press* (15 Sep 1965) 16.
22. *Ibid.*, 16.
23. UN Document S/6685.
24. *Pravda*, 11 Sep 1965.
25. UN Document S/6671.
26. *Ibid.*, S/PV. 1241.
27. *Pakistan Horizon* (1965) 429-30.

28. *Current Digest of the Soviet Press* (13 Oct 1965) 20.

29. *Dawn*, 13 and 14 Nov 1965.

30. S.P. Seth, "Russia's Role in Indo-Pak Politics," *Asian Survey* (Aug 1961) 614-24.

31. *Dawn*, 30 Jul 1965.

32. Raghunath Ram, *Soviet Attitude and Policy Towards Pakistan 1947-1968*, Ph. D. Thesis of Jawaharlal Nehru University, New Delhi, 1973, 189.

33. See J.P. Jain, *China Pakistan and Bangladesh* (New Delhi, 1974) 117-8.

34. Zubeida Hasan, n. 3 31.

CHAPTER 5

1. *Pakistan Times*, 27 Sep 1966.

2. *Times of India*, 30 Mar 1966.

3. *Pakistan Times*, 4 Jul 1966.

4. *Ibid.*, 6 Nov 1968.

5. *Dawn*, 24 Jan 1968.

6. *Pakistan Times*, 5 May 1968.

7. N. Kuznetsov, "Soviet-Pakistan Ties Growing," *Dawn*, 17 Apr 1968.

8. *Pakistan Times*, 17 Apr 1968.

9. H.K. Burki, "Basis of Pak-Soviet Relations," *Ibid.*, 7 Nov 1967.

10. Z.A. Bhutto, *The Myth of Independence* (London, 1969) 58.

11. Mohammad Ayub Khan, *Friends Not Masters* (London, 1967) 118-9.

12. Z.A. Bhutto, n. 10, 145.

13. *Ibid.*, 76-7.

14. Quoted in *Times of India*, 8 Nov 1968.

15. *Pakistan Times*, 16 Feb 1967.

16. Selig S. Harrison, "Troubled India and Her Neighbours," *Foreign Affairs* (New York) (Jan 1965) 326. From 1955 to April 1963, the Soviet Government agreed to give India Rs. 5 billion in aid. In 1965-66, the Soviet Union became the largest single supplier of military weapons to India, while its military aid to India between 1960-65 amounted to over $300 million. On 10 August 1966, Pakistan's Foreign Minister revealed that India's arms purchases included 600 tanks from East European countries. Khalida Qureshi, "Arms Aid to India and Pakistan," *Pakistan Horizon* (1967) 148 and 150.

17. Mohammed Ayoob, "Soviet Arms Aid to Pakistan," *Economic and Political Weekly* (19 Oct 1968) 1613-4.

18. *Morning News*, 27 Sep 1967.

19. *Dawn*, 27 Sep 1967.

20. *Pakistan Times*, 30 Sep 1967.

21. *Keesings, Contemporary Archives*, 22345-6.

22. *Dawn*, 26 Sep 1967.

23. *Pakistan Times*, 11 Feb 1968.

24. *Ibid.*, 8 Feb 1968.

25. *Dawn*, 5 Oct 1967.

26. *Ibid.*, 26 Nov 1966.

27. B. Pyadyshev, "New Developments in Pakistan," *International Affairs* (Moscow) (Jun 1968) 78. Emphasis added.

28. The serving of the notice of termination of the base to the US Government on 6 April 1968 was described by the Pakistani Foreign Minister as "in keeping with our policy of developing bilateral relations of friendship and mutual understanding with all countries." *Morning News*, 22 May 1968. For text of the agreement see *United Nations Treaty Series*, No. 5087. If the notice had not been given, the agreement would automatically have been renewed for another 10-year period. The base, about 675 miles south of Tyuratam—the principal Soviet missile centre—has been used as a major United States advance station for monitoring Soviet missile developments. It served as the take-off point for Maj. Francis Gary Power's ill-fated U-2 flight across the Soviet Union in May 1960, and had also been used for the collection and analysis of electronic intelligence in Soviet radar and codes. *New York Times*, 15 and 20 May 1968.

29. *Morning News*, 18 Apr 1968.

30. *Pakistan Horizon* (1968) 153.

31. *Morning News*, 19 Apr 1968.

32. Bhabani Sen Gupta, *The Fulcrum of Asia* (New York, 1970) 271-2.

33. *Morning News*, 22 Apr 1968.

34. *Dawn*, 22 Jul 1968.

35. *Foreign Affairs Record* (New Delhi) (Jul 1968) 152.

36. Wynfred Joshua and Stephen P. Gilbert, *Arms for the Third World* : *Soviet Military Aid Diplomacy* (London, 1969) 102. According to R. Rama Rao, Pakistan had obtained 250 T-55 tanks, AA guided missiles, field and medium artillery pieces, communication and miscellaneous equipment valued over Rs. 50 crores from Russia. "There is as yet no evidence that these supplies were made on a no-cost basis." R. Rama Rao, "Pakistan Re-arms," *India Quarterly* (Apr-Jun 1971) 141.

37. *Pakistan Times*, 18 Jul 1968.

38. Zubeida Hasan, "Pakistan's Relations with the USSR in the 1960's," *World Today* (Jan 1969) 33. Commenting on the Soviet arms deal with Pakistan, *Pakistan Observer*'s political commentator observed : "One widely held belief is that the arms that would be supplied by Russia to Pakistan would mainly be of a defensive nature—helicopters, transport vehicles and spare parts. But the fact remains that Russia has agreed to supply arms of whatever nature to Pakistan, unthinkable a few years back. This new political equation has great significance for the future. It is interesting and instructive to speculate about the future of the tripartite relation between Russia, India and Pakistan as a result of this latest political development. China does not immediately come in, though its long-term effect on Pak-China friendship cannot be ignored .....If the present trend in Pak-Soviet friendship continues, Russian role as a mediator in the Kashmir dispute will not be liked by India. The Soviet political influence in India has already been eroded a great deal by the arms supply decision. Risking India's friendship by deciding to supply arms to Pakistan will Russia be able to wean away Pakistan from China ? It will depend on the degree of closeness Russia can achieve with Pakistan. It may also be that India may go completely into the arms of the West. The pro-West lobby in India has already started clamouring for still closer ties with the West." *Pakistan Observer*, 15 Jul 1968.

39. Joseph Lelyveld, "Kosygin Brings Smiles But No Concessions," *New York Times*, 21 Apr 1968.

40. *Pakistan Times*, 11 Jul 1968.

41. *Dawn*, 12 Mar 1969.

42. *Ibid.*, 11 Mar 1969.

43. *Pakistan Horizon* (1969) 184.

44. Kosygin's message to Yahya Khan, 9 April 1969. *Ibid.*, 185.

45. *Ibid.*, 186.

46. Pakistan National Assembly, *Debates* (14 Mar 1966) 360.

47. *Pakistan Times*, 17 Dec 1967.

48. *Dawn*, 7 Mar 1968.

49. *Pakistan Times*, 1 Jun 1968. The Soviet Union was linked up with Pakistan with the completion of a modern road in July 1970 which ran through Afghanistan and Quetta. Institute for Defence Studies & Analyses, *India in World Strategic Environment* : *Annual Review, Vol I, 1970-71* (New Delhi, 1972) 416.

50. *Hindustan Times*, 17 Jun 1968.

51. *Dawn*, 17 Jun 1968.

52. Quoted in A.P. Jain, ed., *India and the World* (Delhi, 1972) 195.

53. See J.P. Jain, *China Pakistan and Bangladesh* (New Delhi, 1974) 153-5.

54. *Pakistan Horizon* (1969) 401-2.

55. *Asian Recorder*, 9447.

56. *Ibid.*, 9714.

57. *Dawn*, 27 Jun 1970.

58. *Ibid.*, 26 and 27 Jun 1970. The loan was repayable over a 12-year period in Pakistani goods.

59. *Ibid.*, 10 Feb 1971.

60. *Ibid.*, 15 Apr 1968.

61. *Pakistan Times*, 17 Jan 1963.

CHAPTER 6

1. K. Sarwar Hasan, ed., *The Transfer of Power* (Karachi, 1966) 19-20.

2. India, Ministry of External Affairs, *Bangladesh Documents* (Madras undated) 16.

3. *Ibid.*, 11-2.

4. Sheikh Mujibur Rahman, "6-Point Formula—Our Right to Live," *Ibid.*, 31.

5. *Ibid.*, 715.

6. *Ibid.*, 12

7. *Ibid.*, 32. The position in the Central Secretariat, according to a pamphlet circulated by Opposition leaders in 1966, was as follows :

	West Pakistanis	East Pakistanis
Secretaries	42	None
Joint Secretaries	22	8
Deputy Secretaries	59	23
Section Officers	325	50
Gazetted Officers (Class I)	3769	811
Gazetted Officers (Class II)	4805	884

Times of India, 14 Jun 1966.

8. The former Chief Ministers of East Pakistan, Ataur Rehman Khan and Nurul Amin, welcomed the Tashkent Declaration. A.R. Khan described

it as a "welcome relief in the suffocating atmosphere prevailing between the two countries." Nurul Amin called Lal Bahadur Shastri "a martyr to the cause for peace." The Nizam-e-Islami Party General Secretary, Maulvi Farid Ahmed, declared that it "paves the way and opens broader horizons of understanding between the two great neighbours of Asia." Cited in Sangat Singh, *Pakistan's Foreign Policy* (Bombay, 1970) 66-7. Even Suhrawardy once remarked that for the East Pakistanis neither the Kashmir problems (for which the 1948 and 1965 wars against India were fought) was important nor the canal water dispute. The Awami League mouthpiece, *Ittefaq*, considered the Tashkent Declaration "a positive step towards improving Indo-Pakistan relations" and "a meaningful attempt for restoring peace in this sub-continent." While disagreeing with those who believed that East Pakistan was left untouched by India because of the threat from China, the paper observed: "We do not expect that East Bengal should be taken care of by any super power as it has happened in Vietnam." Tapan Das, *Sino-Pak Collusion and U.S. Policy* (Bombay, 1972) 120.

9. Shabbir Hussain, *Lengthening Shadows* (Rawalpindi, 1970).

10. See Statement by Mazamur Rahmad Chowdhury, Pakistan National Assembly, *Debates,* 15 Mar 1966 and Statement by Aminul Islam Chowdhury, *Ibid.,* 477.

11. *Pakistan Observer*, 18 Feb 1971. Cited in *Bangladesh Documents*, n.2, 163,

12. *Ibid.,* 23-4 and 35.

13. Letter of the Central Committee of the Communist Party of East Pakistan to Fraternal Communist and Workers Parties, 3 May 1971. *Ibid.,* 313-4.

14. *Ibid.,* 718.

15. *Ibid.,* 66-82.

16. Mujib's statement to the press, 24 Feb 1971. *Ibid.,* 172.

17. *Ibid.,* 167.

18. *Ibid.,* 316-7.

19. *Times of India*, 4 Dec 1971.

20. Radio Peace and Progress, Tashkent. Cited in *News Review on China* (Dec 1971) 49.

21. V. Mayevsky, "Tashkent Declaration Serves Peace," *Pravda*, 10 Jan 1971. Reproduced in *Soviet Review* (19 Jan 1971) 31.

22. *Pravda*, 27 Feb 1971. Reproduced in *Ibid.*, (16 Mar 1971) 21.

23. UN Document S/PV. 1607, 112.

24. *Bangladesh Documents*, n. 2, 511.

25. *Komsomolskaya Pravda*, 2 Apr 1971.

26. *Bangladesh Documents*, n. 2, 512.

27. *Times of India*, 12 Aug 1971.

28. L. Rushbrook Williams, *The East Pakistan Tragedy* (London, 1972) 88.

29. *Soviet Review* (18 Jan 1972) Supplement, 10.

30. *Bangladesh Documents*, n. 2, 718-9.

31. Statement at luncheon in Moscow, 28 September 1971. *Soviet Review* (12 Oct 1971) 36.

32. *Ibid.,* 34 and 41.

33. *Amrita Bazar Patrika*, 3 Oct 1971.

34. *New Times*, No. 42 (Oct 1971) 37.

35. K.D. Kapur, *The Soviet Union and the Emegernce of Bangladesh*, M. Phil. Dissertation of Jawaharlal Nehru University, New Delhi, 1973.

36. *Soviet Review* (26 Oct 1971) 29-32.

37. *Ibid.*, (2 Nov 1971) 47.

38. P. Mezentsev, "For a Peaceful Settlement on the Indian Subcontinent," *Pravda*, 23 Nov 1971. Reproduced in *Soviet Review*, n. 29, 32-4.

39. *Ibid.*, 35-8.

40. UN Document A/C.3/SR. 1876, 12.

41. Indian Foreign Minister's written answer in the *Rajya Sabha*, 7 April 1971. *Times of India*, 8 Apr 1971.

42. *Soviet Review*, n. 29, 52-3.

43. *Hindustan Times*, 6 Dec 1971.

44. UN Document S/PV. 1607, 82-5.

45. *Ibid.*, 113-5.

46. *Soviet Review*, n. 29, 41-2.

47. *Ibid.*, 43-5.

48. *Ibid.*, 55.

49. *Pravda*, 9 Dec 1972, as translated in the *Current Digest of the Soviet Press* (4 Jan 1973) 4.

50. *The Statesman*, 10 Dec 1971. Cited in *News Review on China* (Dec 1971) 49.

51. *Ibid.*, 50.

52. *Current Digest of the Soviet Press* (11 Jan 1972) 8-9 and 17.

53. *News Review on China* (Dec 1971) 50-1.

54. UN Document S/PV. 1617.

55. *Ibid.*, 1621.

56. *Soviet Review*, n. 29, 73.

57. UN Document S/PV. 1606.

58. *Bangladesh Documents*, Vol. II, 505-10.

59. UN Document S/PV. 1613.

60. *Ibid.*, 1615.

61. *Soviet Review*, n. 29, 68-72.

62. *Ibid.*, 87-91.

63. Dmitry Volsky, "Now that the Guns are Silent," *New Times*, No. 52 (Dec 1971) 9-10.

64. *Bangladesh Documents*, n. 58, 221.

65. G. Yakubov, "Conflict in Hindustan and the Provocative Role of Mao's Group," *Pravda*, 28 Dec 1971. Reproduced in *Soviet Review* (4 Jan 1972) 38-42.

66. *Ibid.*, (8 Aug 1972) 38.

CHAPTER 7

1. Zubeida Mustafa, "The USSR and the Indo-Pakistan War, 1971," *Pakistan Horizon* (1972) 48.

2. *Dawn*, 12 Jan 1972.

3. D. Vostokov, "The Foreign Policy of the People's Republic of China Since the 9th Congress of the CPC," *International Affairs* (Moscow) (Jan 1972) 27.

4. *Ibid.*, 28.

5. *Patriot*, 15 Mar 1972.

6. *Times of India*, 18 Mar 1972.

7. Institute for Defence Studies and Analyses, *News Review on South Asia* (March 1972) 80-2.

8. *Current Digest of the Soviet Press* (19 Apr 1972) 7-8.

9. *Soviet Review* (New Delhi) (25 Jul 1972) 23-5.

10. *Peking Review* (2 Feb 1973) 27.

11. *Ibid.*, (2 Mar 1973) 20.

12. *Weekly Commentary and Pakistan News Digest*, 9 Mar 1973. Cited in S.M. Burke, "The Post-War Diplomacy of the Indo-Pakistan War of 1971," *Asian Survey* (Nov 1973) 1046-7.

13. *Moscow News* (17 Feb 1973) 6.

14. *Times of India*, 18 Jan and 9 Feb 1973.

15. *Economic Times* (Bombay) 11 Dec. 1972.

16. *Times of India*, 12 Mar 1973.

17. Wayne Wilcox, *The Emergence of Bangladesh* (Washington, 1973) 55.

18. *Times of india*, 23 Mar 1973.

19. *Ibid.*, 27 Feb 1973.

20. Zulfikar Ali Bhutto, "Pakistan Builds Anew, "*Foreign Affairs* (Apr 1973).

21. Saleem M.M. Qureshi, "Pakistani Nationalism Reconsidered," *Pacific Affairs* (Winter, 1972-73). Reprinted in *Strategic Digest* (Aug 1973) 60-1.

22. *Ibid.*, 70-1.

23. Basant Chatterjee, *Inside Bangladesh Today* (New Delhi, 1973) 37-8.

24. *Ibid.*, 79.

25. *Hindustan Times*, 21 May 1974.

26. UN Document A/PV 2122. Cited in J.P. Jain, *China Pakistan and Bangladesh* (New Delhi, 1974) 225-6.

27. *Wilcox*, n. 17, 5.

28. *Moscow News* (28 Apr 1973) 6.

29. Bhabani Sen Gupta, *The Fulcrum of Asia* (New York, 1970) 37.

CHAPTER 8

1. Indo-Soviet Joint Statement, 29 September 1971. See Ministry of External Affairs, *Bangladesh Documents* Vol. II (Madras, undated) 163.

2. UN Document S/PV 1608 (6 Dec 1971).

3. *Ibid.*, S/PV 1613 (13 Dec 1971).

4. *Ibid.*, S/PV 1615 (15 Dec 1971).

5. *Ibid.*, S/PV 1617. (16 Dec 1971).

6. Zubeida Mustafa, "The USSR and the Indo-Pakistan War, 1971," *Pakistan Horizon* (1972) 48.

7. *Soviet Review* (25 Jan 1972) Supplement.

8. *Times of India*, 3 Mar 1972.

9. *Hindu*, 6 Mar 1972. See also *Soviet Review* (7 Mar 1972) 3-10.

10. *Statesman*, 4 Apr 1972.

11. *Soviet Review* (31 Mar 1973) 49. Giving the impressions of his visit to Bangladesh, a Pakistani journalist, Mazhar Ali Khan, had stated that it was explained to him that the assignment of the task of clearing Chittagong harbour to the USSR was not evidence of any special relationship, since this was done because the UN was not able to find the $6 million needed for the job, and after waiting for some time, Bangladesh was compelled to seek Soviet assistance. *Dawn*, 18 to 26 Nov 1972 as reproduced in *Strategic Digest* (New Delhi) (Feb 1973) 22.

12. *Bangladesh Observer*, 10 May 1972.

13. *Hong Kong Standard*, 1 Jun 1972.

14. UN Document S/PV 1659 (24 Aug 1972).

15. *Ibid.*, S/PV 1660.

16. *Ibid.*, A/PV 2093. Emphasis added.

17. Yuri Lugovskoy, "Bangladesh Before Its First Elections," *New Times*, No. 8 (Feb 1973) 22-3.

18. *Times of India*, 23 Mar 1973.

19. *Ibid.*, 10 Mar 1973.

20. *Ibid.*, 24 and 26 May 1973.

21. *Hindustan Times*, 27 May 1974.

22. *Soviet Review* (18 Jan 1972) 92-3.

23. Kirit Bhaumik in *Times of India*, 3 and 5 Jan 1973.

24. *Hindustan Times*, 3 Jun 1974.

25. *Ibid.*, 31 Mar 1973.

26. *Ibid.*, 15 Apr 1973.

27. Justus M. Van der Kroef, "Indian Maoism , Peking and Bangladesh," *Studies in Comparative Communism* (Summer/Autumn 1972). Reprinted in *Strategic Digest* (New Delhi) (Nov 1973) 44.

28. *Ibid.*, 47 and 50.

29. Basant Chatterjee, *Inside Bangladesh Today* (New Delhi, 1973) 78.

30. Cited in *Ibid.*, 38-40.

31. Van der Kroef, n. 27, 52.

32. *Ibid.*, 52-3.

33. Basant Chatterjee, n. 29, 84.

34. Cited in *Ibid.*, 45-7.

35. Dilip Mukerjee, "The 1971 Chapter Ends," *Times of India*, 13 Apr 1974.

CHAPTER 9

1. *Pravda Ukrainy*, 7 Apr 1953. Cited in Raghunath Ram, *Soviet Attitude and Policy Towards Pakistan 1947-1968*. Ph.D. Thesis of Jawaharlal Nehru University, New Delhi, 1973, 62.

2. *Pravda* 9 Aug 1953. Cited in *Ibid.*, 51.

3. Clare Hollings Worth in *Daily Telegraph* (London) 29 Oct 1971.

4. *Economist*, 30 Oct 1971.

5. Dilip Mukerjee, *Zulfikar Ali Bhutto : Quest for Power* (Delhi, 1972) 149.

6. Wayne Wilcox, *The Emergence of Bangladesh* (Washington, 1973) 34.

7. Mohammed Ayoob and Others, *Bangladesh : A Struggle for Nationhood* (Delhi, 1971) 172.

8. Jagdish Bhagwati in *Daedalus* (Fall 1972) 33.

9. Wilcox, n. 6, 34-6.

10. *Ibid.*, 36.

11. *US Foreign Policy for the 1970's : The Emerging Structure of Peace*, A Report by President Nixon to the Congress, 9 Feb 1972 (Washington, 1972) 150.

12. Wilcox, n. 6. 46 and 54.

13. Cited in Mukerjee, n. 5, 152.

14. The official spokesman of Pakistan said that the Treaty would adversely affect the prospects of peace and hinted that a revision of policy towards Moscow might be necesssary if "vital clarifications" sought as regards the Treaty warranted it. *Ibid.*, 152.

15. Statement by Sultan Ahmad Khan, Foreign Secretary of Pakistan, 16 Aug 1971. See *Ibid.*, 152.

16. Cited in *Ibid*, 152.

17. Sheldon W. Simon, "China, the Soviet Union and the Subcontinental Balance," *Asian Survey* (Jul 1973). Reprinted in *Strategic Digest* (New Delhi) (Nov 1973) 22.

18. *Ibid.*, 22.

19. *Hindustan Times*, 9 Jun 1974.

20. Z.A. Bhutto, *The Myth of Independence* (Karachi, 1969) 180.

21. Interview with Dilip Mukerjee. See Mukerjee n.5, 215.

22. *Hindustan Times*, 20 May 1974.

23. *Ibid,*. 8 Jun 1974.

24. *Ibid.*, 14 Jun 1974.

25. Wilcox, n. 6, 40.

26. *Ibid.*, 65.

27. *Ibid.*, 68.

28. *Ibid.*, 72.

29. *Ibid.*, 77.

30. *Hindustan Times*, 11 Jun 1974.

31. *Ibid.*

Appendices

Appendix A
Tashkent Declaration, 10 January 1966

The Prime Minister of India and the President of Pakistan, having met at Tashkent and having discussed the existing relations between India and Pakistan, hereby declare their firm resolve to restore normal and peaceful relations between their countries and to promote understanding and friendly relations between their peoples. They consider the attainment of these objectives of vital importance for the welfare of the 600 million people of India and Pakistan.

I

The Prime Minister of India and the President of Pakistan agree that both sides will exert all efforts to create good neighbourly relations between India and Pakistan in accordance with the United Nations Charter. They reaffirm their obligation under the Charter not to have recourse to force and to settle their disputes through peaceful means. They considered that the interests of peace in their region and particularly in the Indo-Pakistan Sub-Continent and, indeed, the interests of the people of India and Pakistan were not served by the continuance of tension between the two countries. It was against this background that Jammu and Kashmir was discussed, and each of the sides set forth its respective position.

II

The Prime Minister of India and the President of Pakistan have agreed that all armed personnel of the two countries shall be withdrawn not later than 25 February 1966 to the positions they held prior to 5 August 1965, and both sides shall observe the cease-fire terms on the cease-fire line.

III

The Prime Minister of India and the President of Pakistan have agreed that relations between India and Pakistan shall be based on the principle of non-interference in the internal affairs of each other.

IV

The Prime Minister of India and the President of Pakistan have agreed that both sides will discourage any propaganda directed against the other country, and will encourage propaganda which promotes the development of friendly relations between the two countries.

V

The Prime Minister of India and the President of Pakistan have agreed that the High Commissioner of India to Pakistan and the High Commissioner of Pakistan to India will return to their posts and that the normal functioning of diplomatic missions of both countries will be restored. Both Governments shall observe the Vienna Convention of 1961 on Diplomatic Intercourse.

VI

The Prime Minister of India and the President of Pakistan have agreed to consider measures towards the restoration of economic and trade relations, communications, as well as cultural exchanges between India and Pakistan, and to take measures to implement the existing agreements between India and Pakistan.

VII

The Prime Minister of India and the President of Pakistan have agreed that they give instructions to their respective authorities to carry out the repatriation of the prisoners of war.

VIII

The Prime Minister of India and the President of Pakistan have agreed that the sides will continue the discussion of questions relating to the problems of refugees and evictions/illegal

immigrations. They also agreed that both sides will create conditions which will prevent the exodus of people. They further
agreed to discuss the return of the property and assets taken
over by either side in connexion with the conflict.

IX

The Prime Minister of India and the President of Pakistan
have agreed that the sides will continue meetings both at the
highest and other levels on matters of direct concern to both
countries. Both sides have recognized the need to set up joint
Indian-Pakistani bodies which will report to their Governments
in order to decide what further steps should be taken.

The Prime Minister of India and the President of Pakistan
record their feelings of deep appreciation and gratitude to the
leaders of the Soviet Union, the Soviet Government and per-
sonally to the Chairman of the Council of Ministers of the
USSR for their constructive, friendly and noble part in bringing
about the present meeting which has resulted in mutually
satisfactory results. They also express to the Government and
friendly people of Usbekistan their sincere thankfulness for their
overwhelming reception and generous hospitality.

They invite the Chairman of the Council of Ministers of the
USSR to witness this Declaration.

(*Signed*) LAL BAHADUR   (*Signed*) M.A. KHAN, F.M.
Prime Minister of India   President of Pakistan

Simla Agreement on Bilateral Relations Between India and Pakistan, 2 July 1972

1. The Government of India and the Government of Pakistan are resolved that the two countries put an end to the conflict and confrontation that have hitherto marred the relations and work for the promotion of a friendly and harmonious relationship and the establishment of durable peace in the sub-continent, so that both countries may henceforth devote their resources and energies to the pressing task of advancing the welfare of their peoples.

In order to achieve this objective, the Government of India and the Government of Pakistan have agreed as follows :

(i) That the principles and purposes of the Charter of the United Nations shall govern the relations between the two countries.

(ii) That the two countries are resolved to settle their differences by peaceful means through bilateral negotiations or by any other peaceful means mutually agreed upon between them. Pending the final settlement of any of the problems between the two countries, neither side shall unilaterally alter the situation and both shall prevent the organisation, assistance or encouragement of any acts detrimental to the maintenance of peaceful and harmonious relations.

(iii) That the pre-requisite for reconciliation, good neighbourliness and durable peace between them is a commitment by both the countries to peaceful co-existence, respect for each other's territorial integrity and sovereignty and non-interference in each other's internal affairs, on the basis of equality and mutual benefit.

(iv) That the basic issues and causes of conflict which have bedevilled the relations between the two countries for the last 25 years shall be resolved by peaceful means.

(v) That they shall always respect each other's national unity, territorial integrity, political independence and sovereign equality.

(vi) That in accordance with the Charter of the United Nations, they will refrain from the threat or use of force against the territorial integrity or political independence of each other.

2. Both Governments will take all steps within their power to prevent hostile propaganda directed against each other. Both countries will encourage the dissemination of such information as would promote the development of friendly relations between them.

3. In order progressively to restore and normalise relations between the two countries step by step, it was agreed that :

(i) Steps shall be taken to resume communications—postal telegraphic, sea, land, including border posts and air links including over-flights.

(ii) Appropriate steps shall be taken to promote travel facilities for the nationals of the other country.

(iii) Trade and cooperation in economic and agreed fields will be resumed as far as possible.

(iv) Exchange in the fields of science and culture will be promoted. In this connection, delegations from the two countries will meet from time to time to work out the necessary details.

4. In order to initiate the process of the establishment of durable peace, both the Governments agreed that :

(i) Indian and Pakistani forces shall be withdrawn to their side of the international border.

(ii) In Jammu and Kashmir the line of control resulting from the cease fire of December 17, 1971 shall be respected by both sides without prejudice to the recognised position of either side. Neither side shall seek to alter it unilaterally irrespective of mutual differences and legal interpretations. Both sides further undertake to refrain from the threat or the use of force in violation of this line.

(iii) the withdrawals shall commence upon entry into force of this Agreement and shall be completed within a period of 30 days thereafter.

5. This Agreement will be subject to ratification by both countries in accordance with their respective constitutional procedures and will come into force with effect from the date on which the Instruments of Ratification are exchanged.

6. Both Governments agree that their respective Heads will meet again at a mutually convenient time in the future and that, in the meanwhile, the representatives of the two sides will meet to discuss further the modalities and arrangements for the establishment of durable peace and normalisation of relations, including the questions of repatriation of prisoners of war and civilian internees, a final settlement of Jammu and Kashmir and the resumption of diplomatic relations.

(Indira Gandhi)   (Zulfiqar Ali Bhutto)
Prime Minister   *President,*
Republic of   *Islamic Republic of*
India   *Pakistan*

Appendix C

Exchange of Visits Between USSR and Pakisian

1. Soviet trade delegation visits Pakistan — Jul 1949
2. Five-man Soviet Writers' delegation led by M. Mikhonov visits Pakistan — Nov 1949
3. A delegation of Soviet doctors visits Pakistan — May 1951
4. Two Soviet delegates take part in the Epizootics Conference in Karachi — May 1952
5. A Pakistani Cultural delegation and a team of Pakistani doctors visit USSR — May 1952
6. Soviet representatives participate in a conference of Pakistani scientists — Jan 1954
7. A 16-member Soviet Cultural and Goodwill mission visits Pakistan — Mar-Apr 1954
8. Pakistan Economic Delegation, led by Said Hasan, Secretary, Ministry of Economic Affairs, visits USSR — Oct 1954
9. Mikoyan, First Deputy Prime Minister, visits Pakistan — Mar 1956
10. Uzbek philosopher, M. Ibrahim Mouminov, attends Pakistan Philosophy Congress — Apr 1956
11. Prof. A. Gukasayan attends the Conference of the Pakistani Medical Association — Apr 1956
12. Eight-man trade delegation, led by Deputy Minister of Foreign Trade of USSR, M.R. Kuzmin, visits Pakistan — May-Jun 1956
13. Pakistani parliamentary delegation led by Mohammed Ayub Khusro visits USSR — Jul 1956
14. Visit of Sheikh Mujibur Rahman, Special Emissary of Premier Suhrawardy, to the USSR — Sep 1956

15. Pakistani delegation representing the *Jamait Ulema-i-Pakistan* visits USSR — Jul 1957

16. Four-man delegation of scientists, led by Afzul Hussain, visits USSR — Sep 1957

17. Trade delegation, led by Secretary of Ministry of Commerce of Pakistan, Aziz Ahmed, visits USSR — Oct 1957

18. Official delegation, led by Minister of Labour, Abdul Alim, visits USSR to participate on the occasion of the 40th anniversary of the October Revolution — Nov 1957

19. 10-man Soviet parliamentary delegation, led by Minister of Agriculture, I.A. Benediktov, visits Pakistan — Jan-Feb 1958

20. A team of Soviet doctors visits Pakistan — May 1958

21. Bhutto, Pakistan's Minister for Fuel, Power and Natural Resources, visits USSR — Dec 1960

22. Zafrullah Rhan, Pakistan's Ambassador to the UN, visits USSR — Jun 1963

23. 13-man parliamentary delegation, led by Fazlul Qadir Chaudhury, visits USSR — Sep 1964

24. Foreign Minlster Bhutto visits Moscow — Jan 1965

25. President Ayub Khan visits USSR — Apr 1965

26. President Ayub visits Tashkent — Jan 1966

27. Soviet Minister of Geology visits Pakistan to participate in its National Day celebrations — Mar 1966

28. Nine-member parliamentary delegation, led by K.T. Mazurov, visits Pakistan — May-Jun 1966

29. A military delegation, led by Air Marshal Nur Khan visits USSR — Jun-Jul 1966

30. Soviet Deputy Foreign Minister, N.P. Firyubin, visits Pakistan — Sep 1966

31. A Russian tennis star and a football team visit Pakistan — Nov 1966

32. Prof. G. Sverglow visits Pakistan — Nov 1966

33. Three-man Soviet Trade Union Delegation, led by G. Podelshikov, visits Pakistan — Nov 1966

34. Soviet Minister for Geology, A.V.

	Sidorenko, visits Pakistan	—	Jan 1967
35.	Pakistani Foreign Minister Pirzada visits USSR	—	May 1967
36.	Nine-member Pak-National Assembly delegation and two other delegations from East and West Pakistan Assembly visit USSR	—	Aug 1967
37.	President Ayub's second visit to USSR		Sep-Oct 1967
38.	Premier Kosygin visits Pakistan	—	Apr 1968
39.	A high-powered delegation, led by General Yahya Khan, Commander-in-Chief of the Armed Forces, visits USSR	—	Jul 1968
40.	A Soviet Naval Squadron visits Karachi	—	Nov 1968
41.	Marshal A.A. Grechko, Defence Minister of the USSR, visits Pakistan	—	Mar 1969
42.	Premier Kosygin visits Pakistan	—	May 1969
43.	President Yahya Khan visits USSR	—	Jun 1970
44.	Pakistan's Foreign Secretary visits USSR	—	Sep 1971
45.	58-member delegation, led by President Bhutto, visits USSR	—	Mar 1972
46.	Seven-member Pak delegation visits USSR for finalizing agreement for the import of surgical instruments from USSR	—	Apr 1972
47.	Aziz Ahmed, Special Emissary of President Bhutto, visits USSR	—	Jun 1972
48.	A Soviet delegation visits Pakistan to discuss proposals for re-scheduling repayment of Soviet credits totalling $60 million	—	Dec 1972
49.	A.H. Pirzada, Special Emissary of President Bhutto, visits USSR	—	Feb 1973
50.	A six-member Soviet economic delegation visits Pakistan to discuss Pak-Soviet economic cooperation and review the position regarding the unutilized Soviet loans to Pakistan and the rescheduling of Soviet loans granted to Pakistan in 1966	—	Mar 1973
51.	Boris Fedrovik, special Soviet envoy, visits Pakistan	—	Sep 1973

Appendix D

Agreements Between USSR and Pakistan

1. Direct Karachi-Moscow radio-telegraph link established — 6 Jun 1952

2. Barter agreement providing for the supply of 150,000 tons of wheat to Pakistan in exchange for 22,000 tons of raw jute and 13,150 tons of cotton from Pakistan — 16 Sep 1952

3. Gift of Rs. 60,000 for flood victims of East Pakistan from Soviet Societies — Aug 1955

4. Offer of 40 tons of foodgrains for the flood-affected people in East Pakistan by the Soviet Government — May 1956

5. Soviet gift of 16,5000 tons of rice to help Pakistan tide over its food crisis — 15 Jun 1956

6. Trade agreement providing for most-favoured-nation treatment to each other — 27 Jun 1956

7. Cheque of Rs. 10,000 from Soviet Societies to Liaquat Ali Hospital — 14 Mar 1957

8. Second barter agreement signed in Karachi — 30 Nov 1959

9. Pakistan accepts Soviet offer of assistance in the exploitation of mineral resources — Aug 1960

10. Agreement providing for $30 million Soviet credit for prospecting of oil in Pakistan — 4 Mar 1961

11. Five-year contract for the supply of Soviet equipment for oil and gas exploration — 3 Jul 1961

12. Soviet loan of £11 million — Aug 1963

13. Barter trade agreement providing for a total trade of Rs. 10 million a year — 30 Aug 1963

14. Air Transport Agreement   —   7 Oct 1963
15. Agreement on a cultural and scientific exchange programme for 1964   —   11 Jun 1964
16. Credit agreement providing for $11 million Soviet loan for the purchase of earth-moving machinery, rotary drilling machinery, etc.   —   17 Jun 1964
17. A Trade Agreement on commodity-exchange; a protocol on the delivery of Soviet machinery and equipment; an agreement on cultural exchange; a Soviet credit of Rs. 150-250 million for the purchase of Soviet machinery by Pakistan for its Third Five-Year Plan   —   Apr 1965
18. Three-year trade agreement envisaging doubling of Soviet-Pakistani trade by 1967   —   7 Apr 1965
19. Credit agreement providing for $30 million loan (subsequently raised to $50 million) to Pakistan for its Third Five-Year Plan   —   7 Apr 1965
20. Cultural Agreement providing for exchange of scholars, scientists, artists, sportsmen etc.   —   5 Jun 1965
21. Soviet supply of Rs. 1.5 crores worth of machinery on credit for the construction of an airport in Pakistan   —   Aug 1965
22. Barter agreement envisaging three-fold expansion in trade   —   18 Jan 1966
23. Agreement providing for Soviet supply of 140 bulldozers and 20 heavy trailers with prime movers   —   4 Apr 1966
24. Another agreement for Soviet supply of 260 bulldozers with spare parts   —   11 Apr 1966
25. Programme for exchange of writers, journalists, scientists, sportsmen and artists approved   —   22 Apr 1966
26. Contract for the construction of a 110,000 kw Thermal Power Station at Gorzala by the USSR   —   Jul 1966
27. Agreement on economic cooperation providing for Soviet assistance in the construction of 21 projects and a

long-term credit of Rs. 200 million and a commercial credit of Rs. 300 million at 2.5 per cent interest to finance those projects	—	Sep 1966
28. Agreement providing for a "substantial increase" in USSR-Pak trade for 1967	—	30 Jan 1967
29. Soviet assistance for the setting up a factory for the assembly of 5,000 tractors every year announced	—	4 Feb 1967
30. Agreement for technical assistance to work out plans for the proposed heavy electrical complex in West Pakistan	—	1 Apr 1967
31. Agreement for the establishment of a heavy electrical equipment complex in East Pakistan	—	19 Apr 1967
32. Agreement for the supply of 44,000 tons of Pakistani *basmati* rice valued at Rs. 5 crores in return for Soviet supply of edible oil and fertilizers	—	1 Jan 1968
33. Three-year trade agreement providing for Rs. 90 million, Rs. 100 million and Rs. 110 million worth of trade during 1968, 1969 and 1970 respectively. 50 per cent of Pakistan's exports to comprise manufactured goods	—	28 Feb 1968
34. Agreement providing for Soviet technical and economic assistance in the construction of a steel mill at Kalabagh in West Pakistan, a nuclear power station in Roopur in East Pakistan, a radio link between Moscow and Karachi and a fishery development project	—	Apr 1968
35. Cultural and Scientific Cooperation Agreement	—	20 Apr 1968
36. Soviet credit of $66 million for the purchase of capital goods	—	Jul 1968
37. Agreement providing for the exchange of goods valued at Rs. 110 million each way during 1970	—	7 Dec 1969
38. Ten-year agreement on collaboration in the peaceful uses of atomic energy	—	20 May 1970
39. Soviet loan of $200 million for financ-		

ing the cost of machinery and equipment for the Karachi Steel Mill with
a capacity of one million tons of steel
annually   —   Jun 1970

40. Four-year Agreement (1971-75) providing for "considerable growth" in
the volume of trade   —   Dec 1970

41. Trade agreement for the exchange of
a wide variety of goods during 1972   —   5 May 1972

42. Cultural agreement providing for
the exchange of scientists, teachers, students, artists, films, books and radio
and television programmes   —   Feb 1973

43. Agreement releasing Pakistan from
the obligation to repay credits utilized
in Bangladesh when it was East
Pakistan   —   Mar 1973

44. Three-year trade agreement   —   27 Apr 1973

Appendix E

Pakistan's Trade with the USSR
(In millions of Pakistani Rupees)

Year	Pakistan's Imports	Pakistan's Exports
1951-52	1.1	21.5
1952-53	.5	62.5
1953-54	.2	12.0
1954-55	1.0	—
1955-56	.7	.01
1956-57	3.4	6.9
1957-58	6.7	29.1
1958-59	8.8	21.4
1959-60	12.5	30.3
1960-61	25.0	14.2
1961-62	12.5	18.8
1962-63	22.4	39.0
1963-64	40.5	12.8
1964-65	63.0	11.7
1965-66	67.9	80.0
1966-67	179.2	130.4
1967-68	146.3	39.0
1968-69	141.4	109.1
1969-70	135.1	108.3
1970-71	133.2	176.3
1971-72	Not Available	Not Available
1972-73	165.3	222.6

Source : Government of Pakistan, Ministry of Finance Planning and Development, *25 Years of Pakistan in Statistics 1947-1972* (Karachi 1972) 388-9 and 396-7; and *Monthly Statistical Buletin* (Karachi) (July 1973) 595.

Appendix F

Exchange of Visits Between USSR and Bangladesh

1. A Soviet economic delegation, led by V.V. Zverve, visits Bangladesh — Dec 1971
2. A four-member Soviet economic delegation visits Bangladesh — Feb 1972
3. Sheikh Mujibur Rahman visits USSR — Mar 1972
4. Soviet salvage delegation visits Bangladesh — Mar 1972
5. M.R. Siddiqui, Bangladesh's Foreign Trade Minister, visits USSR — Apr 1972
6. A four-member Soviet oil expert team visits Bangladesh — May 1972
7. Syed Nazrul Islam, Minister for Industries, visits USSR to participate in the 50th anniversary of the founding of the USSR — Dec 1972
8. A three-member Bangladeshi delegation visits USSR to attend a meeting of the Preparatory Committee for World Fighters for Peace, Security and National Independence — Mar 1973
9. Soviet delegation, led by Kamalov, visits Bangladesh to attend the Asian Peace Conference — May 1973
10. Sheikh Mujibur Rahman visits USSR — Apr 1974
11. 17-member Soviet economic delegation, led by V. Sergeev, Soviet Deputy Minister for Foreign Economic Relations, visits Dacca — Apr 1974
12. Dr. Kamal Hossain, Foreign Minister of Bangladesh, visits USSR — May 1974

Agreements Between USSR and Bangladesh

1. Barter Agreement : Exchange of Russian materials and equipment for traditional exports of Bangladesh worth Rs. 20 crores both ways — 7 Feb 1972

2. Soviet airline, *Aeroflot*, inaugurates a weekly Moscow-Dacca service — 7 Feb 1972

3. USSR unlocks the flow of aid amounting to 38 million roubles (Rs. 3.80 crores) previously negotiated with Pakistan — 2 Mar 1972

4. USSR earmarks 5 million roubles for commodity assistance to Bangladesh — Mar 1972

5. Agreement for Soviet assistance in the construction of a thermal power station, a radio broadcasting station, an electrical equipment plant and other projects — Mar 1972

6. Agreement for free Soviet assistance for restoring normal conditions for navigation in the seaports of Bangladesh — 22 Mar 1972

7. Three-year Trade Agreement (1972-75) providing for the supply of aircraft and machinery and edible oil by the USSR to Bangladesh for jute and leather — Apr 1972

8. "Imatra," a 1,300-ton ocean-going cargoship handed over to Bangladesh by USSR — May 1972

9. Agreement for the exchange of radio and television programmes — 22 Nov 1972

10. Agreement providing 38 million rouble aid for the exploration

	of oil and gas in Bangladesh	—	17 Dec 1972
11.	Cultural Agreement providing for the exchange of personnel and know-how	—	Dec 1972
12.	Agreement providing for the supply of equipment and materials for the installation of a third generator of 215,000 kw at the Guddu Thermal Power Station	—	2 Jun 1973
13.	Air-service agreement granting air landing facility to *Bangladesh Biman* at Moscow and Tashkent and to *Aeroflot* in Dacca	—	23 Aug 1973

Select Bibliography

BOOKS

Ahmad, Mustaq, *The United Nations and Pakistan* (Karachi, 1955).

———, *Pakistan's Foreign Policy* (Karachi, 1968).

Ahmad, Nafis, *The Basis of Pakistan* (Calcutta, 1947).

Ahmed, Jamiluddin, ed., *Some Recent Speeches and Writings of Mr. Jinnah*, Vol. 1 (Lahore, 1952).

Ahmed, Manzoorddin, *Pakistan : The Emerging Islamic State* (Karachi, 1966).

Ali, Ahmed, *Muslim China* (Karachi, 1949).

Ali, Tariq, *Pakistan : Military Rule or People's Powers* (Delhi, 1971).

Ayoob, Mohammed and Others, *Bangladesh : A Struggle for Nationhood* (Delhi, 1971).

Ayoob, M. and Subrahmanyam, K., *The Liberation War* (New Delhi, 1972).

Balabushevich, V.V., and Dyakov, A.M., *A Contemporary History of India* (Moscow, 1964).

Bhutto, Z.A., *Foreign Policy of Pakistan* (Collection of Speeches) (Karachi, 1964).

———, *Important Speeches and Press Conferences of Zulfikar Ali Bhutto* (Karachi, 1960).

———, *The Great Tragedy* (Karachi, 1971).

———, *The Myth of Independence* (Karachi, 1969).

———, *The Political Situation of Pakistan* (1968).

Binder, Leonard, *Religion and Politics in Pakistan* (California, 1961).

Bol'shaia Sovetskaia Entsiklopediia, Vol. 15 (Moscow, 12 Sep 1952).

Bol'shaia Sovetskaia Entsiklopediia, Vol. 18 (Moscow, 8 Jan 1953).

Bulganin, N.A., and Khrushchov, N.S., *Visit of Friendship to India, Burma and Afghanistan* (Moscow, 1956).

———, *Speeches During Sojourn in India, Burma and Afghanistan* (Representative of *Tass* in India, New Delhi, 1956).

Burke, S.M., *Pakistan's Foreign Policy : An Historical Analysis* (London, 1973).

Callard, Keith, *Pakistan : A Political Study* (London, 1957).

———, *Political Forces in Pakistan : 1947-1959* (New York, 1959).

Chatterjee, Basant, *Inside Bangladesh Today : An Eye-Witness Account* (New Delhi, 1973).

Chaudhri, Mohammed Ahsen, *Pakistan and the Great Powers* (Karachi, 1970).

————, *Pakistan and the Regional Pacts* (Karachi, 1958).

Chopra, Pran, ed., *The Challenge of Bangladesh* (Bombay, 1971).

Choudhury, G. W., *Constitutional Development in Pakistan* (London, 1969).

————, *Pakistan's Relations with India 1947-1966* (London, 1968).

Choudhury, G.W. and Hasan, Parvez, *Pakistan's External Relations* (Karachi, 1958).

Choudhury, Rahmat Ali, *Pakistan : The Fatherland of the Pak Nation* (Cambridge, England, 1947).

Druhe, David N., *Soviet Russia and Indian Communism* (New York, 1959)

Dyakov, A., *India vo Vremia i Posle Vtoroi Mirovoi Voiny 1939-1949* (Moscow, 1951).

————, *The National Problem in India Today* (Moscow, 1966).

Faruqi, M.I., *Jama'at-e-Islami, Pakistan* (Lahore, 1957).

Feldman, Herbert, *From Crisis to Crisis ; Pakistan 1962-69* (London, 1972).

Frederiksen, Oliver J., ed., *The Problem of Soviet Foreign Policy* (Munich, 1959).

Gankovsky, Y.V. and Polonskaya, Gordon, *A History of Pakistan* (Moscow, 1965).

Ghulam Muhammed, Chaudhury, *Jama'at-e-Islami and Foreign Policy* (Karachi, undated).

Goswami, B.N., *Pakistan and China* (New Delhi, 1971).

Government of Pakistan, Department of Advertising, Films & Publications, *Foreign Relations* (Karachi, 1956).

Government of Pakistan, Department of Publications, *Prime Minister's Statement on Foreign Policy* (Karachi, 1956).

Greeve, Fred, *U.S. Policy and the Security of Asia* (New York, 1968).

Hasan, K. Sarwar, *Pakistan and the United Nations* (New York, 1960).

————, *The Strategic Interests of Pakistan* (Karachi, 1954).

————, ed., *The Transfer of Power* (Karachi, 1966).

Husain, Muhammad, *East Pakistan : A Cultural Survey* (Karachi, 1955).

Husain, Syed Sajjad, ed., *East Pakistan : A Profile* (Dacca, 1962).

Husain, S. Shabbir, *Lengthening Shadows* (Rawalpindi, 1970).

Hussain, Arif, *Pakistan, Its Ideology and Foreign Policy* (London, 1966).

Ikram, S.M., *Modern Muslim India and Birth of Pakistan* (Lahore, 1965).

India, Ministry of External Affairs, *Bangladesh : Documents I and II* (Madras, undated).

Jahan, Rounaq, *Political Integration and Political Development in Pakistan* (New York, 1972).

Jain, A.P., ed., *India and the World* (Delhi, 1972).

Jain, J.P., *China Pakistan and Bangladesh* (New Delhi, 1974).

Joshi, Nirmala, *India and the Soviet Union : A Study of Non-Official Attitudes and Contacts 1917-47*, Ph.D Thesis of Jawaharlal Nehru University, New Delhi, 1973.

Joshi, P.C., *The Indian Communist Party* (London, 1942).

Joshua, Wynfred and Gilbert, Stephen P., *Arms for the Third World : Soviet Military Aid Diplomacy* (London, 1969).

Kapur, K.D., *The Soviet Union and the Emergence of the Bangladesh,*

M.Phil. Dissertation of the Jawaharlal Nehru University, New Delhi, 1973.

Kaushik, Devendra, *Soviet Relations with India and Pakistan* (Delhi, 1971).

Kautsky, John H., *Moscow and the Communist Party of India* (New York, 1956).

Khan, Liaquat Ali, *Pakistan : Heart of Asia* (Cambridge, 1951).

Khan, Maj-Gen. Fazal Muqeem, *The Story of the Pakistan Army* (Karachi, 1963).

Khan Mohammad Ayub, *Friends Not Masters* (Karachi, 1967).

————, *Speeches and Statements*, Vol. VII, Jul 1964-Jun 1965 (Karachi, undated).

Khan, Muin-ud-Din Ahmad, *Muslim Struggle for Freedom in Bengal* (1757-1947) (Dacca, 1955).

Malik, Hafeez, *Moslem Nationalism in India and Pakistan* (Washington, 1963).

Mallick, A.R., *British Policy and the Muslims in Bengal 1757-1856* (Dacca, 1961).

Maudoodi, Maulana, *Islamic Law and Constitution* (Lahore, 1967).

Menon, K.P.S., *The Lamp and the Lampstand* (London, 1967).

Moraes, Dom, *The Tempest Within* (New Delhi, 1971).

Mukerjee, Dilip, *Zulfikar Ali Bhutto : Quest for Power* (Delhi, 1972).

Muller, Kurt, *The Foreign Aid Programmes of the Soviet Bloc and Communist China* (New York, 1967).

Murphy, Joseph A., *Pakistan-Soviet Relations with Emphasis on Recent Developments*, Columbia University Thesis, 1955.

Naik, J.A., *India, Russia, China and Bangladesh* (New Delhi, 1972).

————, *Soviet Policy Towards India, From Stalin to Brezhnev* (Delhi, 1970).

National Awami Party, *Resolutions* (Dacca, 1968).

Overstreet, Gene D., and Windmiller, Marshall, *Communism in India* (Berkeley, 1959).

Palit, D.K., *The Lightning Campaign* (Salisbury, 1972).

Pirzada, Syed Sharifuddin, *Evolution of Pakistan* (Lahore, 1963).

Qureshi, Ishtiaq H., *The Muslim Community of the Indo-Pakistan Sub-continent* (The Hugue, 1962).

Raghunath Ram, *Soviet Attitude and Policy Towards Pakistan 1947-1968*, Ph. D. Thesis of Jawaharlal Nehru University, New Delhi, 1973.

Rahman, Fazlur, *Pakistan One and Indivisible* (Karachi, 1960).

Rahman, M., Akhlaqur, *Partition, Integration, Economic Growth and Inter-Regional Trade : A Study of Interwing Trade in Pakistan, 1948-59* (Karachi, 1963).

Rahman, Muhammad Anisur, *East and West Pakistan : A Problem in the Political Economy of Regional Planning* (Cambridge, 1968).

Rajan, M.S., ed., *Studies in Politics : National and International* (Delhi, 1971).

Rajput, A.B., *Muslim League : Yesterday and Today* (Lahore, 1948).

Ray, Jayanta Kumar, *Democracy and Nationalism on Trial* (Calcutta, 1968).

Rose, Saul, ed., *Politics in Southeast Asia* (London, 1963).

Rubinstein, Alvin Z., *The Foreign Policy of the Soviet Union* (New York, 1960).

Sen Gupta, Bhabani, *The Fulcrum of Asia* (New York, 1970).

Sherwani, Latif Ahmed, *Foreign Policy of Pakistan : An Analysis* (Karachi, 1964).

Siddiqi, Aslam, *Pakistan Seeks Security* (London, 1960).

Siddiqi, Kalim, *Conflict, Crisis and War in Pakistan* (London, 1972).

Singh, Sangat, *Pakistan's Foreign Policy* (Bombay, 1970).

Smith, Cantwell W., *Islam in Modern History* (Princeton, 1957).

Soward, F.H. and Fowler, R.M., *The Changing Commonwealth*, Proceedings of the Fourth Unofficial Commonwealth Relations Conference, 1949 (Toronto, 1950).

Spector, Iver, *The Soviet Union and the Muslim World 1917-56* (Washington, 1956).

Stalin, J.V., *Marxism and the National and Colonial Question* (London, 1947).

Stein, Arthur, *India and the Soviet Union : The Nehru Era* (Chicago, 1969).

Stern, J.J., and Falcon, W.P., *Growth and Development in Pakistan* (Cambridge, Mass, 1970).

Suleri, Z.A., *Politicians and Ayub* (Lahore, 1965).

Umar, Badruddin, *Sanskritik Sampradayikta* (*Communalism in Culture* (Dacca, 1969).

US Foreign Policy for the 1970's : The Emerging Structure of Peace, A Report by President Nixon to the Congress, 9 Feb 1972 (Washington, 1972).

Williams, Rushbrook L.F., *The East Pakistan Tragedy* (London, 1972).

——, *The State of Pakistan* (London, 1962).

Wheeler, Geoffrey, *Racial Problems in Soviet Muslim Asia* (London, 1962).

Wilcox, Wayne A., *Pakistan : The Consolidation of a Nation* (New York, 1963).

——, *The Emergence of Bangladesh* (Washington, 1973).

Zafar, S.M., *Through the Crisis* (Lahore, 1970).

Zaheer, Sajjad, *A Case for Congress-League Unity* (Bombay, 1944).

Ziring, Lawrence, *The Ayub Khan Era : Politics in Pakistan, 1958-1969* (New York, 1971).

——, *The Failure of Democracy in Pakistan : East Pakistan and the Central Government, 1947-58*, Ph.D. Thesis, Columbia University, 1962.

ARTICLES

Alexeyer, A., "The Political Situation in Pakistan," *New Times*, No. 510 (1951).

A Group Study, "Pakistan's Relations with the USSR," *Pakistan Horizon* (Oct 1961).

Ashe, B., "Political Parties in India," *World News and Views* (30 Dec 1939).

Ayoob, Mohammed, "Pakistan's Trade Relations with the Soviet Union," *International Studies* (Jul 1969).

——, "Soviet Arms Aid to Pakistan," *Economic and Political Weekly* (19 Oct 1968) 1613-4.

Ayub, M., ' The Foreign Policy of Pakistan,'' *Pakistan Horizon* (1964) 18-24.

Balabushevich, V., "A New Phase in the National Liberation Struggle of the People of Asia,'' *Voprosy Eknomikii*, No. 8 (6 Oct 1949).

Balabushevich, V., and Dyakov, A., "India i Vtoraia imperialisticheskaia Voina,'' *Mirovoe Khoziaistvo*, No. 12 (Dec 1940).

Barton, Sir William, "Pakistan's Claim to Kashmir," *Foreign Affairs* (Jan 1950).

Bhutto, Z.A., "Pakistan Builds Anew,'' *Foreign Affairs* (Apr 1973).

Bose, Tarun C., "American and Soviet Interests in Asia : Conflict and Cooperation,'' *International Studies* (Apr 1969-Jul 1969).

Budhraj, Vijay Sen, "The Evolution of Russia's Pakistan Policy,'' *Australian Journal of History and Politics*, No. 3 (1970).

Burke, S.M., "Sino-Pakistani Relations,'' *Orbis* (Summer 1964) 391-404.

———, "The Post-War Diplomacy of the Indo-Pakistan War of 1971,'' *Asian Survey* (Nov 1973).

Burki, H.K., "Basis of Pak-Soviet Relations,'' *Pakistan Times*, 7 Nov 1967.

Callard, Keith, "The Political Stability of Pakistan,'' *Pacific Affairs* (1956) 5-20.

Caroe, Sir Olaf, "Soviet Imperialism in Central Asia,'' *Foreign Affairs* (Oct 1953).

Chaudhri, Mohammed Ahsen, "Pakistan and the Soviet Bloc,'' *Pakistan Horizon* (Jun 1956).

———,"Pakistan's Relations with the Soviet Union,'' *Asian Survey* (Sep 1966) 492-500.

Chaudhury, G.W., "The East Pakistan Political Scene,'' *Pacific Affairs* (1957) 312-20.

Dyakov, A., "Sovremennaia India,'' *Bolshevik* (Feb 1946).

———, "Indian National Congress Leaders,'' *New Times* (15 May 1946).

———, "The New British Plan for India,'' *New Times* (13 Jun 1947).

———, "The Situation in India,'' *Pravda* (21 Oct 1946).

Dyakov, A.M., "Partitioned India,'' *New Times*, No. 3 (14 Jan 1948).

Franda, M.F., "Communism and Regional Politics in East Pakistan,'' *Asian Survey* (1970) 588-606.

Gladkov, N., "In Pakistan—Travel Impressions,'' *New Times*, No. 21 (1950).

Gopal, S., "India, China and the Soviet Union,'' *Australian Journal of Politics and History* (Aug 1966) 241-57.

Grigoryan, K.H., "The Foreign Policies of the Afro-Asian Countries,'' *International Affairs* (Moscow) (Dec 1961).

Gukasayan, A., "Glimpses of Pakistan,'' *New Times*, No. 29 (1956).

Gupta, Sisir, "Islam as a Factor in Pakistani Foreign Relations,'' *India Quarterly* (Jul-Sep 1962) 230-58.

Harrison, Salig S., "Troubled India and Her Neighbours,'' *Foreign Affairs* (Jan 1965).

Hasan, K. Sarwar, "The Foreign Policy of Mr. Liaquat Ali Khan,'' *Pakistan Horizon* (Dec 1956) 181-99.

asan, Zubeida, "Pakistan's Relations with the USSR in the 1960's,'' *World Today* (Jan 1969) 26 and 35.

————, "Soviet Arms Aid to Pakistan and India," *Pakistan Horizon* (1968) 344-55.

Hyder, Khurshid, "Pakistan's Foreign Policy," *Pakistan Quarterly* (Winter 1964) 4-12.

Imam, Zafar, "Soviet Asian Policy Today," *Contemporary Review* (Jul 1966).

Innes, F.M., "The Political Outlook in Pakistan," *Pacific Affairs* (1953) 311-4.

Ispahani, M.A.H., "Pacts and Aid," *Pakistan Horizon* (1966) 117-26.

Joseph, Ralph, "Pakistan-Soviet Relations," *Eastern World* (Mar 1965).

Kapur, Harish, "The Soviet Union and Indo-Pakistani Relations," *International Studies* (Jul-Oct 1966) 150-7.

Katserikov, D., "Deplorable Results," *International Affairs* (Moscow) (Oct 1961).

Khan, Hajeez-ur-Rahman, "Pakistan's Relations with the U.S.S.R.," *Pakistan Horizon* (1961) 35-55.

Khan, Mohammed Ayub, "The Pakistan-American Alliance," *Foreign Affairs* (Jun 1964) 195-209.

Khan, Nazir Ahmed, "A Commonwealth of Muslim Nations," *Pakistan Horizon* (1961) 103-11.

Klatt, W., "The Indian Sub-continent After the War," *World Today* (Mar 1972).

Kroef, Justus M. Van der, "Indian Maoism, Peking and Bangladesh," *Studies in Comparative Communism* (Summer-Autumn 1972).

Kuznetsov, N., "Soviet-Pakistan Ties Growing," *Dawn*, 17 Apr 1968.

Lambert, Richard D., "Factors in Bengali Regionalism in Pakistan," *Far Eastern Survey*, (1959) 49-58.

————,"Religion, Economics and Violence in Bengal," *Middle East Journal* (1950) 307-28.

Lenin, I., "Fruits of Imperialist Domination in India and Pakistan," *Voprosy Ekanomikii* (Moscow) (Jan 1952).

Lerski, George J., "The Pakistan-American Alliance : A Reevaluation of the Past Decade," *Asian Survey* (May 1968) 400-15.

Levi, Werner, "Pakistan, the Soviet Union and China," *Pacific Affairs* (Fall 1962) 211-22.

Lugovksoy, Yuri, "Bangladesh Before the First Elections," *New Times*, No. 8 (Feb 1973).

Maniruzzaman, Talukdar, "Crisis in Political Development and the Collapse of the Ayub Regime in Pakistan," *The Journal of Developing Areas* (1971) 221-38.

————,"The Leftist Movement in East Pakistan—Leadership, Factionalism, Doctrinal and Tactical Dilemmas" Unpublished paper Rajshahi University, 1970.

Maron, Stanley, "The Problems of East Pakistan," *Pacific Affairs* (1955) 132-44.

Melman, S., "Polozhenie v Indii," *Mirovoe Khoziaistvo i Mirovoia Politika* (Nov-Dec 1942).

Mikoyan, S., "Kashmir, The Apple of Discord," *Literaturnaia Gazeta (Literary Gazette)* (Moscow) (28 Oct 1965).

Mustafa, Zubeida, "The USSR and the Indo-Pakistan War, 1971," *Pakistan Horizon* (1972).

Naik, J.A., "Soviet Policy in Kashmir," *India Quarterly* (Jan-Mar 1968).

Palmer, Norman D., "India's Position in Asia," *Journal of International Affairs* (1963).

Park, Richard L., "East Bengal : Pakistan's Troubled Province," *Far Eastern Survey* (May 1954) 70-4.

Popou, Y., "Kashmir : Artificial Issue," *New Times* (7 Mar 1957) 9-10.

Pronin, A., "Pakistan Affairs," *New Times*, No. 42 (1954).

Pyadyshey, B., "New Developments in Pakistan," *International Affairs* (Moscow) (Jun 1968).

Qadir, Manzur. "The Foreign Policy of Pakistan," *Pakistan Horizon* (1960) 3-12.

Qureshi, Khalida, "The Soviet Union, Pakistan and India," *Pakistan Horizon* (1963) 344-55.

———,"Arms Aid to India and Pakistan," *Pakistan Horizon* (1967).

Qureshi, Saleem M.M., "Pakistani Nationalism Reconsidered," *Pacific Affairs* (Winter 1972-73).

Rashiduzzaman, M., "The Awami League in the Political Development of Pakistan," *Asian Survey* (1970) 574-87.

Reisner, I., "K voprosu o skladyvanii Afghanskoi natsii," *Voprosy Istorii* (Moscow) (Jul 1949).

Rubinstein, Alvin Z., "Soviet Policy in South Asia," *Current History* (Jan 1957).

Sayeed, Khalid B., "The Jama'at-i-Islami Movement in Pakistan," *Pacific Affairs* (Mar 1957) 59-68.

———,"Pakistan's Foreign Policy : An Analysis of Pakistan's Fears and Interest," *Asian Survey* (Mar 1964) 746-56.

———,"Religion and Nation-Building in Pakistan," *Middle East Journal* (1963) 279-91.

Sekhar, Chandra, "The Kashmir Issue," *International Affairs* (Moscow) (Jul 1957).

Seth, S.P., "China as a Factor in Indo-Pakistani Politics" *World Today* (Jan 1969) 36-46.

———,"Russia's Role in Indo-Pak Politics," *Asian Survey* (Aug 1969) 614-24.

Shyam, V., "Implications of Soviet-Pakistan Arms Deal," *United Asia* (Jul-Aug 1968) 227-30.

Simon, Sheldon W., "The Kashmir Dispute in Sino-Soviet Perspective," *Asian Survey* (Jan 1967).

———,"China, The Soviet Union and the Subcontinental Balance," *Asian Survey* (Jul 1973).

"Soviet Arms Supply to Pakistan," AICC *Economic Review* (1 Aug 1968) 3-4.

Suhrawardy, H.S., "Political Stability and Democracy," *Foreign Affairs* (1956-57) 422-31.

Vaidyanath, R., "Some Recent Trends in Soviet Policies Towards India and Pakistan," *International Studies* (Jan 1966) 429-37.

Venkataramani, M.S. and Arya, H.C., "America's Military Alliance with Pakistan : The Evaluation and Course of an Uneasy Partnership," *International Studies* (Jul-Oct 1966).

Volsky, Dimtry, "Pakistan's Worries," *New Times*, No. 28 (1958).

———,"Two Coups," *New Times*, No. 51 (Dec 1958).

Vostokov, D., "The Foreign Policy of the People's Republic of China Since the 9th Congress of the CPC," *International Affairs* (Moscow) (Jan 1972).

Wilcox, Wayne A., "A Decade of Ayub," *Asian Survey* (1969) 87-93.

252 Soviet Policy Towards Pakistan and Bangladesh

——,"The Pakistan Coup d'Etat of 1958," *Pacific Affairs* (1965) 142-63.

——,"Pakistan in 1969 : Once Again at the Starting Point," *Asian Survey* (1970) 73-81.

——,"Political Change in Pakistan : Structure, Function, Constraints and Goods," *Pacific Affairs* (1968) 341-54.

——,"Problems and Processes of National Integration in Pakistan," *The Pakistan Student* (Mar-Apr 1967).

Windmiller, Marshal, "Indian Communism and the New Soviet Line," *Pacific Affairs* (Dec 1956) 347-66.

Zhukov, E., "Velikaia Oktiabr'skaia Sotsialisticheskaia Revoliutsiia i Kolonialnyi Vostok," *Bolshevik* (Oct 1946).

——,"K Polozhenie v Indii," *Mirovoe Khoziaistvo* (Jul 1947).

——,"The Bandung Conference of Asian and African Countries and Its Historic Significance." *International Affairs* (Moscow) (May 1955).

Index

Afro-Asian Muslim Conference, 6-7

Agartala Conspiracy Case, 117-8

Ahmad, M.M., Deputy Chairman of Pakistani Planning Commission, 84

Ahmad, Mustaq, 35

Ahmed, Aziz, 57-8

Ahmed, Muzaffar, 163, 172, 181-2, 191

Al Ahram, 18

Al Azhar, 18

Ali, Choudhury Rahmat, 7

Ali, Mohammed, Prime Minister of Pakistan, 46
  on Kashmir, 21
  on relations with USA, 20-1
  on relations with USSR, 44

Ali, Mohsin, 90

All-Muslim Conference, 36

Asian Peace Conference, 183

Asian Relations Conference, 29

Awami League, 48-50, 121-3, 173, 192

Azad, Abdus Samad, Foreign Minister of Bangladesh, 176

Baghdad Pact, *see* CENTO

Balabushevich, V., 26

Bandung Conference, 23, 44, 47

Bangladesh
  admission into the UN, 177-9, 211
  aid from India, 184
  aid from USA, 184
  aid from USSR, 185
  Crisis, 113-47
  Soviet attitude on, 124-6, 142, 170-1
  relations with China, 189
  relations with India, 183
  relations with Pakistan, 161
  relations with USSR, 170-94
  Soviet recognition of, 173

Beglov, S., 139

Benediktov, I.A., 59

Bhashani, Maulana, 49-50, 103, 117, 119, 163, 185-6, 191, 193

Bhutto, Z.A., 1, 60, 87-8, 103, 148-9, 154-5, 159-60, 164, 203-4
  confrontation with India, 108
  on Kashmir problem, 205
  on military threat from USSR, 44
  on Pakistan's ideology, 2
  on relations with Bangladesh, 161
  on relations with China, 88
  on relations with the West, 87-8
  on Soviet proposal of Regional Economic Cooperation, 108
  on Tashkent Declaration, 89
  on trade relations with USSR, 60
  visit to Afghanistan, 149
  visit to China, 198
  visits to USSR, 60, 151-3, 166

Biswas, Abdul Latif, 116

Borosov, I., 133

Brezhnev, L.I., 77, 83, 153, 195

Bulganin, Marshal A., 59, 62
  on Pakhtoonistan issue, 45

visit to India, 45-6
Burke, S.M., 66-7
Burki, H.K., 86-7, 98-9

Callard, Keith, 19, 22
CENTO, 17, 21, 35, 46, 48-9, 52, 62,
    65-6, 121, 141, 145, 158
Chagla, M.C., 5
China
    and Indo-Pak Conflict of 1965,
        77
    on Indo-Bangladesh relations,
        185
    relations with Bangladesh, 189
    relations with Pakistan, 86
China, Pakistan and Bangladesh, 13
Chou En-lai, 23, 47
Choudhury, Abu Sayeed, 173
Choudhury, G.W., 11-2
Choudhury, Hamidul Huq, Foreign
    Minister of Pakistan, 8,48
Collective Security in Asia, 151-2,
    198
Colombo Conference, 46
Comintern, 25-6
Commonwealth Relations Confer-
    ence, 32
Communist Party of Bangladesh
    (CPBD), 172-3, 181-2, 194
Communist Party of East Pakistan,
    123, 135
Communist Party of India (CPI),
    27, 31, 192-4, 210
    and demand for Pakistan, 27-9,
        31
    and Quit India Movement, 27
Communist Party of India (Marxist)
    (CPM), 190-3
Communist Party of Pakistan, 37
    suppression by Government, 37
    USSR attitude on, 37, 47

Dulles, John Foster, 18, 23
Dutt, S., Indian High Commissioner
    to Bangladesh, 187-8
Dyakov, A., 26, 28, 30-1

East Pakistan Communist Party

(Marxist-Leninist) (EPCP-ML),
    190-1

Farakka Barrage issue, 98, 121
Fedorenko, N., 75
First Islamic Conference, 32
Firyubin, N.P., Deputy Foreign
    Minister of USSR, 83, 132
    visit to India, 199
Foreign aid
    from India to Bangladesh, 184
    from USA to Bangladesh, 184
    from USA to Pakistan, 21-2, 98,
        158, 207
    from USSR to Bangladesh, 185
    from USSR to India, 207
    from USSR to Pakistan, 98, 111-
        2, 157, 174
Foreign trade
    between Pakistan and USSR, 58-
        61, 67-8, 110-1, 153, 157, 174
Friends Not Masters, 72, 87-8
Frye, Richard N., 12

Gandhi, Mrs. Indira, Prime Minister
    of India, 100, 129-30, 135,
    154, 194, 201, 209
    letter to Bhutto, 205
    on "no-war pact," 104
    on Soviet arms aid to Pakistan,
        97
    visit to USA, 199
    visit to USSR, 129, 131
Gankovsky, Yuri, 166
Ghaffor, Abdul, 107
Giri, V.V., President of India, 130
Gon, U. Yan, 9
Great Soviet Encyclopedia, 30
Grechko, A.A., Defence Minister
    of USSR,
    visit to Pakistan, 101
Gromyko, A., Foreign Minister of
    USSR, 68

Haji Pir Pass, 81
Hasan, Said, Secretary in the Pakis-
    tani Ministry of Economic
    Affairs, 58
Hasan, Sarwar, 10

Heikel, Mohammed Hassanein, 18
Hitler, Adolf, 26
Hossain, Kamal, Foreign Minister of Bangladesh, 184
Hsinhua (New China News Agency), 185
Hungarian Crisis
    Pakistani attitude on, 48-9
Hussain, Arshad, Foreign Minister of Pakistan, 99
Hussain, Mahmud, Deputy Foreign Minister of Pakistan, 15

Ikram, First Secretary of the Communist Party of Uzbekistan, 11
Ikrammulla, Begum, 116
India
    aid to Bangladesh, 184
    and US arms aid to, 201
    and USSR arms aid to, 90, 93, 201
    establishment of diplomatic relations with USSR, 29, 31
    peaceful nuclear explosion, 206
    relations with Bangladesh, 183
    relations with Pakistan, 13-5
Indian National Congress, 26
Indian Ocean, 55
Indo-Bangladesh Friendship Treaty, 188-9
Indo-Bangladesh Joint Declaration, 183
Indo-Pakistan Conflict of 1965, 22, 69-82, 118, 133
Indo-Pakistan War of 1971, 136-47
    China's attitude on, 138
    Soviet criticism of China's role, 141, 143-6
Indo-Soviet Treaty, 128, 131-2, 136-7, 147, 150, 162, 200-2
    Pakistan's atiitude on, 137, 202-3
Indus Waters Treaty, 98
Iqbal, Mohammed, 3
Islam, Syed Nazrul, 181
Istanbul Pact, see Regional Co-operation Development
Izvestia, 62, 72, 139, 141, 143, 145, 154

Jamat-i-Islami, 103
Jinnah, M., 13, 15, 26, 44, 115
Joshi, P.C., 27

Kaiptsa, 61
Kashmir Problem,
    use of veto by USSR, 64
    USSR's attitude on, 38-9, 64, 75
    see also Indo-Pakistan Conflict of 1965
Kennedy, John F., 65
Khan, A.R., Defence Minister of Pakistan, 101
Khan, Abdul Qayum Khan, Premier of NWFP, 33
Khan, Aga, 14
Khan, Ataur Rahman, 116
Khan, Ayub, 18, 44, 56, 69, 86, 101-3, 117, 147, 165
    on concept of bilateral equations, 87-8
    on joint defence with India, 57
    on Kashmir, 91
    on Khrushchov's proposal for total disarmament, 55
    on Muslim nationalism, 2
    on Soviet military aid to Pakistan, 94, 96
    on Tashkent meeting, 80
    visit to USSR, 68, 70-2, 81-2, 85, 90-2
Khan, Faizullah, Prime Minister of Uzbekistan, 11
Khan, Liaquat Ali, 17, 33, 35, 37, 115, 195
Khan, Nur, Air Marshal,
    on regional economic cooperation, 109
    visit to USSR, 83, 90
Khan, Samin, 1-2, 5, 12
Khan, Wali, 117, 159
Khan, Yahya, 96, 99, 103-6, 109, 124-5, 131, 134, 148, 166, 198
Khan, Zafrullah, Foreign Minister of Pakistan, 16, 20, 68
Khrushchov, N.S., 61-4, 68-9, 81-2, 195
    on Kashmir, 45, 64

on 1958 military *coup* in Pakistan, 50-1
on partition of India, 34, 45
on two-nation theory, 45
visit to India, 45-6, 57
Kissinger, Henry A., US Secretary of State, 200
Komsomolskaya Pravda, 12
Korea, 16-7
Kosygin, A.N., Prime Minister of USSR, 70, 75, 83, 91, 94, 106, 126, 134, 151-2, 173, 176, 183, 195
    message to Ayub, 74, 147
    message to Yahya, 105
    on Farakka Barrage, 98
    on Indo-Pak Conflict of 1965, 76-7
    on Kashmir problem, 76
    on refugee problem, 129
    on regional economic cooperation, 106-9
    visit to India, 97, 107
    visit to Pakistan, 94-6, 105, 107
Kotelawala, Sir John, Prime Minister of Ceylon, 47
Kransaya Zvedza, 134
Kudryavtsev, V., 139, 141, 143, 145

Lahore Resolution, 113
Lail-o-Nihar, 57
Lenin, V.I., 10

Malenkov, G.M., 196
Malik, Y.A., 38-9, 137-8, 144, 178
Mathai, Dr. John, 41
Mazurov, K.T. First Soviet Vice-Premier, 73, 83
Mikoyan, A., First Deputy Prime Minister of the USSR, 48, 59
Military aid,
    from USA to India, 65, 201
    from USA to Pakistan, 22-3, 201, 210
    from USSR to India, 90, 93, 201
    from USSR to Pakistan, 94-7, 99, 102-3, 112
Mirovaiia Ekonomika, 50
Mirovoe Khoziaistvo, 26

Mohammed, Pir Ali, 2
Molotov, V.M., Foreign Minister of USSR, 48, 59
Morse, Wayne, 59
Motamar-i-Alam-i-Islami, 20
Mountbatten Plan
    USSR's attitude on, 29-30
Mujahid Movement, 7
Mujibur Rahman, *see* Rahman, Mujibur
Mukti Bahini, 190
"Muslim Bengal", 160, 163, 193
Muslim community, 3, 26, 49
Muslim League, 15, 26-8, 34, 63, 113
Muslims
    in Burma, 7-10
    in Soviet Central Asia, 10-3, 23-4, 36, 39, 40
Mustafa, A.T.M., Pakistan's Minister for Education
    on ideology of Pakistan, 3-5
Myth of Independence, The, 87-8

Nasser, G.A., 18-20
National Awami Party (NAP), 50, 159, 163, 181-2, 186, 194, 210
Nazimuddin, Khwaja, Prime Minister of Pakistan, 6, 17
Nehru, Jawaharlal, 29, 47
New Times, 32, 36-7, 51, 66, 127, 133, 145
Nikolaevich, M. Ivan, 31
Nishtar, Abdul Rab, 15
Nixon, Richard N., President of USA
    visit to China, 199
Noon, Feroz Khan, Prime Minister of Pakistan, 22
Novosti Press Agency (APN), 78, 185

Olmstead, General, 18-9

Pakhtoonistan issue
    Soviet attitude on, 43, 63, 196
Pakistan
    agreement with USSR on oil exploration, 60

aid from USA, 21-2
aid from USSR, 61, 71
and Hungarian Crisis, 48-9
and Muslims of Central Asian
    Republics, 40
and Suez Crisis, 49
arms aid from USA, 22-3, 201,
    210
arms aid from USSR, 94-7, 102-
    3, 112
attitude towards Korean War,
    32
attitude towards Soviet arms
    supply to India, 93
defence budget of, 204
disparity between the two wings,
    113-5
establishment of diplomatic re-
    lations with USSR, 31
reaction to India's nuclear ex-
    plosion, 205
relations with Bangladesh, 161
relations with India, 13-5, 56
relations with the West, 15-23
suppression of Communist
    Movement, 37, 46-7
Pakistan-i-Sovetski Souiz, 67
Pakistan Times, 61, 84-6, 92, 98,
    155
Pan-Islamic Movement, 36
Panikkar, K.M., 14
Patel, Sardar, 41
Patriot, 172
Peking Review, 155
People's Party of Pakistan, 122
Pirzada, A.H., 156
Podelshikov, G., 83
Podgorny, Nikolai, President of the
    USSR, 130, 148, 173, 198
message to Yahya, 125
Pravda, 37, 39, 63, 73, 75-7, 80, 124,
    127, 132, 134, 140-1, 144, 146,
    154
Prisoners of War
    Pakistani POWs, 164, 183, 185,
        189, 203

Qadir, Manzur, 57

Qureshi, Saleem M.M., 162-3

Radhakrishnan, S.,
    visit to USSR, 68
Rahman, Fazlul, 44
Rahman, Sheikh Mujibur, 48, 117,
    120, 129, 131, 173-4, 176, 183,
    186, 189-90, 192, 194, 199
    and Six Point Programme, 116,
        122-3
    on exploitation of east wing by
        W. Pakistan, 114, 121
    on Farakka Barrage issue, 121
    on Pakistani POWs, 164
    on relations with China, 123
    on relations with India, 121, 123
    visit to USSR, 174-7
Rajagopalachari, C., 28
Rann of Kutch Crisis, 22, 81
    USSR's attitude on, 72
Rawalpindi Conspiracy Case, 32
Refugees from East Pakistan, 170,
    200
    India's attitude on, 129, 135
    Soviet attitude on, 129
Regional Cooperation for Develop-
    ment (RCD), 4, 69
Regional Economic Cooperation,
    106-9, 198
    reaction of Bhutto, 108
    reaction of Nur Khan, 109

Sadat, Anwar, 20
Salauddin, Mohammed, 188
San Francisco Peace Treaty, 16
SEATO, 17, 21, 35, 47-9, 52, 62, 65,
    72, 94, 121, 141, 145, 158
Second Turkistan Muslim Congress,
    11
Second World Muslim Conference,
    36
Shahabuddin, Khwaja, Information
    Minister of Pakistan, 88-9
Shahi, Agha, 137, 203
Shastri, Lal Bahadur, 77-8, 147
Shurygin, V., 135, 206-7
Sidorenko, Soviet Minister of Geo-
    logy, 85

Simla Agreement, 154, 156, 159,
    180, 203-6, 211
Simenov, V.,124
Sino-Indian Conflict of 1962, 66-7,
    165, 197, 201
Six Point Programme, 116, 118-20,
    122-3
Smetanin, N., 78
Sovietskaya Rossia, 140
Stalin, J., 10, 28, 39-42
Stetsenko, A.C., 32
Suhrawardy, H.S., Prime Minister of
    Pakistan, 6,13, 17, 48-50, 117
Suleri, Z.A., 117
Suslov, M., 65
Sverglov, Prof. G., 83
Syed, G.M., 117

Talbot, Phillips, US Assistant
    Secretary of State, 72
Tameer, 155
Tashkent Declaration, 79-82, 89, 92,
    96, 99, 119, 126, 167
Tass, 73-4, 77, 137, 159
The Basis of Pakistan, 8-9, 13-4
Toynbee, Arnold, 23
Tulu, 89
Turko-Pakistani Pact of 1954, 51

U-2 incident, 65
Ulansky, 127
United Nations
    Security Council, 74, 142, 171
USA
    aid to Bangladesh, 184
    aid to Pakistan, 21-2
    arms aid to India, 201
    arms aid to Pakistan, 22-3, 201,
        210
    relations with China, 151
    trade with Pakistan, 98
USSR
    aid to Bangladesh, 185
    aid to Pakistan, 84-5, 95
    and Chinese role in Indo-Pak
        War of 1971, 141, 143-6
    and establishment of diplomatic

        relations with India, 29, 31
    and establishment of diplomatic
        relations with Pakistan, 31
    and Liaquat Ali Khan's US visit,
        35
    and Maulana Bhashani, 49-50
    and Muslim League, 34
    and Pact with Germany, 23
    and Suhrawardy, 49-50
    and the sub-continent, 158, 168
    and US bases in Pakistan, 51-5
    arms aid to India, 90, 93, 201
    arms aid to Pakistan, 94-7, 99,
        102-3, 112
    attitude during Bangladesh Crisis,
        124-6, 142, 170-1
    attitude towards Indian indepen-
        dence, 30-1
    attitude towards Mountbatten
        Plan, 29-30
    invitation to Liaquat Ali Khan,
        33-4, 42
    on Indo-Pak Conflict of 1965,
        75-6, 78
    on Kashmir, 38-9, 43, 45-6, 68,
        73-5, 78
    on Nehru's visit to USA, 41
    on Simla Agreement, 180
    on suppression of communists in
        Pakistan, 46-7
    protest notes to Pakistan, 51-2
    recognition of Bangladesh, 173
    relations with India, 43, 78-9,
        197
    trade with Pakistan, 58-61, 67-8,
        71, 84-6, 89, 95, 153

Volsky. D., 50
Vostokov, D., 151

Wahab, Maulana, 13
Waqt, 155
Warsaw Pact, 49
Wilcox, Wayne A., 201, 208

Yakubov, G., 146

Zhukov, E., 29
Zorin, V., 39